Cinderella or Cyberella?

Cinderella or Cyberella?

Empowering Women in the Knowledge Society

Nancy J. Hafkin and Sophia Huyer
editors

Kumarian
Press, Inc.

Cinderella or Cyberella?: Empowering Women in the Knowledge Society
Published in 2006 in the United States of America by Kumarian Press, Inc.,
1294 Blue Hills Avenue, Bloomfield, CT 06002 USA

The text of this book is set in 10.5/13 Janson Text.

Production and design by Joan Weber Laflamme, jml ediset
Proofread by Beth Richards
Indexed by Bob Land
Cover design by Laura Augustine

Printed in the United States of America by Thomson-Shore. Text printed with
vegetable oil-based ink.

∞ The paper used in this publication meets the minimum requirements of the
American National Standard for Information Sciences—Permanence of Paper for printed Library Materials, ANSI Z39.48–1984

Library of Congress Cataloging-in-Publication Data

Cinderella or cyberella? : empowering women in the knowledge society / Nancy
Hafkin and Sophia Huyer, editors.
    p. cm.
  ISBN-13: 978–1–56549–219–6
  1. Women in development—Developing countries. 2. Information society—
Developing countries. I. Hafkin, Nancy J. II. Huyer, Sophia. III. Title.
HQ1240.5.D44C57 2006
303.48'33082091724—dc22

                                                            2006009184

15 14 13 12 11 10 09 08 07 06   10 9 8 7 6 5 4 3 2 1   First Printing 2006

Contents

Figures and Tables

Acronyms

AAUW	American Association of University Women
ACP	Africa, Caribbean, and Pacific
AIDMG	Association for the Integral Development of Mayan Guatemala
AISI	African Information Society Initiative
APC	Association for Progressive Communications
APDIP	Asia-Pacific Development Information Programme
APWIN	Asian Pacific Women's Information Network
CEMINA	Communication, Education and Information on Gender
CIDA	Canadian International Development Agency
CLC	community learning center
CTA	Technical Centre for Agricultural and Rural Cooperation
DFID	Department for International Development (UK)
ECA	United Nations Economic Commission for Africa
ECOSOC	Economic and Social Council (United Nations)
ENDA	Environment and Development in the Third World
FIRE	International Feminist Internet Radio
FLOSS	Free/Libre Open Source Software
GICT	gender and ICT
GKP	Global Knowledge Partnership
GTP	Global Teenager Project
ICANN	Internet Corporation for Assigned Names and Numbers
ICT/ICTs	information and communication technology/ies
ICT4D	ICT for development

ICT4E	ICT for education
IDRC	International Development Research Centre
ILO	International Labour Organization
IMC	Independent Media Center
IRI	interactive radio instruction
IT	information technology (related to the employment sector)
ITU	International Telecommunication Union
KRNIC	Korean Network Information Center
MDGs	Millennium Development Goals
NEPAD	New Partnership for Africa's Development
NGO	nongovernmental organization
NICI	national information and communication infrastructure
ODL	open and distance learning
OECD	Organisation for Economic Co-operation and Development
PC	personal computer
S&T	science and technology
SEWA	Self Employed Women's Association
SL	sustainable livelihoods
SMEs	small- and medium-sized enterprises
SMS	short message service
SNA	SchoolNet Africa
SP	stability pact
SP GTF	Stability Pact Gender Task Force
SPEM	State Poverty Eradication Mission (Kerala, India)
TSC	technical service center
VoIP	Voice over Internet Protocol
UNDAW	United Nations Division for the Advancement of Women
UNESCO	United Nations Educational, Scientific and Cultural Organization

UNDP	United Nations Development Programme
UNIFEM	United Nations Development Fund for Women
WSIS	World Summit on the Information Society

Introduction

Sophia Huyer and Nancy J. Hafkin

Cyberella or Cinderella: what is the future for women in the knowledge society? Cyberella is fluent in the uses of technology, comfortable using and designing computer technology and communication equipment and software, and in working in virtual spaces. She can imagine innovative uses for technologies across a range of problems and subjects and finds information and knowledge to improve her life and expand her choices.[1] She is an active knowledge creator and disseminator and, more than a user, she designs information and knowledge systems to improve all aspects of her life. In contrast, Cinderella works in the basement of the knowledge society (if she works in it at all), with little opportunity to reap its benefits. Instead she waits for her prince to decide for her the benefits she will receive.

Cyberellas in countries around the world are using information and communication technologies (ICTs) in creative ways to improve their lives: Women mobile phone operators in Bangladesh help other women get information on registering their land, opening a business, or obtaining a tax certificate. Poor women in Guatemala are learning to repair computers and set up their own ICT-enabled businesses. Teenage girls in Mauritania are using ICTs to find information about sexuality and HIV/AIDS that their society will not discuss. All of these women are Cyberellas who are finding and using information and technologies that were previously inaccessible to them.

It is Cyberella we are aiming for. In order for women to benefit equally from the possibilities of the knowledge society, they need to participate in it actively from a position of independence, choice, capabilities, and action.[2] Gender equality and empowerment are necessary prerequisites for women's participation in the knowledge society.

Much of the work and action on gender equality, women's empowerment, and ICTs has so far emphasized three areas: access to ICTs for

1

women, women's use of ICTs as tools for networking and advocacy, and women's work in the information technology (IT) sector.[3] But there is a wider range of aspects of women's empowerment relating to ICTs that is not as frequently addressed; access to information for health and well-being at the local level, ICT-based small- and medium-sized enterprises (SMEs) for low-income women, and ICT-enabled education for women and girls are just some examples. This book attempts to address this imbalance by calling attention to how ICTs can provide tools to enable individual women or men to make choices about their lives in the household and community. ICTs can be important tools for gender equality and women's empowerment in both society and work, particularly for poor women in developing countries: this book looks at how and why this can happen. Our focus is not on the technology, but rather on women's empowerment in the context of a gendered world and how ICTs can make the most effective contributions to it.

We look at women's social and economic empowerment as supported by ICTs and based in gender and development theory. Our approach to women's empowerment and ICTs builds on an approach to women and development that incorporates an emphasis on gender equality, poverty reduction, and technology for development. The analysis of gender and development theory—including gender and technology for development—as developed over the past thirty years brings clarity to the picture of how ICTs can offer opportunities for women. Bearing in mind the Millennium Development Goals (MDGs) and their focus on poverty reduction, we look especially at the situation of poor women in developing countries and the ways in which ICTs can contribute to their social and economic well-being.

A substantial amount of gender analysis has been done on the role of ICTs in these various sectors, such as their role in promoting women's SMEs and the use of information for women's reproductive and sexual health, but it has not been presented in an integrated manner. This separation of approaches, analysis, and understanding limits the effectiveness of gender advocacy and, therefore, the use of ICTs to support women's empowerment. Calling attention to the possibilities that ICTs present for women's empowerment in all parts of their lives will, we hope, encourage increased connection and collaboration among women and women's advocates across sectors and worlds.

ICTs are not a magic wand or Cinderella's scepter that will do away with centuries of discrimination and inequality. *It is not the technology itself that will empower women.* But because they are an increasingly pervasive force in global life and an increasingly accepted part of what defines the "haves," women need to acquire and use these technologies to prevent further marginalization. Information technologies are tools that can open up a range of possibilities. But they are more than that: they have characteristics and properties that go directly to the roots of women's inequality by transcending invisibility and hierarchy while offering access to information and an escape from cultural isolation.

Finally, women have a great deal to contribute to the design, use, and application of knowledge and information in terms of their local knowledge, innovation, creativity, and perspective. All of these aspects combine to make ICTs not just a means to avoid further marginalization but potentially unique tools for empowerment. *Women should have equal access, use and opportunity to benefit from ICTs in order to improve their lives and increase their status in the household and community as full participants in the knowledge society. Used appropriately, they can be catalysts of gender equality and women's empowerment.*

The world is spinning in an orbit increasingly shaped by knowledge and technology. Countries need to develop their human resources to enter the knowledge society, to include the contributions of all their people. Poverty reduction depends on improving the situation of women and increasing the efficiency of their work: societies that discriminate by gender pay a high price in economic growth (World Bank 2001). Increasingly evidence is emerging of the many opportunities ICTs can provide for women to improve their incomes, gain awareness of their public and private rights, and improve their own and their families' well-being. As a result, promoting women's empowerment through ICTs as a route to their active participation in the knowledge society is one of the critical development challenges of the twenty-first century. As recognized internationally, "when there is an enabling environment, ICT can provide diverse avenues for women's social, political and economic empowerment" (UNDAW 2003). The first phase of the World Summit on the Information Society (WSIS) in Geneva in December 2003 declared gender equality to be a priority for the global information society, to enable "women's empowerment and their full participation on the basis of equality in all spheres of society and in all decision-making processes" (WSIS 2003).

Supporting equitable social development at the local level with ICTs requires a broad understanding of what an ICT is. In an environment where electricity and phone lines are undependable or expensive, computers and the Internet may not be the most appropriate strategy. We adopt Hamelink's functional definition of ICTs as encompassing "all those technologies that enable the handling of information and facilitate different forms of communication among human actors, between human beings and electronic systems, and among electronic systems" (Hamelink 1997). This includes Internet and e-mail, among the new technologies, as well as traditional ones such as community radio. Throughout we use ICTs in this broad sense; we generally refer to the industry that produces ICTs as the IT industry, following North American usage.

To identify the role of ICTs in supporting women's empowerment, we will consider their ability to enable agency, capability, and choices for women and their role in supporting a process of change from a condition of disempowerment. To arrive at full empowerment in the knowledge society, Cinderella needs to become Cyberella.

Chapters in the book are written by practitioners and researchers in the field of gender, ICTs, and empowerment from Africa, Asia, Latin America, and North America. They present examples and analysis of several aspects of women's social and economic empowerment from a variety of viewpoints, including:

- economic empowerment through collective action at the local level and support to women's livelihoods;
- promoting the education of women, both with ICTs and for technological empowerment;
- ICT and telecommunications policy to promote universal access, particularly in rural areas;
- supporting women's social movements at local and national levels; and
- e-governance.

The authors present their perspectives on how ICTs can help to empower women and girls (and men and boys) and support gender equality through both collective and individual approaches. All share the belief that this can be done only if ICTs are implemented in ways that are supportive of local situations and socioeconomic status—in particular, in ways that are cognizant of gender and other social-equality issues. Each chapter also addresses critical factors in the use of ICTs to support women's empowerment, identifying lessons learned and presenting suggestions for next-step issues, research, and actions. All chapters include examples of successful or promising attempts to achieve this goal. ICTs have been used to promote social development only during the past few years, and little large-scale analysis of the results of such efforts is yet available, concerning either gender equality or the benefits and results of these projects. Nevertheless, there are some promising signs of progress, and the chapters in this book attempt to assess these, at the same time presenting a critical view of the potential and actual negative effects of these technologies.

The three opening chapters set the stage for the case studies that follow with global overviews of what we know about the collection of sex-disaggregated data on women's participation in the information society at national and international levels; the involvement of women in ICT policymaking and implementation at international, regional, and national levels; and the educational context affecting the ability of women to benefit from, design, and use ICTs and technology.

They are followed by four case studies that present experience in the gender dimensions of ICT-enabled teaching and learning in Africa as promoted by SchoolNet Africa (SNA); the role of ICTs in supporting women's entrepreneurial activities at the local level (Asia); e-governance at the municipal level (Asia); and the role of ICTs in women's social movements in Latin America.

Two of the cases focus on women who live in grassroots rural and peri-urban remote communities, with particular attention to low-income women. In general, the women in these groups can be expected to have lower levels of literacy, education, and income than other groups[4]—characteristics that tend to inhibit their abilities to use technologies—but these chapters show that ICTs can be used successfully by women and men in marginalized communities.

The use of ICTs by women from a mix of socioeconomic groups is assessed in two cases, ranging from the teachers and leaders in the SNA network and educated technology workers and women leaders in several urban-based social movements in Latin America, to the children in both rural and urban centers who use computers in schools and the rural-based women who learn to use and appropriate ICTs through the work of their social movements.

In Chapter 1, "Understanding Gender Equality and Women's Empowerment in the Knowledge Society," Sophia Huyer reviews the concepts of gender, gender equality, women's empowerment, technology for development, and the global policy environment around these issues, including the MDGs.[5] The questions she asks include What is empowerment for women? What does it mean for women's lives and their relations with men? How can ICTs contribute to women's empowerment, improve their position in life, and increase their well-being? What are the prerequisites for women's empowerment and gender equality in the knowledge society? The purpose is to work toward a theoretical understanding of what women's empowerment in the knowledge society consists of and how ICTs can promote gender equality and women's empowerment toward this end.

While there are many different approaches to and understandings of empowerment, most have in common the concepts of options, choice, control, capabilities, and power. These pertain to women's ability to make decisions and affect events and circumstances around them; benefit from resources and opportunities; exercise control over their own life, body, and resources; and have a say in public life and decision making—all with the result of increasing or achieving autonomy and improving health and well-being. Huyer distinguishes between empowerment approaches that emphasize organized collective action and those that assess women's situation at the individual, local level, and compares related approaches of gender equity, gender equality, and gender mainstreaming.

Huyer then turns to discussions of poverty reduction and technology as they relate to women's role in the household and society, particularly the ground-breaking research by Ester Boserup on women's contributions to economic development and Patricia Stamp's analysis of the effects on women of a technology-as-neutral approach. Finally, she presents a perspective on understanding the interrelations among the range of contributions, approaches, and uses of ICTs as a tool to promote gender equality for social, economic, and political empowerment.

In Chapter 2, "Women, Gender, and ICT Statistics and Indicators," Nancy J. Hafkin assesses the current status of data collection and analysis on the differential impact of ICT on men and women at the global level. Her position is that the availability of quantitative information on how the situation of women compares to that of men in their countries with regard to access, use, and impact of ICTs is a necessary prerequisite to the achievement of a globally equitable information society. Accurate sex-disaggregated data and indicators are necessary to understand gendered trends of participation in the information age, to inform policy, and to develop strategies to address any inequalities and gaps. The current paucity of data in this area makes it difficult, if not impossible, to make the case to policymakers for the inclusion of gender issues in ICT policies, plans, and strategies. Without data, there is no visibility; without visibility, there is no priority.

This chapter surveys the quantitative data currently available on women and gender with respect to ICTs collected by international agencies and national governments (primarily in developing countries) and assesses the strengths and gaps of these data collections. It then presents some current initiatives to develop models and approaches to collect sex-disaggregated data and identifies those areas where data is most needed to come to an accurate understanding of the nature and magnitude of the gender digital divide.

Sonia Jorge looks at the political aspects of empowerment in Chapter 3, "Engendering ICT Policy and Regulation: Prioritizing Universal Access for Women's Empowerment," through involvement in the making of ICT policy and its implementation. She sees socioeconomic empowerment as the goal of political activity in the policy area, envisaging that the greatest results for women will come from universal access to ICTs. Access to means of communication would provide an escape route from women's isolation and lack of "visibility." Her approach establishes the conditions that will allow individual women to use ICTs for their self-defined purposes.

Jorge emphasizes the importance of gender analysis to ICTs for development, especially in the area of policy and regulation. She feels that the analysis needs to be made by gender experts and by gender advocates—men and women who see the need for gender equality in ICTs. She defines ICT policy as providing the vision and the road map for ICT development, whereas regulation is established to implement the policy goals. She shows that much has been accomplished in the last few years in getting gender concerns into ICT policy—by women's groups at WSIS and in national policy in the Dominican Republic, Ghana, Kenya, Mozambique, and South Africa, among other countries. She defines the important gender elements in policy and regulation and stresses that these elements need to be mainstreamed. Jorge then outlines the process by which policy is elaborated and how gender issues can and should be part of the process. While progress is being made in engendering ICT policy, she notes gender concerns tend to fall away in implementation. Jorge also looks at examples of grassroots projects using ICT for women's empowerment, citing examples of women making change themselves instead of waiting for a policy or its implementation. In the quest for women's empowerment through the tool of ICT, she sees universal access to communication as key. As a short-term strategy she advocates working toward universal access policy and funds, supporting grassroots ICT initiatives that empower women, and addressing the issue of ICT affordability. For the long term, she views mainstreaming gender throughout the ICT for development sector, including policy and regulatory bodies, as essential.

In Chapter 4, "Cyberella in the Classroom? Gender, Education, and Technology," Sophia Huyer assesses two complementary aspects of ICTs that can catalyze women's empowerment and gender equality: the enrollment and participation of females in scientific and technological education at all levels, and the potential for ICTs to improve women's and girls' access to formal and non-formal education and improve the quality of the learning experience. Huyer argues that the presence of more girls and women in the technological classroom is an important aspect of turning Cinderellas into Cyberellas at all levels of the information economy and knowledge society. This view calls for organized action (through the education system) to support the ability of women to take economic and social decisions and actions at the individual level.

The shortfall of girls in education is particularly marked in science and technology education in both developed and developing countries for reasons relating to sociocultural, qualificational, and institutional barriers. Huyer points to several strategies that have been put in place to reduce these barriers. While science and technology (S&T) studies are the prerequisite for the empowerment of women in the IT-based professions, ICTs are also an "open sesame" to all varieties of learning and the acquisition of knowledge. Increasingly, computers and ICT-based learning are permeating developing as well as developed countries. The greatest potential for the use of computers in education in developing countries at this time appears to be in teacher education, although more research on this is needed. Similarly, little research exists on gender-differentiated effects and benefits of the use of technologies for education, especially in the use of computers in schools in developing countries. Among the most interesting findings are those of gendered access and use patterns. Huyer sees distance education as a major opportunity for women and girls to overcome many of the obstacles to education that have been placed in their way. She emphasizes that both opportunities and risks associated with ICTs and education need to be clearly understood in order to devise strategies to overcome them and to allow students, teachers, and policymakers to engage in and develop ICT-based education systems that will promote greater equality and empowerment for all groups.

We move from Huyer's overview of gendered issues in the use of ICTs in and for education to a case study. In Chapter 5, "'We Have Womb'—Engendering ICTs in Education: The SchoolNet Africa Experience," Shafika Isaacs presents experience in integrating gender equality concerns into education programming and networking. SNA is an African- and female-led NGO that was set up to promote learning and teaching in schools through ICTs. It works with a network of communities of practice who coalesce around national schoolnet groups and organizations, currently operating in thirty-five African countries. Isaacs's view is that gender equality in ICT-enabled networking involves "more than just numbers" or an access approach that focuses on ensuring girls equal time on computers. Instead, she builds on Derbyshire's framework for gender equality in education, which includes *qualitative* dimensions such as considerations of education content or what learners are learning, as well as the abilities and opportunities open to girls and boys related to their role and status in society (Derbyshire 2003). This approach recognizes that females and males may face different constraints in accessing educational opportunities and in achieving their educational potential. There may also be gendered patterns in interests and priorities when it comes to learning that need to be taken into account in order to enable students to reach their full potential.

The chapter also looks at the role of SNA members in promoting gender equality for women and girls in ICT for education (ICT4E). While SNA has no official gender policy, members of the organization (both male and female) use available opportunities to raise gender equality issues. SNA leaders see these actions as an integral aspect of the group's mandate to promote social equity and development through the promotion of universal access to ICTs in African schools; to advance capacity building in technical, managerial, and pedagogical competencies; and to develop Africanized digital content and curriculum integration. The goal is to produce women and girls who are empowered in their interpersonal actions and can improve their situations and incomes through technological capability in both their working and personal lives.

In Chapter 6, "Improved Livelihoods and Empowerment for Poor Women through IT-Sector Intervention," Shoba Arun, Richard Heeks, and Sharon Morgan address the potential for ICTs to facilitate women's economic empowerment through sustainable livelihoods. This empowerment occurs at the individual level as participating women increase income and skill levels within a collective self-help group that also manages the ICT-based enterprises and provides other forms of support. The authors focus on an assets-vulnerability approach that has been used previously for work on women and anti-poverty initiatives. This approach involves identifying the range of assets that potentially can be used by the poor, rather than relying on baseline financial indicators. It also incorporates the notion of vulnerability as linked to the ability of poor women to own and manage assets to promote livelihoods. In particular, the authors examine the case of women-run Kudumbashree IT units in Kerala in southern India. Core groups are formed on the structure of neighborhood self-help groups, which provide a range of functions and services, including establishment of microenterprises as well as credit, education, and advocacy. Of the 1,206 Kudumbashree units in this study, 56 are data entry and digitization units; 45 provide IT training to local schools and organizations; and 5 are hardware assembly units that build, sell, and maintain personal computers.

The study found that these units contributed to women's empowerment by ensuring a steady income that allowed the members to make expenditures on their children's education, family marriages, and parents' homes. They also gained skills and experience with technologies and business management. Perhaps the greatest value of this experience as expressed by the women members was the confidence and increased social status they gained in both the family and community as a result of increased income and interaction with customers and government officials in the course of their work, and the prestige associated with working with new technologies. The authors conclude that while new vulnerabilities emerge in these units—related to sustainability of the enterprises and the pace of technical change—e-development that directly touches and improves the lives of poor women is possible over a sustained period.

Chapter 7, "Women in Latin America Appropriating ICTs for Social Change," by Maria Garrido and Raul Roman, views women's empowerment through ICTs in the context of social justice movements in Latin America. Their approach focuses on organized, collective action undertaken by women. While concentrating on political aspects of empowerment, they also examine psychological (self-esteem), economic (improved working conditions and opportunities), sociocultural (indigenous knowledge and spaces for collaboration), and legal (women's rights) aspects. They relate the experiences of women, and men working in their behalf, in appropriating ICTs for social change in three different forms of collective action:

- community telecenters;
- participation in social movements, in particular, the Zapatista movement in Chiapas, Mexico; and
- networking and advocacy, especially at the grassroots level.

Among the obstacles they find to women's full engagement with ICTs are rampant poverty, unemployment, wage and labor discrimination, lack of access to education and resources, cultural stereotypes, and poor access to communication infrastructure. They take a cultural approach to technology, seeing technology as functioning in dynamic interaction with the individuals and social groups who use it. Garrido and Roman conclude that ICTs are valuable tools both to empower women in the face of economic globalization and to provide increased collaboration among civil society groups working for social change. In their view the presence of ICTs is a necessary but not sufficient condition for the advancement of women in Latin America and elsewhere.

In his survey of the potential for ICTs to promote women's empowerment through e-governance and ICT-enabled networking in Chapter 8, "Empowerment of Women through ICT-enabled Networks: Toward the Optimum ICT-impact Model," Vikas Nath focuses on the challenge to transform new forms of communication into real opportunities for growth and development, especially for those who are most likely to be bypassed. In this context his understanding of the role of ICTs in women's empowerment is through their use by or for women to develop further their skills and abilities to gain insight about actions and issues that affect them (positively or negatively), as well as to build their capacity to be involved, voice their concerns, and make informed decisions on these issues. This entails building the capacities that will allow women to overcome social and institutional barriers and strengthen their participation in economic and political processes to bring an overall improvement in the quality of their lives.

Individual women are empowered at the local level to access and distribute information and knowledge, experiencing benefits to self-esteem, income, and well-being. This individual level of action and agency is encouraged and supported by more organized collective action in the form of support NGOs at the local or national level.

The chapter assesses how ICT-enabled networking can promote women's participation in the public sphere in the form of participation in governance, access to improved government service delivery, and mobilization and public advocacy. It concludes by suggesting a set of impact and assessment models for visualizing the impact of ICTs on women in three different scenarios:

- ICTs are introduced in a community but benefit only the groups that already have information access;
- ICTs introduce knowledge and information access to new groups in a community, but no gender-targeted activities or programs are undertaken;
- ICTs reach new groups in a community *and* a series of gender-equality and women-targeted activities are integrated into its introduction.

The chapter also focuses on how e-governance can contribute positively to women's empowerment at the local levels through increased access to services and information. The approach is complementary to that of Martinez and Reilly (2002), who point out that e-governance should not be confused with e-democracy, which they define as the use of ICTs by civil society actors to access and use information systems in monitoring, policy advocacy, and democracy building. They focus on "organized women who can use public information as an input to their agendas and put it to the service of women at large" (Martinez and Reilly 2002).

The chapters in this volume reflect a variety of approaches to and understanding of the use of ICT for women's empowerment. Nevertheless, they combine to form a book that reflects a vision of a knowledge society premised on social and gender equality. The chapters present examples of new possibilities and new directions to encourage women to become Cyberellas rather than Cinderellas—able to use fully ICTs as tools for empowerment in the knowledge society.

NOTES

[1] This definition builds on the discussion in Kirkup 2003.

[2] We define *knowledge society* as use of ICTs for development "through empowering the poor and increasing scientific and technical capacity of nations in a way that is consistent with development goals, to support democratic decision-making, more effective governance, and lifelong learning. The benefits are closely associated with establishing equitable policy and regulatory frameworks and with ensuring that understanding, sharing, and partnership-building

are central components of national ICT strategies" (Mansell and Wehn 1998, 8).

[3] The work on access tends to center on comparing men's and women's rates of access to IT and analyzing women's constraints. Much of the promotion of gender issues in ICT came out of pioneering uses of the technology by women's advocacy groups in connection with world conferences in the 1990s and continues now with campaigns for women's rights using innovative technologies such as short message service (SMS). Research, writing, and advocacy on women's employment have looked largely at issues of levels of employment in the IT sector in developed countries and possibilities of its exploitation in developing nations (see Gurumurthy 2004; ILO 2001).

[4] In the case of Kerala, India (Chapter 6), the women participants were comparatively highly educated; with a lack of employment opportunities, however, they remained in the lower income levels.

[5] We address the role of ICTs in contributing to gender empowerment in the context of the MDGs indirectly in that ICTs can contribute to poverty reduction (Goal 1) and to empowering women (Goal 2). For a more detailed assessment of the role of ICTs in contributing to gender equality in the context of the MDGs, see Daly 2003.

REFERENCES

Daly, John. 2003. ICT, gender equality, and empowering women. July 9. http://www.developmentgateway.org (accessed 27 March 2005).

Derbyshire, Helen. 2003. Gender issues in the use of computers in education in Africa. London: Imfundo, DFID. http://www.schoolnetafrica.net/fileadmin/resources/Gender_Report.pdf (accessed 21 September 2005).

Gurumurthy, Anita. 2004. Challenging gender inequalities in the information society. *Gender and Development in Brief, Bridge Bulletin* 15 (September). http://www.bridge.ids.ac.uk/Docs/In%20Brief%20No.15.pdf (accessed 5 December 2005).

Hamelink, Cees J. 1997. New information and communication technologies, social development and cultural change. Discussion Paper no. 86. Geneva: United Nations Research Institute for Social Development.

ILO (International Labour Organization). 2001. *Life at work in the information economy*. Geneva: ILO.

Kirkup, Gillian. 2003. ICT as a tool for enhancing women's education opportunities; and new education and professional opportunities for women in new technologies. Presented at the UN Division for the Advancement of Women Expert Group Meeting on ICTs and Their Impact on and Use as an Instrument for the Advancement and Empowerment of Women. Seoul, Korea, 11–14 November. http://www.un.org/womenwatch/daw/egm/ict2002/index.html (accessed 30 November 2005).

Mansell, Robin, and Uta Wehn. 1998. *Knowledge societies: Information technology for sustainable development*. Oxford: Oxford Univ. Press.

Martinez, Juliana, and Katherine Reilly. 2002. Looking behind the Internet: Empowering women for public policy advocacy in Central America. Background paper, UN/INSTRAW Virtual Seminar Series on Gender and ICTs. Seminar Four: ICTs as tools for bridging the digital gender gap and women's empowerment, 2–14 September. http://www.un-instraw.org/en/docs/gender_and_ict/Martinez.pdf (accessed 30 November 2005).

UNDAW (United Nations Division for the Advancement of Women). 2003. Information and communication technologies and their impact on and use as an instrument for the advancement and empowerment of women. New York: UNDAW. http://www.un.org/womenwatch/daw/egm/ict2002/index.html (accessed 30 November 2005).

World Bank. 2001. *Engendering development—through gender equality in rights, resources, and voice*. Washington, DC: World Bank.

WSIS (World Summit on the Information Society). 2003. Declaration of principles, building the information society: A global challenge in the new millennium. http://www.itu.int/dms_pub/itu-s/md/03/wsis/doc/S03-WSIS-DOC-0004!!MSW-E.doc (accessed 4 December 2005).

1

Understanding Gender Equality and Women's Empowerment in the Knowledge Society

Sophia Huyer

This chapter looks at women's empowerment and the potential of ICTs to contribute to this process. What is empowerment for women? What does it mean for women's lives? How can ICTs contribute to women's empowerment, improve their position in life, and increase their well-being? What are the prerequisites to becoming Cyberella in the knowledge society?

The focus of the chapter, and this book, is on actions and agency for social and economic empowerment at the local level, by both individuals and groups, and how ICTs can be tools to achieve this. The majority of analysis and action to date has emphasized the role of ICTs in promoting political empowerment through organized collective action, primarily at the national, regional, and international levels. I attempt to build on a wider range of approaches, to come to a better understanding of the interrelations and complementarities among them. The focus is on the local level because this area has been neglected in the past and is a necessary part of women's empowerment. However, I fully recognize and support national, regional, and international political efforts, which can often lead to social and economic empowerment at local and individual levels.[1]

The chapter ends with an attempt to link existing approaches on the uses of ICTs as tools to promote gender equality for social, economic, and political empowerment.

BUILDING ON THEORY
AND ANALYSIS:
WHY GENDER AND NOT WOMEN?

Prior to the 1970s, assistance to women in developing countries came in the guise of welfare; women were seen as passive beneficiaries of aid that concentrated on their reproductive and domestic roles. The United Nations Decade for Women launched in Mexico in 1975 called attention to the absence of women's concerns from development efforts and stressed the economic and productive aspects of their contributions. The Decade for Women became the decade of women in development, emphasizing small-scale, income-generating projects for women, often as separate activities from larger development efforts. By the mid-eighties, the women-in-development approach was criticized for its separation of women from the mainstream of development; its addition of economic activities to already overburdened women; and its neglect of the societal context, that is, that women exist in society together with men. The critique led to the gender-and-development approach, which drew attention to the impact of relations between women and men on development policies and aimed at changing the practice of development to promote gender equality.

The gender-and-development approach has become accepted orthodoxy in development theory. It defines gender as the differences between women and men within the same household and within and between cultures that are socially and culturally constructed and change over time. These differences are reflected in roles, responsibilities, access to resources, constraints, opportunities, needs, perceptions, views, and so forth (Moser 1993). Gender differences may vary, according to local circumstances, within a region as well as between regions. Nevertheless, in all cultures of the world women have clearly defined roles and responsibilities in a socially defined gender division of labor. Although in some countries these roles are currently being questioned, in much of the world the division of labor by gender continues to determine the differing roles and responsibilities—and therefore the differing needs and interests—of women and men.

Gender roles are not fixed; they change according to social, environmental, economic, and technological trends. Social factors affecting these gender roles and gender-differentiated interests include:

- Institutional arrangements that create and reinforce gender-based constraints or, conversely, foster an environment in which gender disparities can be reduced.
- Sociocultural attitudes and ethnic and class/caste-based obligations that determine men's and women's roles, responsibilities, and decision making functions.
- Religious beliefs and practices that limit women's mobility, social contact, access to resources, and the types of activities they can pursue.
- The formal legal system that reinforces customs and practices giving women inferior legal status in many countries. (Fong, Wakeman, and Bhushan 1996, 2)

Recognizing that the roles of men and women vary across regions, some general statements can be made about women's roles and responsibilities in their households and communities. Women have a triple role, comprising reproductive activities such as childbearing and care, health care for family members, and subsistence agriculture; productive or income-generating activities outside of the home; and community management or community volunteer work. In most countries women bear primary responsibility for child care and housework, much of which consists of unpaid and uncounted work in the economically invisible non-formal sector. At the same time they make a major contribution to the production of food and the provision of energy, water, health care, and family income in developing countries (ECOSOC 2004).

Gender relations are also conditioned by ethnicity, socioeconomic level, and age; that is, a range of factors affects the relations both *among* and *between* women and men. Educated women who live in urban areas with access to some level of discretionary income are in a much better position to take advantage of opportunities such as ICT than either women or men at lower socioeconomic levels who live in rural areas.

In view of the consistently lower status and access to resources of women globally, and their presence in all disadvantaged groups in a population, a strong focus on women is appropriate for and not inconsistent with the gender-and-development approach. When there are such gender-based inequalities, concern turns to correcting them. Nevertheless, it is recognized that equality for women cannot be accomplished without the support and collaboration of men.[2]

Gender Equality, Gender Equity, and Empowerment

Women's empowerment and *gender equality* are separate but closely related concepts. The World Bank and the Canadian International Development Agency (CIDA) use the term *gender equality*. The World Bank defines it in terms of equality under the law, equality of opportunity (including equality of rewards for work and equality in access to human capital and other productive resources that enable opportunity), and equality of voice (the ability to influence and contribute to the development process). In the view of the World Bank, gender equality implies "equivalence in life outcomes for women and men, recognizing their different needs and interests, and requiring a redistribution of power and resources" (World Bank 2001).

CIDA defines gender equality as equal status for women and men, involving equal conditions for both to realize their full human rights and potential to contribute to national, political, economic, social, and cultural development, and to benefit from the results. Gender equality therefore involves equal choice, control, and opportunities around the resources and benefits of development for both men and women. It is also characterized by the "equal valuing by society of both the similarities and differences between women and men, and the varying roles that they play" (CIDA 1999).

Other organizations use the term *gender equity* rather than *gender equality*. Gender equity is a step on the way to gender equality in that it aims at ensuring "fairness" between men and women, to put both in a position of equal opportunities and actions. Gender equity recognizes that women and men have different "needs, preferences, and interests, and that historical and social disadvantages exist which mitigate against equal opportunities and resources for women and men, so that equality of outcomes may necessitate different treatment of men and women" (CIDA 1999). Gender-equity strategies implement measures to help the less advantaged to reach the level of the more advantaged. Gender equality results when, from this situation of equity, all can act for their own interests at the same level.

Empowerment: Key Concepts and Perspectives

Empowerment is a broader term than either gender equality or gender equity. As such, there are several streams of approach, but as Malhotra, Schuler, and Boender (2002) remark, they hold several concepts in common: options, choice, control, and power. These pertain to ability to make decisions and affect events and circumstanc them; benefit from resources and opportunities; exercise control over their own life, body, and resources; and have a say in public life and decision making, all with the result of increasing or achieving autonomy and improving health and well-being.

Agency or *self-efficacy*, terms that come out of the human rights and feminist perspectives, are also commonly used to refer to a process of inner transformation, seen as essential to formulation of choices. Agency consists of the ability of women to define self-interest and choice, and, importantly, to consider themselves able and entitled to make choices. It also involves, according to Naila Kabeer, "thinking outside the system" or challenging the status quo (Kabeer 2001).

Malhotra, Schuler, and Boender also focus on the idea of process or change from a condition of disempowerment. Women become significant actors in the process of change from inequality to equality, so that empowerment becomes a bottom-up rather than a top-down approach (Malhotra, Schuler, and Boender 2002).

More recently, the United Nations Millennium Project Task Force on Gender Equality has suggested that equality in human capabilities is a critical aspect of gender equality, along with equality in opportunity and agency. It refers to basic human abilities as measured through education, health, and nutrition, which might include acquiring the opportunity to read and write, freedom from infectious diseases, and the ability to eat a nutritious diet. The argument is made that "capability" is the most fundamental of all the three domains and is necessary for achieving equality in the other two (Grown, Gupta, and Kes 2005).

The issue of power and power relations between the sexes is addressed to varying extents and in varying ways, but in general refers to the subordination or disadvantaging of women in public and private relationships. The result is a lack of empowerment or disempowerment. The term *power relations* also refers to the active and powerful assertion of dominance by one group over another, which requires forceful and often (but not necessarily) coordinated collective action to overcome. Keller and Mbwewe use this concept in their description of empowerment as "a process whereby women become able to organize themselves to increase their own self-reliance, to assert their independent right to make choices and to control resources which will assist in challenging and eliminating their own subordination" (cited in Malhotra, Schuler, and Boender 2002, 6).

Several categories of approaches to achieving empowerment with and for women can be identified that build on these identified components. We distinguish between two main categories: a focus on action to change political, legal, and sometimes religious systems to promote rights for women in civil and political contexts, and actions at the community or household level to improve women's access to resources and status. The former approach generally consists of collective organized action, while the latter can consist either of individual actions or larger, organized, collective action that is undertaken by women to gain the ability to assert their independent rights to choices and control over resources. Organized, collective action is usually aimed at institutions at local, national, or international levels. The charge has been made that the political/legal empowerment approach tends to be initiated by educated middle-class women based in urban locations and thus has less relevance to poor women living in remote communities. This trend seems to be changing, however, as illustrated by women in the Zapatista movement presented in Chapter 7, who challenge the model of urban, educated women as the actors in collective action for women's empowerment.

Social and economic actions aimed at improving the situation of individual women tend to be focused on economic opportunities including poverty reduction, livelihoods, and improvement of health, food security, and other basic needs as a step to achieving more strategic gender equality goals (see Carr, Chen, and Jhabvala 1996; Bhattacharjea 2005). Individual strategies involve improving women's access to resources, increasing their individual sense of agency, and improving their status in their household or community.

Despite their differences, the two categories of empowerment approach are interrelated. Social and economic empowerment at the local level may lead to actions to assert political and legal empowerment at higher levels, while political and legal advocacy can provide the macro context for social and economic empowerment.

In answer to the questions of how we know when empowerment is achieved and how we measure or assess it, seven main targets or indicators are generally used (Malhotra, Schuler, and Boender 2002; Lopez-Claros and Zahidi 2005). They are presented under the two main categories of socioeconomic and political empowerment.

Socioeconomic empowerment:

- Economic empowerment: participation and opportunity, including control over income and family resources; increased income and access to employment; and participation in the formal economy and work force at higher levels with higher pay.
- Sociocultural empowerment: freedom of movement, lack of discrimination, visibility in public places, and positive media images.
- Familial/personal empowerment, with respect to status and autonomy in the household and family: right to make choices in one's personal life and in one's family; access to reproductive health and family-planning resources; access to sufficient nutrition and health care; safety, security, and integrity.
- Psychological: including self-esteem, self-efficacy, potential for mobilization, sense of inclusion and entitlement by self and others.
- Education: including access to literacy and education at all levels.

Political empowerment:

- Legal empowerment: knowledge of and ability to exercise one's legal rights, community mobilization and enforcement, the existence of laws and legislation supporting women's rights and offering channels to redress violations.
- Political empowerment: knowledge of the political system and participation in it; the right to vote; representation in regional and national governments; and representation of interests in lobbies and interest groups. The goal is equitable representation in decision-making structures, both formal and informal, with women's voices present in the formulation of policies affecting their societies, and, in the longer run, learning, using, and changing the rules of decision making to reflect all groups.

Although these approaches diverge to a certain extent in their focus and implementation, they nevertheless can be complementary and interrelated in effect. More overt and planned coordination between these approaches could allow them to build on each other and contribute to greater overall achievements.

DONOR APPROACHES TO GENDER EQUALITY

Gender Mainstreaming

In recent years gender mainstreaming has become a favored development agency approach to ensuring gender equality in projects. The concept came into prominence at the 1995 United Nations' Conference on
Women held in Beijing. It then came to be adopted by a number of
governments, international organizations, and NGOs, especially by the
United Nations Development Fund for Women (UNIFEM), the ILO,
the European Commission, and the Nordic states. The term derives
from the criticism that prior efforts left women outside of the mainstream. It is an approach to producing policies and processes that benefit men and women equally, through "the systematic integration of
gender equality into all systems and structures, policies, programs, processes and projects, into ways of seeing and doing, into cultures and
their organizations" (Rees 1998).

Gender mainstreaming involves identifying the ways in which existing systems and structures are androcentric—however unintentionally
and however subconsciously—and to neutralize gender bias. Involving
the application of a gender-and-development approach, inequalities
between men and women are analyzed and programs proposed to eliminate these inequalities on a sector-by-sector and issue-by-issue basis
(Derbyshire 2002).

Critiques of gender mainstreaming are emerging which maintain that,
rather than giving front-line attention to gender, it has become a way of
ignoring gender equality: no gender-specific actions are considered necessary because gender is "already" mainstreamed. For example, a gender review at the Norwegian Agency for Development from 1997 to
2004 found that gender issues had not been mainstreamed in its evaluations (Lexow and Hansen 2005). Other problems with this approach
include a tendency to be under resourced and a lack of appropriate training and expertise. Finally, women's equality units tend to get dismantled
in the process of gender mainstreaming (Rees 2002), so there is no quality control or easy access to expert resources.

Poverty Reduction, Gender Equality, and the Millennium Development Goals

The MDGs define the current major international policy approach to
development. Adopted in 2000, the MDGs grew out of an increasing

consensus that previous development strategies of the 1960s, 1970s, and 1980s, which focused on liberalization and structural adjustment, were not achieving expected results. The MDGs represent an attempt to directly confront poverty (see Table 1–1). Each of the goals contains one to two targets and two to seven indicators to measure progress.

Table 1–1. Gender Equality and ICT-related Targets of MDGs

Millennium Development Goal	Targets Directly Related to Gender Equality or ICTs
1. Eradicate extreme poverty and hunger	
2. Achieve universal primary education	Target 3: Ensure that, by 2015, children everywhere, boys and girls alike, will be able to complete a full course of primary schooling.
3 Promote gender equality and empower women	Target 4: Eliminate gender disparity in primary and secondary education, preferably by 2005, and in all levels of education no later than 2015.
4. Reduce child mortality	Target 5: Reduce by two-thirds, between 1990 and 2015, the under-five mortality rate.
5. Improve maternal health	Target 6: Reduce by three-quarters, between 1990 and 2015, the maternal mortality ratio.
6. Combat HIV/AIDS, malaria, and other diseases	
7. Ensure environmental sustainability	
8. Develop a global partnership for development	Target 18: Make available the benefits of new technologies, especially ICTs.

While gender equality is an explicit goal in itself, many argue that gender equality is necessary for achievement of any and all of the MDGs (Grown, Gupta, and Kes 2005; UNDP 2003). However, it continues to be confined mainly to social development approaches—education (particularly primary education); maternal mortality; and HIV/AIDS— which, although undoubtedly important, reflect a limited recognition of the gender components of economic policies and production strategies. As Kabeer argues, "Closing the gender gap in indicators of health and education not only requires better service delivery. It also means increasing women's economic agency and the value they give themselves and are given by their community" (Kabeer 2003, 7; see also Daly 2003).

THE MYTH OF GENDER-NEUTRAL TECHNOLOGIES

How do these discussions and approaches relate to the question of how ICTs can promote gender equality and women's empowerment? How can ICTs act as important catalysts to this end? I start with an examination of the relationship among women, gender, technology, and development. Lessons learned from earlier analyses of women, gender, and technology for development are directly relevant to current discourse around gender and ICTs; the technology past can help us succeed in the knowledge future.

Ester Boserup's ground-breaking work, *Women's Role in Economic Development* (1970), stressed that new technologies introduced in Africa, as well as in other developing areas, were displacing the labor of women. She noted that when a new technology produced income for women, it was often taken over by men. Boserup's research marked the beginning of the intellectual examination of the effects of new technologies on women's work, especially in developing countries, and the opening of debates about gender gaps in technology. It also moved beyond the generally held view that technologies are gender neutral and that their use is equally available to men and women. In the late 1980s Patricia Stamp's *Technology, Gender and Power in Africa* (1989) brought together an analysis of research on women in development, feminist political economy, and the vast literature on technology transfer to examine the relationship between gender and technology in Africa. Her work followed on Boserup, arguing that technologies are not gender neutral but rather value laden from beginning to end, and that most technologies destined for women in Africa were developed by Western men who did not understand the social, economic, or cultural contexts for use of these technologies. Stamp found that gender biases existed in determining who received technologies as well as who received the education, credit, and other resources for technologies. She also noted a tendency to overlook women's technological skills and use of technologies.

Research elsewhere supports these findings: gendered patterns of health, employment, and access to resources and education mean that technology transfer is not a neutral process. Over the last twenty years of technology transfer the level of poverty for women has *increased relative to men*, and men have benefited more than women from technology programs. Most research and development programs from the 1970s through the mid-1990s only partly recognized women's contributions to the development process and the effect of the process on them. As a result, new technologies often had detrimental consequences, not only for the economic security and social status of women and their families, but also on the ability of these programs and projects to meet development objectives (UN Commission on Science and Technology for Development 1995; Paris, Feldstein, and Duron 2001).

A common theme in the literature is that technology should be developed and transferred in ways that empower women to retain control. Conversely, analysis also shows that technology can be a positive force for women. Stamp (1989) noted that when women in Africa participated in technology transfer, they were empowered by the technologies. Studies on the effects of agricultural technologies have indicated that when developed and transferred appropriately, these technologies can be an important tool to empower women. A study of fishpond development controlled by poor women's groups in Bangladesh found that even though there were some problems in the group, members experienced greater mobility, greater likelihood of working for pay, higher off-farm incomes, and better nutritional status than nonmembers. Women cultivating improved vegetables in Bangladesh reported empowerment in dealing with traders and their husbands, increased freedom of movement, freedom from physical violence, and political knowledge and awareness *specifically related to the adoption of the technology*. In other examples we find that when women earn higher incomes as a result of improved technology or techniques, they gain higher status in the home and community, their children receive education, and nutrition levels for both males and females in the family increase (Meinzen-Dick et al. 2003).

The gendered implications of ICTs follow on the earlier analyses of gender and technology. Women continue to benefit less from technology transfer than men. Statistical evidence shows that, except for a handful of countries, women's participation in the knowledge society, particularly in the developing countries of the world, lags behind that of men and does not correlate with the level of Internet penetration in a country (Huyer et al. 2005).[3] This indicates that a series of factors exists that affects the ability of women to use and benefit from ICTs differently from men. These factors are intricately connected with the factors that relate to women's empowerment overall. As Mitter (2005) comments, "It is the same age-old rationale: women's inferior status in society gives them unequal access to all resources, including to ICTs."

The constraints to women's participation in the knowledge society are in many ways a function of human poverty as well as gender equality (Bhattacharjea 2005). The key elements of this are women's lower levels of education, particularly text literacy (females make up two-thirds of the world's 771 million illiterates), as well as their lower rates of computer and technological literacy. Girls are less likely than boys to enroll in math and computer science courses, while sociocultural barriers to the education of girls and women in science, math, and technology further restrict their interaction with technology as well as their entrance into S&T fields. Other factors restricting use of ICTs by women include prevalence of non-local languages; high costs of equipment and access; lack of time resulting from the burden of domestic and productive activities; socioreligious attitudes restricting public participation and travel; predominance of women in rural areas where ICTs are less available; and the lack of information and knowledge that is relevant to local interests and concerns, particularly those of women (Hafkin and Taggart 2001). As Bhattacharjea (2005) remarks, "To put it simply, if we want to extend the benefits of ICTs in a globalised world, we need to understand that women's information, communication, and technology poverty is mediated by other dimensions of her human poverty."

As has been the case with technology transfer in general, ICTs are often considered both socially neutral and gender neutral. It is assumed that no specific actions are needed to ensure that all groups in a society will benefit from their use. However, as with other technologies, ICTs are implemented in a societal context that is neither value free nor independent of the society that adopts or reinvents it. The case of village phone operators in the Grameen Village Phone Project in Bangladesh is an example of the importance of gender strategies to ensure that services will reach all in the community. In this case, the sex of the village phone operator and the physical placement of the phone within a gendered village context either inhibited or improved women's access to phones; placing one in a woman's home made it accessible to other women. When the operators were women, women were much more likely to be users (Richardson, Ramirez, and Haq 2000). Many other examples exist to show that a recognition of gendered trends of use and benefit rarely emerge "naturally" or during the course of implementation if there are no requirements for gender analysis in project proposals or for sex-disaggregated analysis in reporting (Hafkin 2002). Gender-equality reviews of donor-funded ICT projects undertaken by the authors support this finding. Nath discusses the implications of this approach for the development of ICT-enabled knowledge networking in Chapter 8 while Derbyshire notes that "equity outcomes are not achieved unless they are explicitly stated and operationalised through well thought-out procedures" (2002, 10).

CAN ICTS CONTRIBUTE TO WOMEN'S EMPOWERMENT?

It is clear that ICTs can best support gender equality and women's empowerment by serving as tools to encourage and promote a process of change from disempowerment to empowerment; the ability to assume agency and choice in a situation of authentic, positive, and affordable alternatives; and the possession of fundamental human capabilities. For ICTs to promote the empowerment of women, they need to provide opportunity to gain options, choice, control, and power, or the ability to make decisions based on useful information and affect outcomes in one's life. This involves increased confidence or status at a personal level, which also can lead to actions by women to influence larger political and legal systems.

In the particular context of ICT, agency, choice, and capabilities include the ability to assess, manipulate, and make choices from an informed perspective. Information literacy is important—being able to find and use information. Technological literacy also comes into effect, in terms of the comfort with and ability to use and manipulate computers, videos, cell phones, and other forms of ICTs. But for women to be *active* agents in their empowerment in the knowledge society, as a result of independent and informed choices, it is required that women become creators and developers of the technology and the content it carries. *Therefore, a Cyberella approach needs also to promote the ability to access, use, create, and distribute knowledge.* As Warschauer (2003) argues, the issue is not access or availability of ICTs but rather use of the technology for meaningful social practices, which here are viewed as consisting of practices leading to women's economic, social, and potentially, political empowerment.

A number of existing projects provide examples of how ICTs are contributing to women's empowerment in different areas and make the case that ICTs can contribute to women's socioeconomic and political empowerment.

Economic Empowerment

- Grameen Bank Village Pay Phones. Women operators earned approximately US$700 per year, more than twice the annual per capita income in Bangladesh (Richardson, Ramirez, and Haq 2000).
- e-Seva (e-services) of West Godavari District, Andhra Pradesh, India. Eighty Web-enabled rural information kiosks have been established at the mandal (subdistrict) level, run and managed by women from self-help groups. The centers are becoming self-sustaining, and the women operators are earning between 6,000 and 15,000 rupees per month (GKP 2003).
- Farmwise, Malawi. Improved access to information resulted in increased productivity of women farmers. Output was said to more than double, to between ten and fifteen bags of maize per farmer (Nyirenda 2004).
- Putting ICTs in the Hands of the Poor. Datamation Foundation Charitable Trust, the United Nations Educational, Scientific and Cultural Organization (UNESCO), and Babul-Uloom-Madrasa, an orthodox Muslim religious school in India, set up an ICT center for Muslim women to learn vocational skills and acquire information about small businesses and human and legal rights from interactive multimedia packages. Capacity building, marketing, and financial networking supported the women as they engaged in income-generating activities. A local community website, eNRICH,[4] provided a space for basic computer training and recording concerns on health, education, livelihood, and other matters related to the community's needs.
- Homebiz Management, Home-based Profiles, and IT Tips and Tricks. These enable women to work from home, pursue entrepreneurial ventures, and sustain home businesses in Malaysia. A Forum Board facilitates networking and exchange of ideas and actual experiences, while experts in business development and entrepreneurship respond to questions. The eHomemakers network targets low-income women, including unemployed single mothers with young/disabled children, the disabled, and the chronically ill, to work at home.[5]

Sociocultural Empowerment

- Association with technology seems to convey increased social status to women in their communities in certain circumstances. Poor

Bangladeshi women experienced an enhancement of their social status by virtue of privileged access to a means of communications in the Grameen Village Pay Phones program (Aminuzzaman 2002).

- In Seelampur, India, women who had learned computer skills were seen as worldly, as sources of information, and as having mastered a sophisticated technical device. They gained a position in decision making in their family that previously they did not have (Slater and Tacchi 2004).

- Women participating in the M. S. Swaminathan Research Foundation's Village Knowledge Centre in Pondicherry "have acquired some status and standing in the community. Men—farmers, landless laborers, traders—come and ask them for information and they provide the answers. They have set up self-help groups and micro-enterprises. They have taken part in discussions held at our Foundation and answered questions posed by many overseas delegates. Only a few years ago they would not have ventured out of their village unaccompanied by their husbands or in-laws" (UNITeS 2003).

- Online communities in Saudi Arabia have enabled men and women to communicate in new ways while remaining physically segregated. Results of online communication include greater open-mindedness for both women and men, who became more aware of the personal characteristics of individuals within their society and less inhibited about the opposite gender. Online communication "is disrupting long-established traditions, enabling the mixing of members of both sexes, and making people aware of different ways of living" (Al-Saggaf 2004).

- At a computer education center in India, young women were given the opportunity to enter a mixed public space, move freely around their community, express themselves to men and other authority figures, voice criticism and suggestions, gossip, and have fun, and engage in cultural activities of singing, public debates (held at the center), and using pictures and words (on the computer). Each of these steps in the Sitakund culture is a direct challenge to traditional roles and norms (Slater and Tacchi 2004).

- Female graduates of Cisco's Networking Academy Program in least developed countries said that their completion of the program led to greater respect and autonomy in their families (Hafkin 2005).

- Women use ICTs to confront cultural taboos and challenge cultural prescriptions at the local and personal level. They no longer need to limit themselves to the controlled information and social spaces allowed by their society and families. "We get our freedom from the Internet since in our society girls have limited freedom of movement. We are not allowed to go wherever we want. The Internet . . . takes us out to other people, places and other realities. No one controls where we go with Internet. It is for us a way of escaping from our closed society. It is vital to us; it gives us liberty" (Gadio 2001).

- In Iran, blogs have provided an opportunity for women to talk about taboo subjects in their society, such as the role of women, sex, and other social issues (Hermida 2002).

Psychological

- In six case studies of multi-donor ICT projects, women participants emerged from each project with enhanced self-esteem as a result of successfully using the technologies (Hafkin 2002).
- In a self-evaluation of users at the Sitakund ICT center in India, none of the men mentioned any increase in self-confidence, while every woman user identified this as an outcome. One of the users of the center attested: "But among these changes the most significant change in me has been that I previously used to feel some kind of fear to get out of the house alone, and I used to feel diffidence after coming to the center. But now there is not a bit of that previous fear in me" (Slater and Tacchi 2004).
- Women in ICT projects in Afghanistan said that they experienced a reduced sense of isolation and increased self-esteem and empowerment (World Bank 2005).
- In Bolivia, indigenous Aymara women found that the use of computers considerably strengthened their self-esteem and sense of self-worth (Rodriguez 2001).

Education

- In ICT-assisted literacy classes in India, the majority of the students were women, most from socioeconomically disadvantaged communities with very limited previous exposure to ICTs, if any. Participants were eager to learn to use computers because they associated them with income-earning opportunities and continued to use them beyond the courses (Farrell 2004).

- In a study of computers introduced into primary schools in East Africa, it was found that girls used the computers to expand the range of formal and informal education—they were able to obtain information on sexual and reproductive health issues. While 70 percent of boys saw no impact on their self-esteem from the program, 95 percent of the girls said that they gained both confidence and self-esteem (Gadio 2001).
- Studies of distance and e-learning at tertiary levels indicate that women enroll in these courses for reasons of flexibility of schedules, lower overall costs, comfort with the one-on-one teaching and discussions, and to escape feelings of isolation in male-dominated classrooms (see Chapter 4).

Political

- The Women Information and Communications Technology project empowered poor urban women in Nairobi by enabling them to communicate to policymakers. The women acquired a video camera and negotiated to supply one of the leading broadcasting stations in the country with TV news items and video clips. Material covering several incidences of unrest in the settlement were provided to the media and subsequently used as news items.[6]
- Women in the Mpika district of Zambia negotiated with local politicians for material resources through their involvement with radio listening groups (Warnock 2001).
- In Latin America the Internet has become a powerful tool for NGO activism in gender equity. The "new utility" expands the efficacy and reach of advocacy petitions and action campaigns (Friedman 2004).

Legal

- The Pallitathya Help-Line Centre (Call Centre for the Poor and Underprivileged) in Bangladesh hired women in the community as Mobile Operator Ladies to go from door-to-door with a mobile phone to answer women's questions on livelihoods, agriculture, health, and legal rights, while help-desk operators respond to the women's queries with a database-driven software application and the Internet. The mobile operators were consciously given a crucial role as "infomediaries," increasing their self-worth, their potential to earn, and their knowledge about various issues. Female help-desk operators also enhanced their knowledge of issues and considerably improved their communication skills. Women who took advantage of the help-line service experienced a higher self-assessment and realization of their potential and worth in society, increased incomes, and increased authority over spending decisions.[7]

- "Your Lawyer," a CD-ROM produced in Vietnam, explains to women in simple language the legal issues around starting a business, protecting land rights, and getting a divorce.

These examples reflect an approach that concentrates on the empowering aspects of ICTs. At the same time, one cannot lose sight of the fact that there are many ways in which ICTs can be disempowering to women. These include facilitating increased trafficking of women and children and increased and more violent pornography. In Chapter 7 Garrido and Roman provide examples of a phenomenon they call disempowering empowerment, where women in Latin America have become telecenter managers largely because the men who would normally take on such positions have migrated to cities in search of work. This also happens frequently in labor-migration economies of southern Africa, such as Lesotho, Botswana, and Swaziland. Other disempowering examples include employment in low and insecure positions in ICT-based employment, with little decision-making power and vulnerability to exploitation and harassment (see Barry 2005).

AN APPROACH TO GENDER EQUALITY, ICTS, AND EMPOWERMENT[8]

As we have seen, ICTs have the potential to contribute to the empowerment of women in many ways. But in order for this to happen, several interrelated conditions need to be in place. Five basic enabling conditions, combining the range of social, economic, political, and legal approaches to empowerment discussed earlier, are necessary for ICTs to serve as effective tools for empowering women and building gender equality.[9] The identification of enabling conditions also helps to define the knowledge gaps that need to be filled. Each of the conditions listed encompasses both individual and local strategies for women at the local, community level as well as organized and collective action at regional, national, and international levels.[10] The categories are:

1. creation of an *enabling environment* that supports and encourages strategies to promote women's equal access to and opportunity to benefit from ICT projects, as well as creating a regulatory and policy environment which supports women's use of ICTs *(political, legal, economic)*;
2. development of *content* that speaks to women's concerns, reflects their local knowledge, and is of value for their daily lives, business enterprises, and family responsibilities, including information on health, agriculture or other small-scale production, natural-resources management and SMEs *(social and economic)*;
3. support of increased representation of women and girls in S&T *education*, and using ICTs to promote their increased participation in education at all levels *(social and economic)*;
4. promotion of increased *employment* in the IT sector for women, and ICTs to support women's SMEs and income generation *(social and economic)*;
5. implementation of *e-governance* strategies that are accessible to women, and promoting women's lobbying and advocacy activities in support of a range of civil and human rights for women *(social and political)*.

An Enabling Environment for Women's Participation in the Knowledge Society

Women's low rates of Internet access and the emerging results of ICT project assessments indicate that supporting women's increased access to ICTs is an area for attention (Huyer et al. 2005; Hafkin 2002).

Telecommunication policy and regulation are areas where gender equality concerns are generally considered not to apply. This is despite the significant social and gender implications of access and use of ICTs for income generation and the ability of all to participate in the knowledge society. The question of how women's needs are relevant to regulation is not clearly seen if the understanding of regulation is limited to resolving licensing, spectrum issues, competition acts, and telecommunication codes. In such a framework "women's issues" are not seen as falling within the scope of government interest. However, when long-term goals are taken into account, such as providing connectivity, information, education, consumer protection, poverty reduction, and resolving market failures, then the inclusion of social concerns becomes relevant (Huyer and Sikoska 2002). Similarly, ground-level approaches to technology choice and implementing technologies in line with social practices and infrastructure conditions are also part of an enabling environment.

A recent Asia-Pacific Development Information Programme (APDIP) review of research on the role of ICTs in poverty reduction since 2002 makes the distinction between two categories of conditions required for ICTs to be effective: government interventions and program implementation. A set of conditions was identified as prerequisites for ICTs to play this role at each level. The conditions for government interventions include reform of public services for e-government; conducive telecommunications regulations and environment; decentralized decision-making; complementary infrastructure; education; and monitoring and evaluation. On the side of program implementation, a series of conditions include mainstreaming or embedding of ICTs; creativity and innovation in program design; partnerships; local entrepreneurship; content development; participation and ownership by the poor; and evaluation (APDIP 2005).

APDIP (2005) further notes that there is little discussion of the implications for poverty reduction for the evolution and convergence possibilities of ICTs. A focus on computers, Internet, and telephones mean that little attention is paid to mapping applications onto the most suitable technologies, new or old, existing or emerging.

This approach can include community access centers or telecenters as well as blended technologies. Telecenters are widely promoted as a low-cost and effective way to provide accessible community access to ICTs, although preliminary evidence suggests that telecenters in developing countries will not be effective in helping women gain access to better economic, educational, and other opportunities unless specific women-targeted strategies and services are implemented (see Etta and Parvyn-Wamahiu 2003).

Blended technologies can provide technologies that are adapted to local conditions and requirements, such as unreliable electricity or low literacy rates, and allow sharing, packaging, and presentation of information in ways that women understand and appreciate. CEEWA (Council for Empowerment for Women of Africa)-Uganda uses laptops, the Internet, e-mail, scanners, telephones, binding and faxing services, photocopiers, CDs with audio-visual material, radio, and video in its women's training program on best practices in agriculture. Radio has proven to be an important communications technology for women; it does not require literacy, it is affordable, and women can work while listening.

Radio is used for literacy, information on food production, and making women's concerns known to local policymakers (see Girard 2003).

Analysis of telecommunications policy and regulation and advocacy for inclusion of gender-equality concerns are important elements in this category, which Sonia Jorge addresses in more detail in Chapter 3.

Areas for more work include greater in-depth analysis of the socio-economic relations and environments that impede adoption of ICT for poverty reduction; analysis of existing models of ICT use to reduce poverty; clearer definition of the facilitating conditions in which ICTs will be effective; monitoring the use of telecenters and other kinds of community access points by women; development and dissemination of models for blended technologies that are appropriate to local conditions and educational levels of the users; comparison of women-friendly training programs; and evaluation of ICT projects concerning gendered opportunities to benefit and lessons learned.

Appropriate and Relevant Content

More research is needed on identifying, developing, and disseminating women-appropriate content, that is, content that is developed by women and reflects their knowledge and perspectives; increases their capabilities and helps them more effectively fulfill their daily tasks and responsibilities; increases their well-being and that of their families; and generates income. Access to information in general contributes to women's income-earning capacity—even access to reproductive health can increase women's productivity (ILO 2001; Rodriguez 2001).

This is an area where strategically allocated resources and support could produce enormous benefits. Particularly important is the recognition and valuing of women's local knowledge.

Further research and analysis is needed on how ICTs can be used to ensure that women's knowledge is not lost; that ICTs ensure that women benefit from the proceeds (financial and otherwise) of this knowledge; and that dissemination of women's knowledge is beneficial in ways that do not disempower them or allow the theft of this knowledge.

Content to Support Women's Productive and Reproductive Activities

In order for ICTs to contribute to poverty eradication, it is important that they help women fulfill their daily productive and reproductive activities, which support the health and well-being of their families and communities. There are several sectors in which ICTs can make an important contribution that have been comparatively overlooked to date, including provision of health information targeted to women; support for women's agricultural, food production, and related natural-resources management activities; and increased access to education for women and girls.

Information for Women as Health Practitioners

The use of ICTs by health practitioners in developing countries is well established. Satellife,[11] for example, provides health information and connections to colleagues in other parts of the world for developing-country health professionals.

While this kind of project shows how ICT can contribute to improving health conditions in developing countries, the provision of health information to women directly has been given less attention. It is unknown to what extent women benefit from health information made available through ICTs. How many doctors and health workers participating in these programs are women? Further, how many women on the ground gain access to this information? Comparatively few ICT-based health-information projects to date have targeted women users, despite the fact that they are the primary users of health information. As found by the AfriAfya health information initiative in Kenya, health information made available is often not easily understandable at the local level (Nyamai 2002). The Association of Uganda Women Medical Doctors has begun a pilot project to disseminate electronically information on reproductive health to women-oriented NGOs for advocacy and personal use. Women constituted a significant number of visitors to the Technology Access Community Centre in Egypt who sought health-related information they were unable to find elsewhere. The presence of women staff encouraged rural women to travel a long distance to access the center and health-related information in Arabic on immunizations, breast cancer, breast feeding, and family planning (Nath 2001).[12]

The use of personal digital assistants by health workers is another area with much promise. Several examples indicate that if implemented in a gender-sensitive manner, they can act as empowering tools as well as improve health care in rural areas. In rural Uganda midwives use them to learn of illness in other communities before it arrives in their home community; send data on illness in their home community for analysis and specialist assistance; and access information on medical conditions, expanding their own knowledge. The technology not only improves health conditions in the local area but also contributes to the increasing education and status of the health worker who uses it (Fuchs 2005).[13]

Software that gathers health information in new ways and presents new kinds of health-related information can make an important contribution to the way women's health concerns are perceived and addressed. For example, the Tanzania Essential Health Interventions Project worked with rural health offices and policymakers to draw out and present raw data on the health status of rural populations. Planners were able to focus on curative and preventative interventions to identify locally important diseases so that resource allocation matched more closely the actual prevailing burden of disease. Infant and child mortality rates have decreased substantially (Reid 2002).

Knowledge gaps include better understanding of which models of information and IT transfer are most effective in getting health information to women users. What are the most effective strategies for reaching young women and men regarding reproductive health and HIV/ AIDS issues with ICTs?[14] What kind of health information do women find most useful? What format and approach to content is most effective? Which software and ICT-based data-collection frameworks can increase the accuracy of morbidity and mortality assessments for decision makers on health issues of importance to women?

Women as Food Producers and Natural Resources Managers

Women are responsible for 60–80 percent of food production across the developing world and for half of the food production worldwide. Nevertheless, they do not tend to own or control key resources, such as land, credit, technological productivity-enhancing inputs, and services on which their agricultural activities depend. The effects on gender relations of ICTs are particularly important with respect to agricultural production, because subsistence agriculture remains an important part of many developing country economies. Agriculture also provides, both directly and indirectly, an opportunity for women to improve nutrition and increase income for themselves and their families (Carr and Huyer 2001).

Mobile telephones allow farmers to verify prices, arrange transport, and communicate with distributors and clients. Rural radio programs use e-mail, fax, and mobile telephone to enable sharing and dissemination of agriculture-related information. For example, the Zambia Federation of African Media Women facilitates advocacy and communication between farmer radio-listening groups and politicians through these technologies.

Important knowledge gaps include how best to support the creation and exchange of local and locally relevant information by rural women themselves, or information customized to their needs, language, literacy abilities, and interests, and how to synthesize existing and disparate work and research on gender, ICTs, and agriculture for rural development (Hambly et al. 2002).

Education

ICTs can promote increased opportunities for education for both females and males at all levels, from primary education to adult distance learning. Computers and other ICTs, such as video and radio, in schools can promote access to learning for girls and boys in remote regions and increase the quality of learning through expanded curriculum and teaching resources. Distance education through ICT can provide a real opportunity for women and girls to overcome many educational obstacles. The flexibility of access and study times and the potential to reach women in rural areas can make this a very positive educational approach for women and those living in remote rural areas.

At the same time, for women to be active participants in, creators of, and contributors to the knowledge society, it is important that women enter and succeed in technical education at all levels. This is an area where much more work and support is needed (see Chapters 4 and 5 for further discussion on ICT-enabled education).

Promoting Employment and Income Generation for Women

ICTs can support the employment and income generation of women in several ways: they can provide increased opportunities for employment in the IT sector in call centers, data processing, and similar enterprises (see Mitter 2003; 2005). They can support women's professional activities through provision of new sources of employment, flexible work schedules, and telework. At the same time, they support women's SMEs and other economic activities through access to information and services and development of small ICT-based enterprises. The use of ICTs as a tool for production also needs more attention. Women continue to lack access to the technologies that could help them to improve farm yields and to increase the quality and diversity of their non-farm economic activities.

Important areas of research include the relation of telework to career advancement, rate of pay, and work performance of women; the quality and sustainability of work in new institutions such as call centers; models for telecommunications policy and infrastructure development that will support small-scale IT-based and IT-enabled businesses in both urban and rural areas; collection and assessment of case studies of ICTs for women's micro and SMEs, including use of ICTs for business training and development; expanding connections to producers and customers; IT equipment as a basis for income generation; strategies to provide women with information on international markets, e-commerce techniques, and practices, international and regional trade policies, and how their business can benefit (Mitter 2003).

E-governance, Networking, and Lobbying

The use of ICTs to promote e-governance, especially at the local level, is undoubtedly an important enabling condition. The ability to influence external decisions that affect our lives is a sign of empowerment. Women face more barriers and restrictions than men in influencing governance at local and national levels. ICT-enabled governance approaches can facilitate the direct participation of women in the governance of their societies, including in areas where they have previously been insufficiently engaged. Further, these new models can lead to more interactive forms of communication, characterized by greater transparency and accountability, with officials in local governance. This can occur

- by bringing improved access to government services, in that services available online do not require either extensive travel or representation of women by family members.
- by providing improved and increased interaction with government officials and local electoral representatives, leading to greater accountability, responsiveness, and transparency.
- by networking with advocacy groups and organizations regarding issues of interest and concern, both locally and across regional and national borders.

- by making possible increased public profiling of local level officials and policies, which increases the accountability of public officials.

Work on the use of ICTs to promote collective organizing and advocacy for the political, legal, and rights empowerment of women is well
represented in the literature at large. Some examples, in addition to the
ones in this volume, include Martinez and Reilly (2002), the work of the
Association for Progressive Communications Women's Networking
Support Program (Villaneuva 2000), and Harcourt (1999).

CONCLUSION: TURNING CINDERELLA INTO CYBERELLA

Rosser's theory of phases of gender and ICT inclusion is useful in de-
scribing the stages that women pass through in order to experience
empowerment through the use of new information technologies. In the
first stage the absence of women's concerns and presence from the IT
sector are not noted. In the second stage women's issues and concerns
are "added on" to existing structures and designs but are seen as problems or anomalies that deviate from the norms of ICT. A major step
toward empowerment occurs when women are seen as workers, users,
and designers of ICTs. The final stage is the full inclusion of women in
all these aspects (Rosser 2005).

Unfortunately, in most countries of the world, and particularly in
developing countries, far from being able to exploit the power of the
technology for their empowerment, women are still at the first stage of
inclusion, with their absence not noted. This absence is borne out both
by their invisibility in statistics and indicators and in results of reviews
of major donor-funded ICT projects undertaken by the author and editor.

Applications of ICTs for social development are receiving attention
by both multilateral agencies and NGOs, as is ICT-supported networking and advocacy for women's political and human rights.[15] But the use
of ICTs to support women's social and economic empowerment at both
the local and individual levels is less understood and promoted. Funding assistance and credit for women's social and economic development
tend to be concentrated in sectors such as literacy or health and fertility
programs (targeted at women), for example, while projects to make agricultural information available through the Internet and other ICTs

tend to focus on male farmers. Few donors are entering the arena of enterprise training for women or investment in ICT use by women that goes beyond the establishment of public access centers.

But ICTs provide the base for an increasingly pervasive knowledge society—that is, a society characterized by the creation and exchange of knowledge and information. If women do not have the ability to develop, use, and access knowledge as well as the technologies that carry this knowledge, they will lose an important resource for their own and their communities' development. We need more Cyberellas if we are to have an knowledge society that addresses the social, environmental, and economic well-being of all.

I suggest that the centrality of women to poverty reduction and social development requires a widening of our approaches, both to ICT for development and to gender and development, in order to understand the broader range of uses that can benefit women and the contributions that women can make to the development and application of ICT systems. New approaches are needed also to widen the range of partners in this endeavor; governments and donor agencies must be involved, but also the private sector and the NGO community.

The Cyberella approach to ICTs and development includes gender equality and women's empowerment, while recognizing that women's empowerment includes the contributions that ICTs can make to social and economic development.

NOTES

[1] We use the term *political empowerment* to refer to actions taken to address institutional and personal politics, including civil and human rights and related legal mechanisms.

[2] There are cases where men or boys are disadvantaged in comparison with women. Decreasing school enrollments of boys in several regions and their susceptibility to violence as related to social exclusion, unemployment, and curtailed educational opportunities are examples (Barker 2005).

[3] For example, in some countries with high levels of Internet penetration, such as the United States and Canada, usage rates for women and men are roughly equal, but in Germany, the UK, France, and Norway women make up less than 40 percent of Internet users. Conversely, some countries with very low overall Internet penetration rates do not have a gender divide to the same extent. In Mongolia, the Philippines, and Thailand, female ICT use exceeds male (Huyer et al. 2005).

[4] http://enrich.nic.in.

⁵ http://www.ehomemakers.net/en/index.php.

⁶ www.itdg.org/docs/shelter/wuf04_kenya_wict.pdf.

⁷ http://www.dnet-bangladesh.org/achievements.html.

⁸ This section builds on previous work for the Gender Advisory Board, UNCSTD (see http://gab.wigsat.org/policy.htm).

⁹ This approach is inspired by the UNDP model for mainstreaming ICTs in the MDGs, which combines poverty reduction, education, health, environment, and gender equality in four main categories of activity: (1) creating economic opportunities and contributing to poverty reduction; (2) managing the processes of providing basic services (e.g., health care, education) at lower cost and with greater coverage; (3) facilitating access to information and the involvement of stakeholders through greater transparency and support to networking at every stage; and (4) enhancing the capacity to measure, monitor, and report progress on the goals and strategize (UNDP 2001).

¹⁰ Political-empowerment approaches, in the sense of advocating that governments set gender-appropriate policies and incentives, apply to all categories. The empowerment approaches related to each category are set in italics and inserted in parentheses.

¹¹ http://www.satellife.org.

¹² http://www.auwmd.interconnection.org/.

¹³ Other studies, however, have noted the negative gender effects of providing such technologies only to female or male field workers (see Hafkin 2002).

¹⁴ For a recent assessment of the use of ICTs for mitigating HIV/AIDS in Southern Africa, see SPIDER 2005.

¹⁵ It should be noted, however, that the percentage of official development assistance for ICT infrastructure has actually decreased over the last fifteen years, from $1.2 billion in 1990 to $194 million in 2002. Over the same period aid to the communications sector dropped from 4.5 percent of all official development assistance to 0.16 percent (DAC 2005).

REFERENCES

Al-Saggaf, Yeslam. 2004. The effect of online community on offline community in Saudi Arabia. *Electronic Journal of Information Systems in Developing Countries* 16, no. 2, 1–16. http://www.is.cityu.edu.hk/research/ejisdc/vol16/v16r2.pdf (accessed 2 December 2005).

Aminuzzaman, M. 2002. Cellular phones in rural Bangladesh: A study of the village pay phone of Grameen Bank. Univ. of Dhaka.

APDIP (Asia-Pacific Development Information Programme). 2005. ICT for poverty reduction: Necessary but not sufficient. APDIP e-Note 6. http://www.apdip.net/apdipenote/6.pdf (accessed 30 November 2005).

Barker, Gary T. 2005. *Dying to be men: Youth, masculinity and social exclusion.* London: Routledge.

Barry, Idrissa. 2005. Pressions sur les filles des cybercafés. *L'Evénement*. 29 January. http://www.lefaso.net/article.php3?id_article=5738 (accessed 21 March 2005).

Bhattacharjea, Roma. 2005. Achieving the MDGs: Overcoming women's human poverty. 18 August. http://www.digitalopportunity.org/article/view/117343/ (accessed 5 December 2005).

Boserup, Ester. 1970. *Woman's role in economic development*. London: St. Martin's Press.

Carr, Marilyn, Martha Chen, and Renana Jhabvala. 1996. *Speaking out: Women's economic empowerment in South Asia*. London: Intermediate Technology Publications.

Carr, Marilyn, and Sophia Huyer. 2001. Information and communications technologies: A priority for women in developing countries. *Gender, Technology, and Development* 6, no. 1.

CIDA (Canadian International Development Agency). 1999. Policy on gender equality. Gatineau, Canada.

DAC (Development Assistance Committee). 2005. Financing ICTs for development efforts of DAC members: Review of recent trends of ODA and its contribution. Report to the UN Task Force on Financial Mechanisms for ICT for Development, OECD. http://www.oecd.org/dataoecd/41/45/34410597.pdf (accessed 2 December 2005).

Daly, John. 2003. ICT, gender equality, and empowering women. 9 July. http://www.developmentgateway.org (accessed 27 March 2005).

Derbyshire, Helen. 2002. *Gender manual: A practical guide for development policy makers and practitioners*. London: Department for International Development.

ECOSOC (United Nations Economic and Social Council). 2004. Promoting the application of science and technology to meet the development goals contained in the Millennium Declaration. Report of the Secretary-General to the Seventh Session of the Commission on Science and Technology for Development. 24–28 May.

Etta, Florence Ebam, and Sheila Parvyn-Wamahiu, eds. 2003. *The experience with community telecentres*. Vol. 2, *Information and Communication Technologies for Development in Africa*. Ottawa: IDRC/CODESRIA.

Farrell, Glen. 2004. *ICT and Literacy: Who benefits? Experience from Zambia and India*. Vancouver: Commonwealth of Learning.

Fong, Monica S., Wendy Wakeman, and Amjana Bhushan. 1996. *Toolkit on gender in water and sanitation*. Gender Toolkit Series no. 2. Washington, DC: World Bank.

Friedman, Elisabeth Jay. 2004. The reality of virtual reality: The Internet's impact with gender equality advocacy communities in Latin America. http://www.ssrc.org/programs/itic/publications/friedman.pdf (accessed 2 November 2005).

Fuchs, Richard. 2005. How will it help Veronica . . . ? In *Access, empowerment and governance: Creating a world of equal opportunities with ICT*, ed. Rinalia Abdul Rahim, Daniele Waldburger, and Gabriele Siegenthaler Muinde. Kuala Lumpur: Global Knowledge Partnership. http://www.globalknowledge .org (accessed 27 November 2005).

Gadio, Coumba Mar. 2001. Exploring the gender impact of World Links. Washington, DC: World Links.

Girard, Bruce, ed. 2003. *The one to watch: Radio, new ICTs, and interactivity*. Rome: Food and Agriculture Organization. http://comunica.org/1-2-watch/ (accessed 22 July 2003).

GKP (Global Knowledge Partnership). 2003. Youth, poverty, gender: ICT for development success stories. http://www.globalknowledge.org/ gkps_portal/index.cfm?menuid=201&parentid=179 (accessed 2 December 2005).

Grown, Caren, Geeta Rao Gupta, and Aslihan Kes. 2005. *Taking action: Achieving gender equality and empowering women*. UN Millennium Project Task Force on Gender Equality and Empowering Women. London: Earthscan.

Hafkin, Nancy J. 2002. Are ICTs gender neutral? A gender analysis of six case studies of multi-donor ICT projects. INSTRAW Virtual Seminar Series on Gender and ICTs. Seminar One: Are ICTs Gender Neutral? http:// www.un-instraw.org/en/docs/gender_and_ict/Hafkin.pdf (accessed 30 November 2005).

———. 2005. Community impact assessment of the Cisco/CLI Gender Initiative: Synthesis of country case studies.

Hafkin, Nancy J., and Nancy Taggart. 2001. *Gender, information technology and developing countries: An analytical assessment*. Washington, DC: USAID.

Hambly, Helen Odame, Nancy Hafkin, Gesa Wesseler, and Isolina Boto. 2002. Gender and agriculture in the information society. ISNAR Briefing Paper 55. International Service for Agricultural Research. September.

Harcourt, Wendy, ed. 1999. *Women@internet*. London: Zed.

Hermida, Alfred. 2002. Hindi chatbot breaks new ground. *BBC News Online*. 27 August. http://news.bbc.co.uk/1/hi/technology/2209775.stm (accessed 2 December 2005).

Huyer, Sophia, Nancy Hafkin, Heidi Ertl, and Heather Dryburgh. 2005. Women in the information society. In *From the digital divide to digital opportunities: Measuring infostates for development*, ed. G. Sciadis. Montreal: Orbicom. http://www.orbicom.uqam.ca/orbi_info/vol03_no13/tire_en.html (accessed 22 November 2005).

Huyer, Sophia, and Tatiana Sikoska. 2002. INSTRAW virtual seminar series on gender and information and communication technologies. Presented at the UN Division for the Advancement of Women Expert Group Meeting on ICTs and Their Impact on and Use as an Instrument for the Advancement and Empowerment of Women. Seoul, Korea, 11–14 November. http://www.un-instraw.org/en/docs/gender_and_ict/Synthesis_paper.pdf (accessed 10 November 2005).

ILO (International Labour Organization). 2001. *World employment report: Life at work in the information economy.* Geneva: ILO.

Kabeer, Naila. 2001. Reflections on the measurement of women's empowerment. In *Discussing women's empowerment: Theory and practice.* SIDA Studies No. 3. Stockholm: Novum Grafiska AB.

————. 2003. *Gender mainstreaming in poverty eradication and the Millennium Development Goals.* London: Commonwealth Secretariat.

Lexow, J., and S. Hansen. 2005. Gender and development: A review of evaluation reports 1997–2004. Norwegian Agency for Development Cooperation, Oslo. http://www.eldis.org (accessed 30 November 2005).

Lopez-Claros, Augusto, and Saadia Zahidi. 2005. Women's empowerment: Measuring the global gender gap. Geneva: World Economic Forum. http://www.weforum.org/pdf/Global_Competitiveness_Reports/Reports/gender_gap.pdf (accessed 5 August 2005).

Malhotra, Anju, Sidney Ruth Schuler, and Carol Boender. 2002. Measuring women's empowerment as a variable in international development. Commissioned by the Gender and Development Group, World Bank. http://www.aed.org/LeadershipandDemocracy/upload/MeasuringWomen.pdf (accessed 2 December 2005).

Mansell, Robin, and Uta Wehn. 1998. *Knowledge societies: Information technology for sustainable development.* Oxford: Oxford Univ. Press.

Martinez, Juliana, and Katherine Reilly. 2002. Looking behind the Internet: Empowering women for public policy advocacy in Central America. Background paper, UN/INSTRAW Virtual Seminar Series on Gender and ICTs. Seminar Four: ICTs as Tools for Bridging the Digital Gender Gap and Women's Empowerment, 2–14 September. http://www.un-instraw.org/en/docs/gender_and_ict/Martinez.pdf (accessed 30 November 2005).

Meinzen-Dick, Ruth, Michelle Adato, Lawrence Haddad, and Peter Hazell. 2003. *Impacts of agricultural research on poverty: Findings of an integrated economic and social analysis.* FCND Discussion Paper 164. International Food Policy Research Institute. Washington, DC.

Mitter, Swasti. 2003. Globalisation and ICT: Employment opportunities for women. Prepared for the Gender Advisory Board, UN Commission on Science and Technology for Development. http://gab.wigsat.org/policy.htm (accessed 30 November 2005).

————. 2005. Interview on ICT and gender. 21 October. Development Gateway. http://topics.developmentgateway.org/gender/rc/ItemDetail.do~1049577 (accessed 23 October 2005).

Moser, Caroline. 1993. *Gender, planning and development: Theory, practice and training.* New York: Routledge.

Nath, Vikas. 2001. Technology access community centres (TACCs): Evaluation mission report. United Nations Volunteers EGY/99/V01. http://www.unites.org/html/resource/knowledge/taccs.htm (accessed 5 December 2005).

Nyamai, Caroline. 2002. Harnessing ICTs for community health: Lessons from the AfriAfya initiative. Presentation at workshop on Exploring the Role for ICTs in Health. CIDA. Ottawa. 5 December.

Nyirenda, Bessie. 2004. Malawi: Farmwise. *ICT Update*, no. 21 (October). http://ictupdate.cta.int/index.php/article/articleview/366/1/69/ (accessed 2 December 2005).

Paris, Thelma R., Hilary Sims Feldstein, and Guadalupe Duron. 2001. Technology. In Empowering women to achieve food security. 2020 Focus, no. 6. August. http://www.ifpri.org/2020/focus/focus06/focus06_05.htm (accessed 2 December 2005).

Rees, Teresa. 1998. *Mainstreaming equality in the European Union*. London: Routledge.

———. 2002. Gender mainstreaming: Misappropriated and misunderstood? Paper presented to Department of Sociology, Univ. of Sweden. http://www.sociology.su.se/cgs/ReesPaper.doc (accessed 24 October 2005).

Reid, Graham. 2002. Entry points for ICTs in the health sector: Practical experience from Tanzania. Presentation at the Seminar on Exploring the Role for ICTs in Health. CIDA. Ottawa. 5 December.

Richardson, Don, Ricardo Ramirez, and Moinul Haq. 2000. Grameen Telecom's VillagePhone programme in rural Bangladesh: A multi-media case study. Telecommons Development Group. Final Report. http://www.telecommons.com/villagephone/index.html (accessed 2 December 2005).

Rodriguez, Nidia Bustillos. 2001. ICTs for the empowerment of indigenous women in Bolivia: An experience in Omak. http://www.eldis.org/fulltext/ict_bolivia.doc (accessed 1 April 2005).

Rosser, Sue V. 2005. Global issues and actions in academia. Presentation to International Symposium on Women and ICT. 11 June. Univ. of Maryland, Baltimore County.

Slater, Don, and Jo Tacchi. 2004. *Research on ICT innovations for poverty reduction*. New Delhi: UNESCO. http://cirac.qut.edu.au/ictpr/downloads/research.pdf (accessed 2 December 2005).

SPIDER (Swedish Program for ICT in Developing Regions). 2005. ICT for mitigating HIV/AIDS in Southern Africa. Stockholm.

Stamp, Patricia. 1989. *Technology, gender and power in Africa*. Ottawa: International Development Research Centre.

UN Commission on Science and Technology for Development. 1995. Gender Working Group. Introduction. In *Missing links: Gender equity in science and technology for development*. Ottawa: IDRC and Intermediate Technology Publications.

UNDP (United Nations Development Programme). 2001. *Human development report: Making new technologies work for human development*. New York: UNDP.

———. 2003. *Millennium Development Goals: National reports—A look through a gender lens*. May. http://www.undp.org/gender/docs/ResourceGuideGenderThemeGroups_eng.pdf (accessed 5 December 2005).

UNITeS (United Nations Information Technology Services). 2003. Information Village Research Project—India. http://www.unites.org/cfapps/WSIS/story.cfm?Sid=2 (accessed 2 December 2005).

Villaneuva, Pi. 2000. *Women in sync—Toolkit for electronic networking*. Association for Progressive Communications Women's Networking Support Programme (APCWNSP).

Warnock, Kitty. 2001. DTR radio listening clubs. Zambia: Impact Evaluation Report. For Panos Southern Africa. http://www.comminit.com/pdf/zambiaDTR.pdf (accessed 2 December 2005).

Warschauer, Mark. 2003. *Technology and social inclusion: Rethinking the digital divide*. Cambridge, MA: The MIT Press.

World Bank. 2001. *Engendering development: Through gender equality in rights, resources, and voice*. World Bank Policy Research Report. Oxford: Oxford Univ. Press.

World Bank. 2005. ICTs and economic empowerment of women in South Asia. Gender Digital Divide Seminar. 2 March. http://web.worldbank.org/WBSITE/EXTERNAL/TOPICS/EXTGENDER/0,,contentMDK:20363909~menuPK:489311~pagePK:148956~piPK:216618~theSitePK:336868,00.html (accessed 2 December 2005).

2

Women, Gender, and ICT Statistics and Indicators

Nancy J. Hafkin

IMPORTANCE OF GENDER AND ICT STATISTICS AND INDICATORS

A major prerequisite for discussing ICTs for women's empowerment in developing countries is having clear knowledge of their situation. Data are needed to determine whether and how ICTs affect men and women differently. What is the situation of women and ICTs in developing countries with regard to access, use, and impact of ICTs? Without the data to answer this question, the situation of over 50 percent of the world's people with respect to these questions may be overlooked. The collection and analysis of information on the differential impact of ICT on men and women are necessary prerequisites to the achievement of a globally equitable information society.

Unfortunately, we know very little about the situation of women and ICTs in developing countries because in many cases the data—sex-disaggregated statistics and gender indicators on ICTs in developing countries—are not there. This chapter surveys the quantitative data situation on women and gender with respect to ICTs (primarily in developing countries), investigates the problems that arise from this lack of data, and presents some current attempts to remedy the problem. It concludes with some recommendations for further action.

To Inform Policy: Without Data, There Is No Visibility

The major reason for collecting and disseminating ICT statistics and indicators by sex is to inform policy and to set policy goals. Observation

49

and anecdotal evidence have identified a gender component to the digital divide in several developed and many more developing countries, but there is little data to document it. The paucity of data makes it difficult, if not impossible, to make the case to policymakers for the inclusion of gender issues in ICT policies, plans, and strategies. As the UNDP puts it, "Without data, there is no visibility; without visibility, there is no priority" (cited in Huyer and Westholm 2000). The Measuring the Digital Divide project also put it succinctly: "Comprehensive ICT data with a gender dimension across a large number of countries do not currently exist" (Huyer et al. 2005, 137). WSIS in its first phase (Geneva, December 2003) recognized this gap and recommended corrective action:

> Gender-specific indicators on ICT use and needs should be developed, and measurable performance indicators should be identified to assess the impact of funded ICT projects on the lives of women and girls. (WSIS 2003, no. 28d)[1]

Regrettably, although the WSIS Plan of Action cited above talks about gender analysis being included in a digital divide index and the statistics generated to set up the index, the Plan of Action makes no reference to the collection of sex-disaggregated data, which are the basis for developing gender-specific indicators, including project-level performance indicators. It is the lack of data disaggregated by sex that makes it impossible at present to assemble gender-specific indicators of ICT in developing countries.

In *From the Digital Divide to Digital Opportunities* (Sciadas 2005) the followup report on the digital divide index by Orbicom (the International Network of UNESCO Chairs in Communications),[2] the problem is expressed thusly:

> Much remains to be done in order to understand better why gender gaps exist and why they matter, as well as to initiate actions as to how best to close the gender digital gaps and how this links to more general disadvantages facing women. To this end, proper quantification and analysis become critical. Such efforts, however, continue to be hindered by a dearth of adequate and reliable statistical information. Much like the digital divide, a statistical divide exists where the need is greatest—in developing nations. (Huyer et al. 2005, 194)

Project-level qualitative data has established that ICTs are not gender neutral. ICTs affect men and women differentially, and in almost all cases women have many disadvantages that result in their having less access to and use of the media (see Hafkin 2002; Hafkin and Jorge 2002). The policy implication of this is that unless special interventions are made, most women will not benefit from the information society to the same extent as men. This situation is most sharply felt in developing countries.

If ICTs were gender neutral, affecting men and women equitably, then special attention to women would not be necessary. Nor would sex-disaggregated statistics be needed for policy making. As ICTs are not gender equal, both data and special attention are needed. Without both, women will continue to have fewer opportunities to benefit from the myriad possibilities of the information age.

Data are needed both at micro (project) and macroeconomic levels. At the project level the major reason for collecting sex-disaggregated data is to ascertain if men and women are benefiting differently from project interventions and to take corrective action if this turns out to be the case. At macroeconomic levels it is needed for ICT planning, policy, and strategies. Unfortunately, neither national-level nor project-level sex-disaggregated data are being collected regularly in most countries of the world.

The paucity of sex-disaggregated information on the information society, the norm in developing countries, reflects the more general dearth of statistical information on women's activities across all sectors that might lead to an improved understanding of the "different worlds men and women live in" in terms of access to education, work, health, personal security, and leisure time (United Nations 1995, xvii).

OFFICIAL STATISTICS AND INDICATORS ON ICT

Michael Minges explains why there is so little sex-disaggregated data on ICT use:

> First many government organizations do not collect national ICT statistics in a consistent and regular manner. Of those government agencies that compile [ICT] statistics, most do not provide a breakdown by gender. Second, traditional ICT statistics are either obtained from telecommunication organizations

> (e.g. telephones) or estimated based on shipment data (e.g. personal computers). These organizations have their own operational or analytical reasons for maintaining the data, and gender is not one of them. (Minges 2002)

The major sources of sex-differentiated statistics and gender indicators on women and gender and ICT are official government statistics, for a few countries, and market research surveys, for a larger number of countries where Internet commerce is already significant or expected to be so shortly.

As with statistics and indicators in general, the collection of sex-disaggregated statistics is more developed in rich countries than in poor countries. Where the gender digital divide is generally thought to be most marked, virtually no official statistics are available. It is also in these countries that the digital divide is hardest to document. The few countries that collect sex-disaggregated ICT statistics are typically countries where Internet penetration is high and the gender digital divide tends to be the least marked. The United States, Canada, Hong Kong, Thailand, Iceland, Sweden, Chile, Singapore, Finland, Ireland, and Denmark all collect sex-disaggregated ICT usage statistics. In all of these countries the percentage of female Internet users as a percentage of total Internet users is 45 percent or more. In most African countries, where such data are not collected by official statistics sources, estimates of female Internet use as a percentage of total use are 25 percent or less.

Among the major market-research firms engaged in sex-differentiated data collection are Ipsos-Reid, ComScore Media Metrix, and Neilsen/NetRatings. However, all of these firms carry out their research in a limited number of developed countries and in those developing countries with major markets, such as India and China.

ITU Activities in Sex-Disaggregated Statistics

Until 2003 the only sex-disaggregated ICT data that the International Telecommunication Union (ITU) published was the percentage of female employees in telecommunications administrations. This in itself was a relatively recent addition to the ITU's annual questionnaire. Only one-third of all countries supplied these data, and a number of developed nations, including France, Germany, Japan, and the United States, did not do so. However, these data are not very significant because they simply reveal that in most countries the majority of positions within the public telephone companies—telephone operators—are held by women. The percentage of female personnel among telecommunications staff is not an indicator of gender equality in employment in the telecommunications or the ICT industry as a whole. Many of the reporting countries maintain old telephone networks that require heavy operator intervention, and telephone operators have traditionally been women, except in places such as the Gulf states where cultural prohibitions restrict women from most employment outside the home. These data on female employees say nothing about the level of employment in the sector as a whole or about the comparative access to or use of ICT by men and women.

Since 2003 ITU has increased to three the number of sex-disaggregated indicators included in its annual questionnaire to member states and in its *Handbook of Key Indicators of the Telecommunications/ICT Sector*, adopted by the third World Telecommunications/ICT indicators meeting held in Geneva in January 2003. The two new indicators are:

- female Internet users as a percentage of total users
- female Internet users as a percentage of females

The definitions in Table 2–1 were adopted for these indicators:

Table 2–1. Key Gender Indicators of the Telecommunications/ICT Sector

ITU Code	Indicator	Definition
16.1	Percent female Internet users	Share of females in the total number of Internet users. This is calculated by dividing the number of female Internet users by the total number of Internet users.
16.2	Female Internet users as percent of female population	Share of female Internet users in the total number of females. This is calculated by dividing the number of female Internet users by the total number of females.

Additionally, the UN MDGs monitoring report and database has also begun to include female Internet users as a percentage of total Internet users.

In its 2003 World Telecommunication Development Report, ITU presented data on female Internet use for thirty-nine countries (see Figure

2–1).[3] Of the data from these countries, only thirteen cases are indicated as coming from country sources, presumably national statistical offices that collect sex-disaggregated data. There was disappointingly little data available on female Internet use in developing countries. Of the thirty-nine countries that supplied data, twenty were outside Europe and North America. There is data available on only one African country—South Africa, a country atypical of the region. Only five Latin American countries are represented, and they, too, are among the richest countries of the region (Argentina, Brazil, Chile, Mexico, and Venezuela). Of the Middle East countries, only Israel is represented. While the highest number of countries from any region outside Europe and North America is from Asia, the list is heavily weighted toward wealthy countries and does not include India, an important omission in view of the country's initiatives in gender and ICT.

Korean Work on Gender and ICT Statistics

Some of the most interesting and substantial work in gender and ICT statistics has come from Korea. Since the first quarter of 2000, the Korean Network Information Center (KRNIC), has undertaken and published quarterly surveys of Internet use, averaging fifty-seven hundred users, with some twenty categories of data collected and disaggregated by sex, and in addition, in most cases, age. KRNIC's categories for which data are available by sex are shown in Table 2–2.

In 2001 the Ministry of Gender Equality released a research report entitled "Women's Informatization Survey and Index Development" to document and examine the gender digital divide in Korea. The ministry based its research on five categories, from which it developed an index of women's rate of "informatization," defined as the extent to which women are part of the process by which information technologies have transformed economy and society. The categories covered are *awareness*, *access*, *utilization*, *skill*, and *effects*, disaggregated to measure comparative informatization by sex. The results showed that women's informatization measured 88 percent that of men's. Although women scored very high on awareness, skills, and effect, the overall situation of women was less—particularly in terms of access and usage. Women's rate of access was only 22.9 percent that of men, and their use of the Internet 28.2 percent that of men.

Figure 2–1. Key Gender Indicators of the Telecommunications/ICT Sector

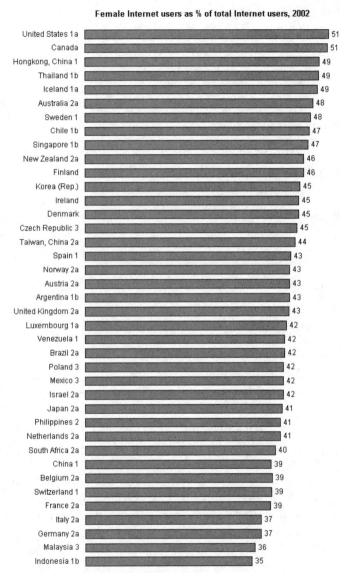

Female Internet users as % of total Internet users, 2002

United States 1a	51
Canada	51
Hongkong, China 1	49
Thailand 1b	49
Iceland 1a	49
Australia 2a	48
Sweden 1	48
Chile 1b	47
Singapore 1b	47
New Zealand 2a	46
Finland	46
Korea (Rep.)	45
Ireland	45
Denmark	45
Czech Republic 3	45
Taiwan, China 2a	44
Spain 1	43
Norway 2a	43
Austria 2a	43
Argentina 1b	43
United Kingdom 2a	43
Luxembourg 1a	42
Venezuela 1	42
Brazil 2a	42
Poland 3	42
Mexico 3	42
Israel 2a	42
Japan 2a	41
Philippines 2	41
Netherlands 2a	41
South Africa 2a	40
China 1	39
Belgium 2a	39
Switzerland 1	39
France 2a	39
Italy 2a	37
Germany 2a	37
Malaysia 3	36
Indonesia 1b	35

Note: 1=National source. 2=Nielsen//NetRatings. 3=TNS. a=2001. b=2000.
Source: International Telecommunication Union (ITU).

Table 2–2. Sex-Disaggregated ICT Indicators, Republic of Korea

Rates of Internet usage (by sex and age)

Main reasons for Internet usage (10 reasons cited)

Age of first Internet usage

Frequency of Internet usage

Average duration of Internet use

Anticipated (projected one year) Internet use

Modes of Internet access (e.g. LAN, IDSN, DSL)

Time of main Internet usage

Places of primary, secondary, tertiary Internet usage

Average cost of Internet connection

Main purpose of usage

Main purpose of Internet surfing

Numbers of e-mail addresses

Rate of possession of homepage

Problems with using Internet

No. of hours weekly reading newspapers, watching television

Reasons for not using Internet

A report comparing men and women's rates of informatization followed the development of the index (Republic of Korea 2001). The findings reported a serious digital divide by age, with women's scores on all categories in the index decreasing from the age of twenty, and a serious gap appearing in the group over fifty years of age. Not surprisingly, higher-income women showed a higher rate of informatization than those at lower income levels.

In 2002 the Asian Pacific Women's Information Network Center of Sookmyung Women's University, the leader in this research, organized a workshop entitled "Survey of Women's Informatization in Asia and the Pacific." The intent was to develop indicators for the extension of the survey on women's involvement in information technologies throughout the Asian region (APWIN 2002). Work continues in this area.

Identifying Desirable Data and Indicators—More than Internet!

Despite the acknowledged importance of initiatives such as the Korea informatization program, no single indicator can capture all the gender-equality issues of the information society. Limiting data collection and analysis to male/female differentials in access to or even use of the Internet provides a very limited picture of the information society. Among the questions it leaves unanswered are these: What are the relative difficulties that women experience in accessing the Internet? Once connected, does content exist that is accessible in terms of language, literacy, and interest to women of the world, particularly poor women in developing countries? Which media are most available to women? For example, access to other communication media such as radio, which addresses issues of cost, time, and language, among others, is particularly important for women in developing countries.

As the information society also encompasses the knowledge economy, it is important to know the extent to which the women of the world are participating. As the basis for both the information society and the knowledge economy, entry and progress in the IT industry are particularly important for women as well as men. Participation in this sector is based on education, in particular scientific and technological education, so that comparative data on men's and women's education in S&T and employment in technological fields are necessary. Data are particularly needed to answer the important questions of the participation of girls and women in computer and communications education, including nonformal education, which provides the basic skills needed for participation in the information society at all levels.

In addition to formal-sector employment, ICT enables a host of new employment opportunities, including e-commerce and communications-based businesses. Are women starting these sorts of businesses? Are national ICT policies sensitive to gender issues relating to development as well as the gender divide in ICT decision making? Given the large number of development projects globally in the broad area of information society and development supported and implemented by international and national agencies, to what extent are gender issues being considered in these projects, and what has their impact been on women? The impact question remains open: how to define and collect data on a composite indicator that can measure the comparative impact of the information society on men and women globally.

Critical areas for the collection of sex-disaggregated statistics and development of gender-specific indicators are detailed below.

Access Data

In addition to Internet usage by sex (the most widely available statistic), sex-disaggregated data on access to a range of ICTs are very important. Among other reasons, availability of such data can inform regulators in the application of universal access to telecommunications. To date, most universal access strategies have been based on geographical factors (rural or urban location) or income (low-income areas are more likely to be under-served). It is important to add gender as an important variable in determining universal service obligations, achieving universal access, and enabling the universal right to communicate. To date the only telecommunications access statistics or indicators disaggregated by sex relate to mobile phone ownership in some countries. These data would be highly desirable for all developing countries, in view of the increasingly dominant position of cell phones in ICT use, particularly in Africa, where their growth exceeds that of any other region. Access to radio by sex would also be very valuable, in view of the fact that the presence of a radio in a household does not ensure its availability to the women in the household.

Content

Gender indicators of content need to be developed, and data collected. Some data is emerging to indicate that women and men access and use different kinds of materials on the Internet. These data are available in sex-disaggregated form for many developed countries where market research firms are interested in sex-differentiated content access patterns. For developing countries, content access data are completely unavailable. Data could be presented on the specific sites or types of sites most commonly accessed by men and by women. Other content questions relate to format and language: do they need to be different for men and women, and are they available?

Employment

Valuable statistics and indicators in employment include gender-related employment differentials within the IT and telecommunications industries, and employment by sex and level in the IT field, relating both to jobs in which IT is used and in the IT manufacturing industry. As discussed above, this is the only area where the ITU, the major collector and disseminator of ICT statistics, currently collects sex-disaggregated ICT statistics—the employment of women in telecommunications service providers by country. Other useful statistics would disaggregate by sex the rates and levels of employment in telecommunications, including telecommunications manufacturing and ICT industries (both IT manufacturing and IT using).

Few data are available on women's participation in computer science and engineering research and employment in either the private sector or in research institutions. However, the available data indicate that the participation of women in higher-skilled, higher-ranking, and higher-paid positions remains very low. There is a progressive decline in the number of women in ICT-related employment at increasing levels of complexity. Many women operate computers, largely for word processing and related office programs, and enter data. Far fewer are programmers and systems analysts, and the smallest number of women is found in software and hardware engineering. The participation of women in IT design and development is particularly low; data collected by the European Union indicates that while women's participation is increasing as researchers in certain science disciplines, such as agricultural and medical sciences, the percentage of female researchers in engineering and technologies is at 19 percent (European Commission 2003). Figures collected in the United States and Canada show that enrollment figures for women in computer-science courses, never over 35 percent, are actually declining.

Concentrated in the low or unskilled end of employment, women are not getting the training that the new and higher-level jobs require to the same extent that men are. This is leading to fears of the global feminization of labor, whereby occupations in which women predominate experience a decline in salaries, status, and working conditions. Readily available statistics and indicators in this area would help make the case for encouraging girls' and women's education in S&T in order to make them eligible for higher-level IT positions.

Education

Questions of women's technical education and their participation in S&T professions are important for sustainable development, in view of the role of science, technology, and innovation for economic growth and national development (see Juma and Lee 2005). While more governments are collecting data on the use of IT in public education, it is still not possible to obtain data on the number of men and women studying IT and computer science in both formal and non-formal educational settings in most countries and in nearly all developing countries. Although few sex-disaggregated data are collected concerning women's participation in S&T education, the data we do have indicate consistently low participation by women and girls. Data on differential access to and participation in education for use of and employment in telecommunications and ICT are significant in determining the future of the gender digital gap and in the formulation of strategies to remedy women's under-representation. For example, in response to data that indicated continuing and increasing declines in the numbers of women studying computer science, Carnegie Mellon University in the United States successfully undertook corrective actions that resulted in increased female enrollment (Margolis and Fisher 2002).

Gender Issues in ICT Policy

The inclusion of gender issues in ICT policies would be a useful indicator. To date, few developing countries have included gender concerns in their national ICT policies, plans, or strategies. South Korea is a notable exception, with a well-developed gender strategy in the national ICT plan. In Africa, there has been much progress on this issue in recent years, quite likely in response to the efforts by the United Nations Economic Commission for Africa to encourage countries to develop gender-aware national information and communication infrastructure (NICI) plans. However, as Sonia Jorge shows in Chapter 3, evidence from Africa and elsewhere indicates that inclusion of gender issues in policies is not sufficient in itself and that the crucial element is inclusion in ICT policy implementation. An indicator should be developed to capture this as well.

Participation in Telecommunications and ICT Decision Making

An examination of the extent to which women are represented in decision making in IT reflects the progress of women in the field and the possibility that women in positions of power serve as role models for others, facilitate the entry of other women, and alleviate some of the negative impacts of new technologies on women. Available data indicate that women are conspicuously absent from decision-making structures in IT in both developed and developing countries. These structures include boards and senior management of IT companies, senior management and advisers of policy and regulatory organizations, technical standards–setting organizations, industry and professional organizations such as the Internet Society, national policy and regulatory organizations, line ministries responsible for the IT sector, and international development organizations and agencies. Indicators in this area could include numbers of women in senior management positions at selected IT firms, in ministries of communication and IT (or their equivalent), in the Internet Corporation for Assigned Names and Numbers (ICANN), and in ITU study groups.

Impact of ICT Projects on Women: Measuring Participation in ICT Projects

As noted above, the WSIS Plan of Action called for the development of measurable performance indicators to assess the impact of donor-funded ICT projects on the lives of women and girls. Given project-level qualitative data indicating the differential impact of IT on men and women, quantitative data relevant to this area would be highly useful.

One key quantitative performance indicator of whether men and women are participating and benefiting equitably from an ICT project or component in a project is participation by sex in the activities of the project. Another essential element for measurement is whether the project affects men and women differently. Indicators of this would include number of participants in the project by sex; users of project services by sex—for example, participants in training, or participants at a conference, seminar, or workshop; users of credit facilities; and users of information services. Breakdowns of project staff by sex would also be useful. As these indicators are the standard project data normally collected for both monitoring and evaluation, the essential element is to ensure that they are disaggregated by sex. Surprisingly, this is rarely done. Analysis of the data could then indicate whether there were serious gender imbalances to be addressed in the project.

NEW EFFORTS IN GENDER STATISTICS
AND INDICATORS IN ICT

Two efforts completed in 2005 have brought significant advances to the collection and analysis of statistics and indicators of gender and ICT. They are the gender and ICT network Régentic (Réseau genre et technologies de l'information et de la communication) and work on the gender digital divide undertaken as part of Orbicom's Monitoring the Digital Divide project.

The Gender Digital Divide in Francophone West Africa

Researchers in West Africa recently completed pioneering field research attempting to measure the gender digital divide. Under the sponsorship of the International Development Research Centre (IDRC), Régentic[4] undertook research in six francophone countries of West Africa (Benin, Burkina Faso, Cameroon, Mali, Mauritania, and Senegal) that are among the leaders in the region in the widespread use of ICTs.[5] The survey comprised a sample of 6,743 individuals and 380 institutions. Respondents were equally divided among men and women and representative of the population distribution by sex, age, and residence. The study covered only those areas that were served by ICTs: 63 percent of those surveyed lived in urban areas, 18.6 percent were peri-urban, and 19 percent rural. Because of the topic, those with more education were over-represented: 52 percent had achieved at least secondary level education, and 29.2 percent had gone beyond that. The research, undertaken in the fourth quarter of 2004, gathered data on eighteen indices relating to the use of computers in general, the Internet, and cell phones.

The study defined and constructed a composite indicator of the gender digital divide, based on four components (decision making and policy, content, skills, and connectivity). While the South Korea index described above also assembled a composite indicator of women's informatization, and both examined content and use, the Régentic index alone looked at the elements of content and representation in decision making and policy. The research concluded that men overall are much more likely than women to benefit from the African information society.

The findings of the study included the following:

- A gender digital divide exists in the six francophone countries. The composite indicator of women's participation in the information society is 0.65, meaning that women experience 35 percent fewer opportunities and benefits than men with regard to ICT. The summary index, however, masks some larger disparities. While there is some gendered disparity in access (on the order of 10 percent), it is much larger in terms of capacity to use ICTs and the knowledge conveyed by content, and larger still in participation in ICT decision making (where women are 68 percent less well represented than men).

- There was no negative gender gap in connectivity or usage among young women educated to secondary school level and beyond. These girls and women were more likely to undergo training in computer use and more likely to go on to work in a computer-use field than young men. However, there were differences in usage related to levels of skill: women tended to work at entry-level positions and, while they were educated in computer use, it tended to be at elementary levels. The young women in this study generally were not involved in creating content, or using it at high levels, and were not involved in developing systems.

- While young women secondary school graduates have become the *majority* of those working in ICT enterprises in these countries, they do not become managers or technical analysts. They gain computer skills as an entry tool for secretarial or data-entry jobs but rarely advance beyond this level.

- Women tend to use the Internet and cell phones more for personal and social use in the six West African countries, while men use them more for professional or work-related reasons.

- Cases emerged where men tended to feel threatened by women's use of cell phones and Internet access, seeing it as destabilizing to relationships and providing women with inappropriate and unsupervised freedom. Many cases were reported of men monitoring the cell phone and Internet use of their partners. According to one woman from Cameroon: "My husband won't let me have a cell phone; I have asked him several times to get me one. He answers that if I want a divorce, I just have to say so."

- The major connectivity obstacles for women relate to place of access (particularly safety and security of location), time constraints, and technophobia.

- Very little local content was available on gender issues.
- Few people were aware of gender issues in ICT.

Among the recommendations made by the study were that

- ICT policy should move beyond access—where the gender gap was not large—to control, content, and capacity building, in order to contribute to reduction of the gender digital divide.
- Young women should be encouraged to enroll in advanced computer training.
- Before gender-equitable ICT policy can be elaborated, tools need to be developed to monitor and evaluate differential impacts of ICT on men and women. Universal access strategies should be implemented to enable access to ICTs for adult women in low-income and rural areas.

Measuring the Digital Divide

Orbicom, the International Network of UNESCO Chairs in Communications, released its second report on measuring the "infostate"[6] of 192 countries in the world in September 2005, in the framework of its project *From the Digital Divide to Digital Opportunities: Measuring Infostates for Development.* The report quantifies the gender digital divide by constructing a pilot statistical database that identifies where pockets of sex-disaggregated ICT data exist. Among the problems encountered in the course of the work were lack of consistent sex-disaggregated statistics in a large number of countries, lack of common definitions and concepts, and a mixture of public and private sources.

The report finds that the gender divide is large and generally larger in developing countries, although it exists in both developing and developed countries. It recognizes that in addition to statistical data, large amounts of a different type of information are also needed, relating to the context of individual countries, social norms, histories, and cultures (among other factors) in order to address the many dimensions and nuances of the gender digital divide. The second part of the study contains qualitative analysis, with in-depth information from fieldwork experiences, case studies, and anecdotal and contextual evidence. The qualitative analysis also sets the stage for the development of additional non-quantitative indicators to give a full picture of the situation of women in ICTs.

The study found that, with a handful of exceptions, the proportion of female Internet users in most countries is well below 50 percent. While there was found to be a gradual increase in the percentage of Internet users who are female, there was no evidence of a direct correlation between increasing Internet penetration and higher percentages of women users. In other words, the gender divide and the overall digital divide do not move in tandem. If the gender divide did mirror the overall deployment and use of ICTs across countries, countries with higher infostates should have smaller gender gaps, and those with lower infostates would have larger gender gaps. If this were the case, policies and actions undertaken to improve the diffusion and use of ICTs and help close the digital divide in general would suffice to a large extent to close the gender divide over time. This would run counter to voices that call for specific targeting of the gender divide as a path to economic and social development.

However, we know that although the gender divide is generally more pronounced in developing countries, it persists even among developed nations with high Internet penetration. The gender gap has vanished in a few countries with high Internet penetration, such as the United States and Canada, but it remains in other countries with high infostates, such as Norway, Luxembourg, the UK, Netherlands, Germany, and France—all of which have rates of female Internet users that resemble those of low infostate countries such as Brazil, Mexico, Zimbabwe, and Tunisia. Italy's gender gap is similar to that of Kyrgystan, with one-tenth the Internet penetration. Relatively rich countries such as Greece and Portugal are fairly close to the bottom on the measure of percent of female Internet users, while some poor countries such as Mongolia and the Philippines are close to the top, despite widely diverging infostates.

While the gender divide is narrowing somewhat, this is occurring only in women's access to and use of ICTs, which are only "entrance" issues—necessary but not sufficient conditions to close the gender digital divide. Even in countries where access is no longer an issue and overall penetration is high, inequalities in use can hamper women's economic and social development and constrain women's equal and active participation in the information society. The study also found that the gender gap increases with newer technologies. The differences between men and women with respect to Internet access are consistently higher than for computer access, gradually decreasing as penetration increases. It was also found that there is a need to look at the whole range of ICTs, from older ones (including basic telephone, radio, and television) to the cell phone and the Internet, depending on the country context.

For these reasons the specific country context emerged as a crucial variable in assessing gender trends in ICT use. Other important variables include access options (home, office, cybercafe, or other public access), labor-force participation, government policies, and sociocultural norms. While the gender divide tends to narrow at higher levels of education, a gap remains nonetheless. In addition to education, other factors that affect ICT use by sex are labor-force status, age, and urban/rural location. Comparing these factors, it was found that the gender divide associated with labor force status is more pronounced than the difference between rural areas and metropolitan centers. It was also clear that the proportion of female Internet users declines steeply with age everywhere (Huyer et al. 2005).

CONCLUSIONS

The major challenges with respect to sex-differentiated statistics and indicators on ICT are that few sources are collecting these data and there is no systematic approach or coordinated method to its collection. Not many government organizations collect national ICT statistics in a consistent and regular manner; of those that do, very few provide a breakdown by sex. It is vital to all countries to have these data in an increasingly globalized world and to ensure that the information society that develops is an equitable one.

How is it possible to encourage countries that do not currently collect sex-disaggregated and gender-specific ICT data to do so? The first phase of WSIS identified the collection of gendered ICT data as an important area for action by member states. Sex-disaggregation of all relevant data—not only data on female Internet users—related to the information society must be encouraged. Perhaps the best hope for the collection of gender-specific and sex-disaggregated data comes through household and enterprise surveys undertaken by national statistical agencies. In order for this to happen, there needs to be pressure from gender advocates at the national level, on both national statistical agencies and national ICT policymakers. There is also an important role for the ITU in encouraging national statistical agencies to collect ICT data and to disaggregate the data by sex wherever relevant.

An encouraging initiative in measuring ICT for development is the partnership of UN bodies—including UNESCO and the regional commissions, the Organization for Economic Co-operation and Development (OECD), and national statistical agencies—that aims at closing the gap in information society statistics and that has taken on a commitment to collecting sex-disaggregated data. The partnership's objectives include developing a set of core indicators and the construction of a database, as well as offering training for capacity building in data collection in developing countries.

While efforts are under way to address the situation, it may be years before satisfactory progress is achieved. In the meantime, the best alternative is to compile all existing data, despite its incompleteness and heterogeneity, and combine it with contextual knowledge as a means to deepen understanding, support much-needed policies, and monitor progress. Doing so will also have the effect of keeping in plain view the need for better sex-disaggregated ICT statistics and indicators.

NOTES

[1] See also Hafkin 2002. Gender-specific indicators point out gender-related changes in society over time.

[2] Jointly created in 1994 by UNESCO and University of Quebec at Montreal, Orbicom comprises twenty-eight chairs and over 250 associate members in seventy-one countries in the fields of communications research, ICT for development, journalism, multimedia, public relations, and communications law. See http://www.orbicom.uqam.ca (accessed 30 November 2005).

[3] Regrettably, ITU has not updated its published statistics on female Internet use since the 2003 report, which used data from 2000–2002.

[4] The gender and ICT network Régentic is a joint initiative of Environment and Development in the Third World (ENDA), the Observatoire des systèmes d'information, réseaux et inforoutes du Sénégal (OSIRIS), and the Senegalese Telecommunication Regulation Agency. Its members are individuals and organizations working to promote gender justice in the national, African, and global information society in partnership with public, private, national, and global development cooperation actors.

[5] The study was published by ENDA as *Fracture numerique de genre en Afrique francophone: une inquiétante realité* (The gender digital divide in Francophone Africa: A harsh reality). http://www.famafrique.org/regentic/indifract/fracturenumeriquedegenre.pdf (accessed 4 December 2005).

[6] A country's infostate is the measure of its uptake and intensity of the use of ICT based on an aggregated index of information networks, education, and skills (Sciadas 2005).

REFERENCES

APWIN (Asian Pacific Women's Information Network Center). 2002. Survey on women's informatization in Asia and the Pacific. http://www.itu.int/ITU-D/pdf/5196-007-en.pdf (accessed 4 December 2005).

European Commission. 2003. Directorate-General for Research. *She figures: Women and science statistics and indicators.* Luxembourg: European Communities. http://europa.eu.int/comm/research/science-society/pdf/she_figures_2003.pdf (accessed 31 October 2003).

Hafkin, Nancy. 2002. Is ICT gender neutral? A gender analysis of six case studies of multi-donor ICT projects. Background paper prepared for the INSTRAW Virtual Seminar Series on Gender and ICTs. June–July 2002. http://www.un.instraw.org/Docs.Hafkin.doc (accessed 30 November 2005).

Hafkin, Nancy, and Sonia Jorge. 2002. Get in and get in early: Ensuring women's access to and participation in ICT projects. *Women in action* 2 [Isis International-Manila]. Special issue on women and communications. http://www.isiswomen.org/pub/wia/wia202.getin.htm (accessed 4 December 2005).

Huyer, Sophia, Nancy Hafkin, Heidi Ertl, and Heather Dryburgh. 2005. Women in the information society. In *From the digital divide to digital opportunities: Measuring infostates for development*, ed. George Sciadas. Orbicom/ITU: Ottawa. http://www.orbicom.uqam.ca/index_en.html (accessed 2 December 2005).

Huyer, Sophia, and Gunnar Westholm. 2000. *GAB/UNESCO toolkit on gender indicators in engineering, science and technology.* Paris: UNESCO. Updated 2006. http://gstgateway.wigsat.org/ta/data/toolkit.html (accessed 30 November 2005).

Juma, Calestous, and Lee Yee-Cheong. 2005. *Innovation: Applying knowledge in development.* United Nations Millennium Project Task Force on Science, Technology, and Innovation. London: Earthscan.

Margolis, Jane, and Alan Fisher. 2002. *Unlocking the clubhouse: Women in computing.* Cambridge, MA: The MIT Press.

Minges, Michael. 2002. Gender and ICT statistics. Presented to third World Telecommunications/ICT indicators meeting. Geneva. 15–17 January 2003. http://www.itu.int/ITU-D/ict/WICT02/doc/pdf/Doc07_E.pdf (accessed 4 December 2005).

Republic of Korea. 2001. Study of women's informatization survey and index development. Ministry of Gender Equality.

Régentic (Réseau genre et technologies de l'information and communications). 2005. *Fracture numerique de genre en Afrique francophone: une inquiétante realité.* Enda: Dakar. http://www.famafrique.org/regentic/indifract/fracturenumeriquedegenre.pdf (accessed 4 December 2005).

Sciadas, George, ed. 2005. *From the digital divide to digital opportunities: Measuring infostates for development.* Ottawa: Orbicom/ITU. http://www.orbicom.uqam.ca (accessed 2 December 2005).

UN. 1995. *The world's women: Trends and statistics.* New York: UN.

WSIS. 2003. Plan of Action. Document WSIS-03/GENEVA/DOC/5–E. 12 December 2003. http://www.itu.int/dms_pub/itu-s/md/03/wsis/doc/S03 -WSIS-DOC-0005!!MSW-.doc (accessed 4 December 2005).

3

Engendering ICT Policy and Regulation

Prioritizing Universal Access for Women's Empowerment

Sonia N. Jorge

THE LONG ROAD TOWARDS GENDER EQUALITY IN ICT

The world of ICT for development is marked by innovation, entrepreneurship, dynamic communities and community leaders, and increasing demand for services and applications that serve the needs of communities around the world. Women should be critical players in this world, as producers, consumers, advocates, entrepreneurs, and users. However, especially at the grassroots level, the needs and roles of women in ICT are not often noticed or recognized. ICT for development needs more people trained and experienced in gender awareness and analysis in order to bring beneficial outcomes that include as many women as possible. This is particularly the case in the critical areas of ICT policymaking and regulation.

ICT policy and regulation set the stage for developments in the sector. Policy and regulation can promote access and use of ICT but can also increase barriers, depending on how they are formulated. The decisions made in policy and the choices made in regulation affect women's lives and their chances for the empowerment that ICTs offer. Gender analysis and awareness in policy and regulation can facilitate those possibilities. This chapter will examine how to arrive at gender-aware policy and regulation that can translate into affordable and equal universal access to ICT for men and women alike.

ICT policy and regulation cover an array of issues, all of which have gender dimensions—from competition policy, market structure, licensing, universal access, development funds, price and tariff regulation, to consumer protection, and spectrum management, among others (see Jorge 2000; Hafkin 2002a). To better understand the gender component in ICT policy and regulation, it is helpful to look at policy and regulation from two perspectives: from the process by which policy develops, and from the implementation of that policy, that is, the specific programs and projects defined to implement policy, often by means of regulations and regulatory frameworks to address each particular telecommunications market.

Policy and regulation are interrelated, and it is often difficult to distinguish them. In general, policy provides the vision for the ICT and telecommunications sector and is established by the ministry of communications in coordination with other agencies and stakeholders involved in the field, such as an ICT commission, the ministry of science and technology, universities, civil society organizations, and industry associations, among others. Such a vision should provide a road map for the development of the sector and reflect the short-term and long-term goals of society for that sector. Regulation normally focuses on telecommunications markets and services and is established to implement the goals of the policy and facilitate development toward the vision that policy sets out. For example, a policy normally provides a vision for universal access in all areas of the country, including rural areas, and often defines what is meant by universal access.

Universal access in telecommunications is a recent concept. The magnitude of the access gap, particularly in the developing world, has led to a rethinking of universal service policies, shifting the focus from the traditional "telephone per household" measure to wider "community access" to telecommunications services. A telephone per household is a target that is unlikely to be achieved or even be commercially desirable in developing countries. Universal access can be measured in many ways, such as time to reach a telephone or distance to a community access point. Universal access to telecommunications goes beyond access to telephones and focuses on community access to ICTs (that is, the provision of shared telecommunications and ICT services at a community access point or location). As telephone availability is taken as the usual prerequisite for access to ICTs, although wireless and satellite technologies no longer require it, those concerned with ICT for development have adopted universal access to telecommunications as a goal.

Regulations or specific programs can be established within a regulatory framework to facilitate and promote universal access by, for instance, defining requirements for deploying infrastructure and goals for each existing communication services operator; establishing special licenses for rural operators, including community-owned networks; approving discounted tariffs for community access points or rural customers; and establishing funds to subsidize infrastructure development and access in remote areas. Many countries finance the expansion of telecommunications into under-served and rural areas through telecommunication development funds, financed from telecommunications operators' revenues and managed by regulatory bodies.

The development of public policies differs from country to country, based on the type of government, the degree of public participation, and the influence of the various stakeholders. In most democratic countries the policy process follows a basic sequence of tasks, which includes an assessment and study of the issues at stake, formulation of policies, public consultations, the drafting and release of a final policy document, and often an implementation strategy and monitoring and evaluation plan.

From the viewpoint of equity, the most basic ICT policy goal should be to increase affordable access to ICT for all women and men, regardless of geographic location, language, age, race, and social class. For this to happen, gender considerations need to be specific and timely. When policies neglect the specific context of the lives of over half of the targeted population, then they are likely to fail, at least in meeting the needs of the ignored group. In order to have meaningful inclusion of gender considerations, they need to be part of the process from the start and at all levels of the policymaking process (Jorge 2000). Regrettably, this rarely happens.

Despite extensive evidence of the significant impact of gender analysis in development work, it has made little headway in the ICT for development area, particularly at policy and regulatory levels.

GENDER IN ICT POLICY AND REGULATION

Understanding the importance of gender analysis in ICT policy-planning and implementation stages is fundamental. Greater awareness and recognition of gender issues in policy, including goals toward gender equality, particularly within the context of the MDGs, are meaningless if they are not translated into action in projects and programs. Recommended actions around gender and ICT may include gender-specific projects and programs, regulations that facilitate affordable access to women and the poor, establishment of universal access programs targeting women, licensing regimes that favor companies with gender-equality policies, and programs that consider women's needs and realities (where illiteracy is widespread, where information in local languages is critical, where technology may be intimidating, where ICT need to be affordable, where training is always required, and where ICT may already have a role that needs to be improved or supported instead of modified).

Gender equality is not simply an overarching issue that relates to all areas of human endeavor; it is a variable to be considered when addressing pricing and tariffs, network deployment, technology choices, licensing, projects to increase access, and capacity-building activities, among others. For example, pricing and tariff regulation should consider income inequality (based on gender, rural-urban divides, race, and so forth) in determining economic demand for services. If such analysis is not conducted, those decisions will keep a large percentage of the potential market outside of the information society. A long-established dictum of policy and regulation theory is that high prices for short-term gain do not result in growth and development. Far preferable is a strategy that focuses on larger markets and higher demand as a consequence of lower prices. Limiting technology choice—by prohibiting low-cost alternatives such as wireless networks and Voice Over Internet Protocol (VoIP) telephone—may prevent many poor women from accessing communications technology. Network deployment may focus on expensive, high-capacity, specialized access rather than an affordable technology. Infrastructure deployment may be limited in geographical areas where women are the majority. If mobile and Internet Service Provider (ISP) licensing fees are set high, they are likely to be passed on to users, limiting their affordability to women (Jorge 2000; Hafkin 2002a).

ICT for Gender Equality at International, Regional, and National Levels

Despite the prevailing absence of gender considerations in ICT policy and regulation, gender advocates are helping to shape ICT policy in a way that is gender aware in a number of cases at international, regional, national, and local levels.

International Level

Over the last ten years gender advocates have become better equipped to participate and influence ICT policy development at international, regional, and national levels. The preparation for the first phase of the WSIS held in 2003 was a process of both advocacy and lobbying as well as a laboratory for learning for all involved. The road of advocacy is a long one and results happen in increments, often small but always significant. Those interested in ICT for development came to realize the importance of policymaking processes and the need to educate themselves to participate in them. The experience of gender advocates at WSIS illustrates those efforts, including the challenges associated with lobbying, the frustrations, and also the victories. It also demonstrates that advocates need to be persistent and innovative in their advocacies.

Gender advocates were among the most visible and consistently active groups during the preparation for the first WSIS. The results of their work are reflected directly in both the WSIS Declaration and its Plan of Action (Hafkin 2005). Karen Banks analyzes that effort:

> The success of gender advocates . . . cannot be seen or measured solely by an assessment of the language of the official documents, which was largely disappointing, but in specific partnerships and collaborations with certain governments, intergovernmental agencies and other stakeholders as a result of increased networking, awareness and knowledge sharing which has emerged from the WSIS process.
>
> After 2 years of intense lobbying, all references to gender equality and women's empowerment disappeared from the documents in the period just prior to the last preparatory meeting. . . . The majority of stakeholders did not prioritise gender concerns, and the language that had been successfully incorporated into official regional documents was ignored. The references to gender equality were reinserted only after a good old-fashioned 't'-shirt campaign, which secured one strong paragraph in the first section of the political declaration—paragraph 12:
>
> *"We affirm that development of ICTs provides enormous opportunities for women, who should be an integral part of, and key actors, in the Information Society. We are committed to ensuring that the Information Society enables women's empowerment and their full*

participation on the basis on equality in all spheres of society and in all decision-making processes. To this end, we should mainstream a gender equality perspective and use ICTs as a tool to that end."

The Action Plan contains references to the special needs of women in relation to capacity building; participation of women in formulating ICT policies; ICT applications (e-health and e-employment); cultural diversity and identity; media; and follow-up and evaluation. There is a special reference to the need for "putting in place the conditions for mobilizing human, financial and technological resources for inclusion of all men and women in the emerging Information Society" in the document outlining the work of the Task Force on Financing Mechanisms. (Banks 2005)

Experience at the international policymaking level, such as WSIS, is informing national processes and providing greater credibility to gender advocates previously not involved in the process. As a result of the WSIS experience and the momentum it created around national efforts to develop ICT policies (also referred to as e-strategies or connectivity agendas), gender advocates are becoming more active at the regional and national levels. Experience at the international level has been valuable for sharing knowledge and gaining experience that can be applied at the national level. Most of those involved still face tremendous resistance and are often faced with their own lack of knowledge or experience in the field, particularly when it relates to the more technical telecommunications issues.

Regional Level

At regional levels the work of the UN Economic Commission for Africa (ECA) has been significant in promoting gender awareness in ICT policies of African countries. ECA has developed the NICI Policies and Plans process, by which it assists African countries to develop national ICT strategies (e-strategies) for accelerating socioeconomic development. Working within the context of the MDGs and the New Partnership for African Development (NEPAD), the NICI process emphasizes a participatory and consultative method and aims at developing inclusive policies appropriate in the context of the specific country's development plans. The process specifies gender as an important social dimension to be addressed in the elaboration of national ICT policies. The consultative process in many countries has included a number of gender advocates, women's organizations, and governmental bodies responsible for gender equality. As a result, most of the national ICT policies developed with ECA assistance refer to and, to a certain extent, address gender issues.[1]

National Level

There are a number of positive examples of gender awareness in ICT policymaking from Africa, Asia, and Latin America, with more examples coming from Africa than other regions, possibly because of the influence of ECA and the NICI process with its emphasis on gender. The following cases are examples of the inclusion of gender issues in ICT national-level policymaking by region and country.

Africa

The ICT policy and strategy in *Benin* (République du Bénin 2003) includes the objective of making Benin an information-literate society made up of men and women active in and benefiting from the information society. Actions include increasing women's capacities to use ICTs, promoting ICTs among women's organizations, and using ICTs to develop an information system that promotes women and women's concerns.

The *Guinea* national ICT policy sees gender as an important component of equitable human development and aims at contributing to greater awareness of gender.

The *Ghana* national ICT policy addresses gender issues and gender-equality goals "to accelerate the development of women and eliminate gender inequalities in education, employment, decision making through the deployment and exploitation of ICT by building capacities and providing opportunities for girls and women" (Republic of Ghana 2003, 9). Bridging the gender inequality gap in social, economic, and political development is considered a strategic focus, while objectives and priorities include increasing women's access to ICTs by ensuring gender balance in training; promoting women's rights to expression and communication through ICT; and the development of a system to monitor progress to gender equality in ICTs. The telecommunications policy also addresses gender equality in its vision and more specifically within the universal access policy. Women's groups in Ghana were actively involved in shaping the ICT policymaking process, with national forums in person and online to discuss the issues from a gender perspective.

In *Kenya*, too, women's groups organized and educated themselves to take part in the national ICT policy debates.

The national ICT policy in *Mozambique* (Mozambique 2002) addresses gender by a commitment to include a gender dimension in ICT development projects and by recognizing the specific needs of women and youth with respect to capacity building, affordable access, online spaces, capacity for self employment, e-commerce, applications, and content development, among other areas. The national telecommunications policy addresses gender issues primarily within its universal access policy.

The *South Africa* Telecommunications Act of 1996 includes gender-specific language, in line with other national legislation based on gender-equality principles. South Africa's 1999 Telecommunications Act established the Universal Service Agency and provided the policy and legislative frameworks to redress gender imbalance. During the consultative process leading up to the act, the 1996 White Paper on Communications (Republic of South Africa 1996) stated that "besides referring to those who were disadvantaged by the apartheid system in the past, the term 'disadvantaged' also applies to those South Africans who have been historically disadvantaged through discrimination on the grounds of gender and/or disability." It also stressed the need to ensure gender equality in issues such as licensing, procurement, and training. Additionally, the national research-and-development strategy includes a chapter on human capacity building in S&T, with many references to the importance of gender equality (Gillwald 2001).

Uganda's National Information and Communication Technology Policy includes references to the need for policy to stimulate industrial growth, commerce, infrastructure, and linkage of rural and urban communities "as well as uplifting of disadvantaged groups, while taking care of gender balance" and making available communications at affordable costs "which match the ability of their users to pay, so as to reduce gender and spatial disparities in information access." In addition it states that one of its policy objectives is to ensure gender mainstreaming in ICTs for development and associated strategies (Republic of Uganda 2002).

In *Zambia* the first draft of the national information and communication policy in 2003 made several references to gender and youth. Its guiding principles include mainstreaming youth and gender into policy formulation, review, and implementation.

The ICT policy in *Tanzania* mentions "gender," "women," and "equitable" five times in total, mostly in relation to discussions of human capital for a well-educated and learning society, but every ministry is required to have a women's desk (Etta 2004).

Latin America

The Dominican Republic stands out in Latin America as an example of the consideration of gender issues in its ICT policy, which was finalized in September 2005. The telecommunication development-fund policy document addresses gender issues and the needs of women and women's organizations in determining project location, project staff and management, and funding awards, among other areas. The national ICT policy, E-Dominicana, places great emphasis on gender issues in the information society and establishes clear goals toward gender equality in ICT development as well as specific gender projects and programs.

The government website, edominicana.gov, presents the policy in this way:

> The final version of the Dominican ICT Policy reflects a commitment to gender and gender equality not previously seen in any national ICT policy. The policy profiles gender as an issue in the information society (as it does with health, education, and other areas), establishes specific gender objectives and, more importantly, it proposes a number of gender-specific projects for the policy implementation phase. These include, among others, a gender-sensitization project, a gender-content portal, a gender-based indicators project, a project to adapt telecenters and education programs to the needs and constraints of women, including illiteracy, and a directory of telework employment opportunities.

Asia

In Asia the best example of the inclusion of gender issues in ICT policy is Korea. Korea has mainstreamed the use of ICT by women in its overall development plan for women—and provided a plan and a budget for it, an essential step that has happened virtually nowhere else.

Other countries of the region have evidenced a modicum of gender awareness in national ICT policy, but without addressing specific issues.

In *Samoa*, gender equality is considered a crosscutting issue in the ICT policy document. The policy also proposes a project to develop gender and ICT indicators and to prepare a baseline study on gender equality in ICT. However, gender is not directly addressed in any of the specific policy activity areas.

The final draft of the *Indonesia* e-strategy (which was still pending approval at the time of this writing) reflects a general acknowledgment of gender issues and of gender equality within the context of the MDGs. However, the policy does not reflect a commitment to gender, and gender is only addressed as a dimension of ICT for development.

The ICT policy for *China* addresses women and ICT as part of the overall development of women.

The ICT policy process has made a contribution in raising public awareness about the sector itself. In Mozambique, Kenya, Uganda, South Africa, Sri Lanka, India, Estonia, Bolivia, Peru, and Ecuador, among other countries, the ICT policy process and the countries' commitment to the sector have not only increased knowledge about the sector itself but also increased the interest of the general populace and many civil society groups in ICT policy and the area of ICT for development. ICT projects in many countries have been featured in the media and have benefited from a certain level of exposure. Civil society organizations, including women's organizations, have been actively engaged in the national policy debate, but in general their efforts have focused on addressing the access gap, on investments in ICT for development, and on promoting a communications rights agenda.[2] One hopes that the increasing awareness and interest in ICT policy may lead to more serious attention to gender issues.

Not Including Gender Is the Rule

Despite these developments at the national level, there are many countries—the vast majority, in fact—where gender issues are simply not addressed in ICT policy. In Latin America a number of countries have developed ICT policies (also called connectivity agendas). A brief review of the policy documents[3] and the government websites for the policies shows that, with the exception of Dominican Republic, cited above, gender issues are not addressed. The policies of Colombia, Ecuador, and Bolivia make no mention of gender issues. Analysis of the current projects and policies on ICTs and digital inclusion in Brazil shows no gender perspective as a main issue in any of them (Selaimen 2005). Regional efforts to direct the process in Latin America, such as the connectivity agenda for the Americas, the Quito Action Plan, a document and policy developed by the Inter-American Telecommunications Commission, also makes no mention of gender issues, although it does focus on issues of poverty reduction, needs of rural people, and economic equity (CITEL 2003).

In Asia the strategic framework for ICT development in India, Malaysia, and the Philippines is silent on gender issues and considerations (Ramilo and Villaneuva 2001). In Africa the policies of Botswana, Malawi, and Madagascar contain no references to women or gender equality. And in Senegal telecommunications policy formulation has focused almost exclusively on the performance of the operator and the structure of the sector. Women's NGOs and other stakeholders concerned about gender issues are active in Senegal but have not been able to influence the development of the national ICT policy (Mottin-Sylla 2002).

Although the challenge remains to secure gender considerations in ICT policy in most countries, policy is insufficient in itself to realize gender equity in ICT. Securing the inclusion of gender in policy implementation and regulatory decisions is an even greater challenge. Gender advocates, civil society organizations, and those interested in working toward gender equality in ICT need to develop a strategy that tackles gender within this crucial area. It is implementation that counts, and for the most part it isn't happening there.

IMPLEMENTATION: WHERE GENDER ANALYSIS FALLS SHORT

Once policies are developed, the real test is the process of implementation, the commitment to the policy goals, and the actual impact of the policy. Policies that recognize gender equality as a goal need to develop implementation programs that address gender, develop gender-specific projects appropriate to the context of the country, and integrate gender considerations in any project or program. The harsh reality is that to date there is a huge gap between policy and goals, and what actually is implemented. Despite advances in the inclusion of gender considerations in policy, few if any concrete results are turning up on the ground. While many ICT policies have been in place for two to three years, there are very few projects and programs where one can see the results of thorough gender analysis and/or a commitment to gender equality.

When Mozambique's ICT policy was approved in December 2000, there was much hope that this would become a best practice on gender issues. However, despite an admirable ICT policy in terms of gender, an implementation strategy that addresses critical areas of need, including gender, and an ICT commission that is working hard to advance access, there is only one mention of women in the implementation document— with respect to violence against women. None of the projects planned for the first five-year implementation period focuses on women or gen- der issues (Mozambique 2002). Significantly, no women's organizations participated in the national consultative forum that led to the imple- mentation strategy. If gender equality is truly a goal, as the policy states, gender analysis needs to be part of the implementation process and ad- dressed seriously. Without such consideration the policy will most likely have a less than desirable effect on the lives of women in Mozambique (Hafkin and Jorge 2002). There are numerous examples of the neglect of gender when gender issues are not clearly spelled out (Hafkin 2002b).

Some Examples of Good Implementation

Based on the evidence so far, and among developing countries, Korea has been the most successful country from the implementation as well as the policy perspective. The Korean experience illustrates the impor- tance of the leadership role taken by the Ministry for Gender Equality (which is responsible for mainstreaming gender among all government institutions) in working closely with the telecommunications and sci- ence and technology ministries to ensure that women would benefit equally with men from the country's ICT-related policies. In addition, a national commitment to the information society—embodied in the Informatization Policy, the Digital Divide Act of 2001, and the Master Plan for Closing the Divide, 2001—and a coordinated effort among different government agencies have been key to ensuring access and to educate women to be effective users of ICT in Korea. As a result of these efforts, various programs have been implemented, which include, among others, capacity building and training programs for women (es- pecially housewives and women small-business owners) and a widespread universal access program providing free access to ICTs in rural and ur- ban telecenters.

The Department of Communications and the Universal Service Agency in South Africa are actively working to integrate women and gender issues in their work and in project implementation. The Univer- sal Service Agency, which was set up through the regulatory process, has established more than forty telecenters and cyberlabs throughout the country with the aim of providing universal access to ICTs. Some telecenter projects have been notably successful in increasing access to and use by women and other disadvantaged groups. In some instances, as a result of policy decisions resulting in new regulations and licensing requirements focusing on serving disadvantaged communities, ensuring affordable services, and having some women owners of communication services, operators have set discounted tariffs for services provided by community telecenters or other access points.

Other countries' experience with implementation is still limited, but evidence shows that the majority of projects to implement ICT policy fail to integrate gender-equality goals and concerns. While some positive steps are being taken in a number of countries, they are far from enough. Gender considerations are still seen as an add-on aspect of a social dimension rather than an integral part of the process as a whole. In general, gender-equality and gender issues that are mentioned and acknowledged in policy receive no further attention in regulation and implementation. Unless gender analysis is done in a systematic manner, ICT policy and its implementation will not contribute to gender equality and will fail to meet the MDGs in different respects. Systematic gender analysis means its inclusion in all levels of policy decisions as well as in planning for implementation, allowing gender issues to be tackled in practice. Lack of sex-disaggregated data at all levels is a further barrier to the incorporation of gender issues in ICT planning.[4]

Development Projects and Programs: Action by Civil Society

If one looks only at the results of the ICT policy and regulatory processes, it would be easy to completely miss a dynamic and innovative aspect of gender in ICT for development. From Latin America to Africa, from East Europe to Asia, a large number of innovative projects and programs are being developed and implemented with gender concerns as their focus and women and girls as the main targets. Women's organizations all over the world have developed ICT projects focusing on issues from health to education, from business development to e-commerce, from community radio to networking and Internet use, and from economic empowerment to political and democratic participation in society. Many of these projects, a majority of them at the grassroots level, have had substantial social and economic impact, despite operating with limited support from their governments, donors, or philanthropic organizations. Most of them have no support at all from the development funds established by national ICT or telecommunications policy and are often struggling to stay in operation. Yet they are small-scale examples of what implementation of gender-aware ICT policy could bring.

Several gender and ICT awards and programs have been established to recognize and promote these seminal projects to improve women's lives by using ICT. Among these is the GenARDIS grants fund (an initiative of the Technical Centre for Agricultural and Rural Cooperation [CTA], the International Institute for Communication and Development, IDRC, and Hivos), which supports work on gender-related issues in ICTs for Africa, Caribbean, and Pacific (ACP) agricultural and rural development. As described on the GenARDIS website:

> The programme was developed in recognition of the constraints and challenges encountered by rural women in ACP countries with respect to ICTs. The challenges include cultural factors that hinder women's access to ICTs, limited time availability to participate in training and use of ICTs, minimal access to technology such as radios, mobile telephones or computers, and inadequate availability of information in local languages that is relevant to local contexts.[5]

The Gender and ICT (GICT) awards, co-sponsored by the Association for Progressive Communications (APC) Women's Networking Support Program and the Global Knowledge Partnership (GKP), were established to recognize innovative and effective projects by women to use ICT for the promotion of gender equality and/or women's empowerment. The collaborating organizations have produced a gender and ICT projects database, which includes all eligible and nominated projects for the awards. The number and diversity of projects illustrates the extent of the work being done in the gender and ICT for development area.[6] These awards have helped to raise awareness on gender in ICT for development and have contributed to the exposure and promotion of these projects. Many of these projects have received considerable media attention, have become the subjects of films, and in several cases have led to the establishment of new networks and support mechanisms.

Among the award winners are the following:

Isis-Women's International Cross Cultural Exchange (Isis-WICCE), Uganda
This Isis-WICCE project records and disseminates the stories of women living in situations of armed conflict in Uganda and elsewhere in Africa.

Since 1997, Isis-WICCE, a globally activist women's resource center, has documented the experiences of women in situations of armed conflict in ten countries in Africa. In addition to raising awareness about the consequences of armed conflict for cultural, social, economic, and political development, and particularly for women's well-being, the project also provides tools for victims of conflict to help them secure redress, and for decision makers to formulate laws and policies to reduce conflicts in Africa. The project also lobbied for programs to meet the emergency needs of women war survivors, including their reproductive health.[7]

The Pallitathya Help-Line: Helping Women Help Themselves Project
GICT selected the Pallitathya Call Centre for the Poor and Underprivileged, a project of development through access to network resources, as the winner of its 2005 award. With the objective of empowering women economically, the project was based on an assessment that showed that the lack of timely and relevant information was a major bottleneck to rural development in general and to women in particular.

The project deployed women in the community as Mobile Operator Ladies who move from door to door with mobile phones to enable other women, mostly housewives, to pose questions related to their livelihoods, agriculture, health, and legal rights; help-desk operators answer the queries using a database and the Internet. To expand the information base, resource persons from government, NGOs, and health and human rights groups provide responses to frequently asked questions.

An evaluation revealed that the mobile operators who serve as information intermediaries experienced an increase in their self-esteem, their earnings potential, and their knowledge about various issues. Women help-desk operators also enhanced their knowledge and improved their communication skills. Women who used the service said that they, too, gained in self-esteem and increased their incomes and involvement in domestic spending decisions.[8]

Gender and ICT: The Power of Community Radio in Brazil
Communication, Education and Information on Gender (CEMINA) was founded by Brazilian women who wanted to improve and promote communication, education, and information on issues of concern to Brazilian women. CEMINA developed a successful community radio program, "Fala Mulher" (Women speak up), broadcast to selected communities in Brazil, on issues relevant to women and community life, including women's rights,

HIV/AIDS, violence against women, health, and sexuality. The program has a website, develops new content, and makes audio files freely available for broadcasting by other community radio stations and networks. CEMINA's success with "Fala Mulher" led it to set up training workshops for community women on radio program production, content development, and other areas. The organization also started a women's radio network, which currently supports about four hundred radio programs for women produced by women for local community radio.

CEMINA's website describes its projects to promote digital inclusion, including:

- a mobile radio studio transmitter that allows people from rural and poor urban areas to access CEMINA's training activities;
- a radio production center that produces programming for partner radio stations across Brazil;
- a radio and ICT project that provides ICT facilities for radio program production, ICT training, and information sharing across the network;
- a community radio telecenter project that provides shared access to ICT for community radio stations and poor communities across the country;
- Rede Cyberela (Cyberela Network), which provides ICT training and access, including broadband, to women community radio producers to help them develop content and share it among the network;
- a youth project that supports hip-hop youth groups in developing music with messages about health and gender issues.

UNIFEM and UNESCO have given awards to CEMINA for its use of community radio as a tool for women's empowerment. CEMINA has developed from a strong women's community radio project to a wider ICT-access and capacity-building project for Brazilian women, testifying to the power of community radio as a tool for information dissemination and women's empowerment.

These programs and projects show that civil society organizations, particularly women's organizations, play a critical role as developers and implementers of ICT projects that can empower women through the use of ICTs. They provide women with ICT access and teach women about the benefits of using ICT. Their work has been innovative and has contributed to the improvement of women's lives, to women's empowerment in society, and to socioeconomic development in their communities and regions. As grassroots organizations, they are close to the public they serve, with an understanding of the needs of their constituents as well as effective strategies to reach them.

These projects are gaining recognition from international organizations and support from a number of sources. The APC Women's Networking Support Program and its regional projects, the Isis International Network, and many other women's organizations provide a number of resources, support project implementation, and promote various capacity-training initiatives. However, such projects tend to remain small scale, with their sustainability in doubt. With resources, many civil society organizations could implement projects that not only complement their government's policy goals but also in fact contribute to development in the country. Much more needs to be done to develop strong financial and organizational support from local, national, regional, and international sources for women's civil society organizations working in gender and ICT for development.

Civil Society as a Crucial Element in Gender-Aware ICT Project Implementation

On the basis of their experience with gender-aware ICT projects, civil society organizations could provide useful lessons for national ICT policy and implementation. These organizations could also play a crucial ICT policy role by assisting in building capacity for advocacy in behalf of women and gender issues at policy and regulatory levels. While it requires a comprehensive and technical understanding of policy and regulatory issues, this task has the potential to open opportunities for gender and ICT projects and programs around the world to benefit from new and existing resources for communications development.

Getting Gender Analysis into Policy and Implementation: The Need for Gender and ICT Expertise

As highlighted above, gender advocates, largely women's groups, have raised awareness of the need for gender equality in ICT policy at the national and international level. Gender equality is emerging as a principle mentioned in a number of ICT policies, but gender issues are not coming through in specific policy aspects.

To give reality to the inclusion of gender considerations in ICT policy, more than gender advocacy is necessary. Professional expertise in both gender and ICTs, a fairly rare combination, is needed to deal with the technical aspects of ICT policy, which dominate policymaking and which often tend to intimidate gender advocates. Certain aspects of policy-making, such as telecommunications policy (which covers such issues as infrastructure development, licensing, pricing of services, and subsidies allowed) still largely lack a gender perspective, although each of these issues has a clear gender aspect. Unless someone with a gender and tele-communications background is involved in the policy process, it is likely that gender concerns will not be part of technical decisions, although they have clear implications for women's empowerment through the use of ICTs. Unfortunately, it is rare to see a gender expert involved in such processes.

Even in those cases of ICT policies where gender is recognized, it tends to be addressed in a general manner—as an obligation and a goal but not as in relation to specific policy issues. The cases of South Africa, Mozambique, the Dominican Republic, and a few others illustrate this. They incorporate gender awareness and gender analysis, to a certain extent, as a result of active involvement of gender experts in the process. However, the process to engender policy and regulation is not system-atic, but rather ad hoc, dependent on the random and occasional par-ticipation of gender experts or professionals concerned with gender issues. Such an approach does not result in a fully informed engendered process. Even when the policy and regulations are clear as to how to integrate and consider gender—by covering such issues as human re-sources needs, capacity-building initiatives, community access, and pric-ing issues from a gender perspective—those implementing the programs are ultimately responsible. If they are not trained in gender analysis, they may have difficulty in effecting gender-aware implementation.

There is also a critical need for experienced gender experts to work in the field with policymaking agencies and at regulatory bodies. Efforts to employ women in those areas are necessary but not sufficient; being a woman does not guarantee gender awareness. Gender and ICT training should be required for all women and men working in the ICT policy and regulatory areas. Otherwise, even as policies appear to be gender aware because of the inclusion of the references to gender and women, they may not look at gender from a technical perspective, and implementation of those policies will fall short of providing equal access to women and men.

For ICT development efforts to become successful from policy to regulation to implementation, it is absolutely necessary to ensure that women representatives and gender experts not only participate in the development of policy and regulations, but also that the number of women and gender experts employed in policymaking and regulatory institutions is significant and sufficient to ensure that gender analysis is integral to their work and that gender issues are considered at all levels of implementation.

Again, Korea serves as a useful model for such a systematic approach to the inclusion of gender considerations in ICT policy, since gender advocates and government officials with a gender background were involved at all levels of development of the ICT sector. The Korean experience shows that gender mainstreaming ideally should occur in a coordinated manner and that there is a need for a respected institution in the country, such as the Ministry for Gender Equality, to play a gender leadership role. Fortuitously, Korea had ICT experts in its Ministry for Gender Equality who were aware of the gender issues in technical aspects of ICT policy. Unfortunately, this is not the case with many other countries.

Problems of Universal-Access Implementation

While a number of countries have universal-access policies as well as universal-access programs to implement those policies, implementation often runs into obstacles that prevent the services from reaching women and men alike. Lack of support, limited regulatory capacity to implement the programs, and political impediments often lead to delays in implementing universal-access projects; funds can get tied up in bureaucratic nightmares of political interests. Brazil and Bolivia are cases in point, where large amounts of money have been accumulated in telecommunications development funds, but nothing has been done to implement universal-access projects. Such inaction by the regulator may lead to loss of these funds. These kind of problems delay disbursement of resources to the organizations and institutions that reach unserved and under-served areas of the country and keep needed programs from being implemented.

PRIORITIZING UNIVERSAL-ACCESS PROGRAMS FOR WOMEN'S EMPOWERMENT: KEY ACTION ITEMS

- In view of the multiple obstacles cited above to realizing gender equity in ICT policy and implementation processes, gender advocates need to develop both short-term and long-term strategies.

They need to refocus their efforts and invest their resources where they are most needed, particularly around issues of access.

- Women's ability to benefit from ICTs as tools for their socioeconomic empowerment is limited by many factors, including income levels, social and cultural determinants, levels of literacy, and lack of knowledge of ICTs and their benefits, among others.

In addition, Anita Gurumurthy points out some of the key sociocultural factors that constrain women's use of ICT, particularly in rural areas:

- Cultural attitudes discriminate against women's access to technology and technology education.
- Women are less likely than men to own communication assets—radio, mobile phones.
- Women in poor households do not have the income to use public [ICT] facilities.
- Information centres may be located in places that women are not comfortable visiting.
- Women's multiple roles and heavy domestic responsibilities limit their leisure time. Centres may not be open when it is convenient for women to visit them.
- It is more problematic for women to use facilities in the evenings and return home after dark. (Gurumurthy 2004)

ICT policies, regulations, and resulting projects should focus on addressing these constraints by either decreasing their impact or by developing programs that directly address them. For example, a universal-access program could develop a scheme to subsidize women's ownership of basic ICTs (such as radios and mobile phones) and provide training on how to use the technologies. The same program could also support the development of locally relevant content and information necessary for women's lives in their local language. And most important, universal-access programs need to address the ICT needs of women and of the poor, who will not be able to pay for services.

A long-term strategy should focus on a coordinated effort to mainstream gender through all ICT for development work, including national policy and regulatory bodies. Such a strategy should include a long-term capacity-building plan on gender sensitization and gender analysis for all organizations, governmental and nongovernmental, involved in ICT for development work. Work should also focus on developing systems to support initiatives for gender equality, women's empowerment, and development.

In the short term, gender advocates in many countries need to develop a plan to influence universal-access policy and access the funds that have been allocated to effect such access at national level. Such a strategy would have direct impact on ensuring access to and use of ICT by women. This could be complemented by an organized campaign to promote ongoing gender and ICT initiatives. This strategy needs to address seriously the issue of affordability and provide alternatives for access in low-income areas. Such alternatives can include fully subsidized services, establishment of community access points with lower access rates, and, in some cases, introduction of innovative technologies to facilitate widespread ICT access in remote areas.

Some areas for specific focus in the short term include:

- Pricing policy—gender-based income inequality and income levels among regions are critical variables; community or discounted tariffs should be promoted.
- Network deployment—issues such as security and technology choice, including energy-saving communication technologies are central.
- Location of community access points—women's access is critical and often determined by income and cultural barriers.
- Licenses—critical changes can be made to ensure that women's organizations and institutions with gender-equality policies are given priority (such as women or rural community cooperatives in some countries).
- Subsidies—criteria for allocation of subsidies need to consider gender equality both for implementation of subsidized projects and from the recipient's organizational plan.
- Project criteria/selection—projects that consider and integrate gender can be given priority and support if necessary; gender statistics and sex-disaggregated data should be provided.
- Content development—resources are urgently needed to develop gender-specific content in local languages.
- Capacity building—policy and regulatory agencies that promote capacity-building activities need to be gender aware and address gender constraints (such as schedules, women only classes, incomes, and child care).

Many countries would welcome a program under the universal-access mandate whereby civil society organizations could tap into available financial and human resources to improve and expand their operations. It is in the government's interest to have a strong and able civil society, capable of implementing development programs and working with it toward meeting its MDGs, including gender equality and women's empowerment at all levels of society.

CONCLUSION

ICT policy and regulation are very important areas to women in their quest for empowerment. However, little gender awareness has yet permeated this area. While gender awareness is growing with regard to ICT policy, as examples from international, regional, and national levels illustrate, it is frequently limited to general references to women or gender equality as a goal, without further consideration when technical issues are raised. The balance sheet is less positive in the case of regulation, where there are few examples of gender-aware policy implementation. One bright spot on the gender and ICT scene is that of innovative projects using ICTs for women's empowerment, largely implemented by civil society organizations. All possible encouragement should be given to these organizations to continue their work and to involve themselves in national policy and regulatory processes. Both the field experience of these organizations and the expertise of gender and ICT specialists are needed to arrive at gender-aware policy and its implementation through the regulatory process.

NOTES

[1] See http://www.uneca.org/disd/ict/ and http://www.uneca.org/aisi/nici/nici_term.htm.

[2] See, for example, a number of national ICT policy sites by civil society organizations at http://rights.apc.org/policy_sites_list.shtml; see also the Communications Rights in the Information Society (CRIS) campaign at http://www.crisinfo.org/.

[3] The author reviewed the connectivity agendas of Colombia, Bolivia, Ecuador, and the Dominican Republic.

[4] For a detailed discussion of the problem of the paucity of statistics and indicators on gender, women, and ICT, see Chapter 2.

[5] "GenARDIS Round 2 Update," 22 April 2005. http://www.cta.int/about/genardis2_winners.htm.

[6] "Gender and ICT Awards." http://www.genderawards.net/gict_pr_db.shtml (these were projects eligible for the 2003 awards).

[7] "Documenting Experiences of Women in Situations of Armed Conflict." http://www.genderawards.net/winners/wicce.htm.

[8] http://www.genderawards.net/the_awards/2005.htm.

REFERENCES

Banks, Karen. 2005. World Summit on the Information Society: Potential for addressing the gender digital divide? http://www.genderit.org/en/beginners/wsis-fulltext.shtml (accessed 4 December 2005).

CITEL (Inter-American Telecommunications Commission). 2003. Agenda de Connectividad para las Americas. Plan de Acción de Quito.

Etta, Florence. 2004. ICT policy and governance: Challenges and opportunities for women. Paper presented to conference on Women and ICT: Challenges and opportunities on the road to Tunis. Arusha, Tanzania. 20–22 October.

Gillwald, Alison. 2001. Telecommunication policy and regulation for women and development. *The Southern African Journal of Information and Communication* 1, no. 1.

Gurumurthy, Anita. 2004. Gender and ICTs: Overview report, Bridge Cutting Edge Pack. Brighton: Institute of Development Studies. http://www.bridge.ids.ac.uk/reports/cep-icts-or.pdf (accessed 4 December 2005).

Hafkin, Nancy J. 2002a. Gender issues in ICT policy in developing countries: An overview. Prepared for the UN Division for the Advancement of Women Expert Group Meeting on ICTs and Their Impact on and Use as an Instrument for the Advancement and Empowerment of Women. Seoul, Korea, 11–14 November. http://www.un.org/womenwatch/daw/egm/ict2002/reports/Paper-NHafkin.pdf (accessed 30 November 2005).

———. 2002b. Is ICT gender neutral? A gender analysis of six case studies of multi-donor ICT projects. Background paper prepared for the INSTRAW Virtual Seminar Series on Gender and ICTS. June-July. http://www.un-instraw.org/en/docs/gender_and_ict/Hafkin.pdf (accessed 30 November 2005).

———. 2005. Gender issues at WSIS. *Information Technologies and International Development* 1, no. 2 (Summer).

Hafkin, Nancy J., and Sonia Jorge. 2002. Get in and get in early: Ensuring women's access to and participation in ICT projects. *Women in action* 2 [Isis International-Manila]. Special issue on women and communications. http://www.isiswomen.org/pub/wia/wia202.getin.htm (accessed 4 December 2005).

Jorge, Sonia. 2000. Gender perspectives in telecommunications policy. A curriculum proposal prepared for the ITU-BDT Task Force on Gender Issues.

Mottin-Sylla, Marie-Helene. 2002. Participation of Senegalese civil society in the formulation of ICT policies. APC Africa ICT Policy Monitor Project.

Mozambique. 2002. ICT Commission. ICT policy implementation strategy. http://www.infopol.gov.mz/ (accessed 15 October 2005).

Ramilo, Chat Garcia, and P. Villanueva. 2001. Issues, policies and outcomes: Are ICT policies addressing gender equality? Paper presented at United Nations Economic Commission for Asia and the Pacific Expert Group Meeting to Review ICT Policy from a Gender Perspective. Bangkok.

Republic of Ghana. 2003. *The Ghana ICT for accelerated development (CTAD) policy*. Accra: Government Publishing Corporation.

Republic of South Africa. 1996. White paper on telecommunications policy. The Ministry for Posts, Telecommunications, and Broadcasting. http://www.polity.org.za/html/govdocs/white_papers/telewp.html?rebookmark=1 (accessed 4 December 2005).

Republic of Uganda. 2002. National information and communication technology policy. Ministry of Works, Housing and Communications. The President's Office. National Council for Science and Technology. http://www.logos-net.net/ilo/150_base/en/init/uga_1.htm (accessed 4 December 2005).

République du Bénin. 2003. Politique et stratégies des TIC au Bénin. http://www.gouv.bj/textes_rapports/textes/politique/politiquetic.php (accessed 4 December 2005).

Selaimen, Graciela. 2005. ICT public policies and gender equity—the gaps and the bridges. GenderIT.org. 15 March. http://www.genderit.org/en/index.shtml?w=a&x=91234 (accessed 4 December 2005).

4

Cyberella in the Classroom?

Gender, Education, and Technology

Sophia Huyer

Women and girls are poorly placed to benefit from the rise of the knowledge society. While those who are technologically literate and electronically connected are dynamic and creative actors, they remain in the minority. Overall, females have less access than males to education in general and to S&T education specifically. They also have less access to the skills training and development that will enable them to gain employment in the IT sector.[1]

To become Cyberellas, to be fully empowered in the knowledge society, involves not only the ability actively to use and benefit from ICTs and information, but also to design, create, and contribute to the production of knowledge and new technologies as well as to understand their implications for life and society. To realize this empowerment, we need to ensure that women and girls are equally represented in scientific and technological education and training so that they can contribute actively to the knowledge society.

In order to secure equal representation and to ensure that ICTs do not become tools of disempowerment and increasing marginalization for women, they need to be implemented in ways that are gender and socially appropriate. If this is done, they can be tools of empowerment to provide access to education at all levels, including technical education. As part of a non-formal educational approach that provides women and men with information, ICTs can also supply tools and skills both to use technologies and improve well-being.

In this chapter complementary aspects of the interrelations among gender, ICTs, and education are presented and discussed: the enrollment and participation of females in S&T education at all levels; and the potential for ICTs to improve access to all groups (but particularly women and girls) to formal and non-formal education and literacy, as well as to increase the quality of the learning experience.

SETTING THE STAGE:
WOMEN AND GIRLS IN S&T EDUCATION

While education rates for girls at the primary level are increasing—and approaching parity with boys in some countries—fewer girls than boys overall are enrolled in primary grades. Two out of three of the 110 million children in the world who do not attend school are girls, with 42 million fewer girls than boys at the primary level. Girls also do not tend to go to school for as many years as boys. A six-year-old girl in South Asia will typically spend six years in school, compared with nine years for a boy. Living in the countryside widens the gap; a girl living in a rural area is three times more likely to drop out of school than a boy in the city. Literacy levels of females are lower than males in almost every region, with the notable exception of the Caribbean. Overall, women make up two-thirds of the world's 771 million illiterate adults (UNESCO 2003).

As we move up the educational ladder, the gender gap tends to widen, with regional and national variations. The enrollment of girls at the secondary level has increased in all developing regions since 1990, although there continue to be discrepancies in some countries, especially those with very low female enrollments in primary grades—such as Cambodia, India, Iraq, Nepal, Pakistan, and many sub-Saharan African countries. The trend is to parity in Latin America, especially in the Caribbean. Enrollment levels average around 30 percent of youth in sub-Saharan Africa and 70 percent in Latin America and the Arab States, while OECD countries and Central and Eastern European countries are at or close to universal secondary enrollment (UNESCO 2003).

A range of factors affects the lower enrollment of girls and young women, including parents' choices to invest in boys' education over that of girls and preconceptions that girls do not need education as much as boys because they are often not expected to move into paid employment outside of the home. The trend to early marriage and motherhood in many areas is another factor: in Nepal 40 percent of girls are married before age fifteen (UNESCO 2003). Factors beyond the household include lack of acceptable or appropriate sanitation facilities at schools (such as latrines); situations of armed conflict in which girls are more vulnerable to rape, sexual violence, and exploitation than boys,[2] and sexual harassment within schools. However, there are also trends to increasing dropout rates for boys and young men in certain countries, for reasons of violence, gang activity, and war (UNESCO 2003; Barker 2005).[3]

At the tertiary level, the enrollment of women has increased to 46.8 percent globally. However, there are wide regional variations in participation. In OECD countries and Central and Eastern Europe, gross enrollment rates are 45 percent, while in the great majority of developing countries they are under 30 percent (UNESCO 2003). This encouraging sign of increasing numbers of women at higher levels of education disappears when one looks at the enrollment of women in S&T subjects. Girls tend not to enroll in S&T subjects at the secondary level. In Chile, of those students enrolled in secondary-level technical streams, 82.2 percent of girls chose a commercial specialization, while 58.5 percent of boys (and 13.1 percent of girls) chose the industrial specialization. The International Mathematics and Science Study undertaken in forty-one nations in 1995–96 revealed a gender gap in math and science courses that increases during the academic process. In France, although girls perform better than boys in science at the secondary level, they make up less than half of the students in science baccalaureate streams (44.2 percent). In the United States, while gaps between girls and boys in math and sciences courses seem to be diminishing, likely as a result of more attention paid to gender equity issues in science and math courses, boys nevertheless continue to take more advanced courses (UNESCO 2003; AAUW 1998).

At the tertiary level, while in many regions the participation of women in biological and life sciences has increased and continues to increase, the level of representation of women in "hard" sciences such as physics and engineering is low around the world. In the United States, for every five-to-six men who graduate from an engineering program there is one woman, and while the percentage of women in chemical and agricultural engineering is slightly higher, in electrical and mechanical engineering there are fewer women—less than 14 percent (NSF 2003). In Europe, male graduates tend to outnumber women graduates in science, mathematics, and computing (except in Belgium and Spain), and in engineering programs. The average percentage of women graduates in science, mathematics, and computing in the European Union is 35.7 percent, down from 41 percent in 2000 (European Commission 2003).[4]

The numbers for undergraduate level computer science degrees awarded to females in computer science courses in the United States declined slightly (from 28.6 percent in 1994 to 27.6 percent in 2001); at the master's level women earned 33.7 percent of degrees in 2001 and only 18.8 percent of Ph.D.s (NSF 2004). In Canada, women made up 27.6 percent of the computer and information systems professionals work force in 2001, 9 percent of full-time faculty in engineering and applied sciences, and 23.1 percent of university students (at all levels) in engineering and applied sciences (CCWEST 2004).

EXPLAINING THE NUMBERS: BARRIERS TO FEMALE PARTICIPATION IN S&T EDUCATION

Barriers to participation in S&T education, including computer education, fall into roughly three categories: sociocultural/socioeconomic, qualificational, and institutional.[5]

Sociocultural barriers include lack of family commitment to female education by spouses and parents. Sociocultural attitudes about what is considered appropriate for girls and women affect family members' support of girls' choice of subject or discipline.[6] For example, some reasons given by women and men in Nigeria for the low participation of women in IT were that IT and IT-related careers were unsuitable for the female personality, too strenuous for women, and limited their chances for marriage (Ajayi and Ighoroje 1996).

Girls and women often experience a lack of comfort with or interest in S&T subjects. Studies in both the North and South show that teachers in math and science classes tend to answer boys' questions more often than those of girls and pay more attention to girls in non-science classes, thereby sending messages about gender capacities (see Margolis and Fisher 2002). Teaching materials, textbooks, and lectures tend to depict S&T as a male domain, depriving girls of role models. It is also found that a narrow technology focus in the curriculum, while appealing to boys, can alienate girls, who are more interested in understanding how the technology fits into a larger social, environmental, or work context (AAUW 2000; Bissell et al. 2003).

At the tertiary level, while the narrow technology focus of computer science courses seems to discourage women, they tend to enroll in larger numbers when courses are introduced that place technology in a larger context of society, occupation, history, or use (Margolis and Fisher 2002;

Bissell et al. 2003). This is also supported by Rajagopal and Bojin, who found that women students learn IT best in the context of their courses: "They seem to be more purposeful or course-oriented learners" (2003).

Socioeconomic class is also a factor in women's access to higher and technical education. Women in higher social classes are more likely to have family support for continuing their education and to have access to the resources to cover the cost of higher education (Gajjala 2002; Evans 1995).

Barriers to female enrollment specific to computers and IT subjects are also evident at early stages. Many studies show that girls are turned off early on by the intensely masculine nature of technology. They reject computer games as violent, redundant, and tedious. They also reject the nonsocial, technical obsession they see in their fellow male students (AAUW 2000; Rajagopal and Bojin 2003). As result, girls are less comfortable with computers. At later stages, preconceptions about computer scientists or software developers on the part of teachers and professors, as well as social stereotypes, may alienate or discourage women from pursuing studies in this area (Margolis and Fisher 2002).

Ufomata's study of the use of computer games by children in Nigeria found that many children believed that they are designed for boys, who supposedly like violence and action. When asked who plays the games most, with almost no exception the children responded that boys do. Ufomata lists the reasons given in order of response:

- Boys are more interested.
- Boys have a lot of time to spare because they have no work to do.
- Girls are always busy in the kitchen or with housework.
- Computer games are designed for boys.
- Boys like action games.
- Boys like violence.
- Boys are more adventurous.
- The games have mostly male characters; only boys and men are heroes of the games.
- Boys understand such things more easily.
- Mostly boys are found in computer clubs; girls are scared of such places. (Ufomata 1996)

Qualification barriers include lack of formal math and science education or experience in computer programming, which is often perceived as a barrier for continuing education in S&T and IT, although increasing evidence is emerging to suggest that lack of previous training in these subjects is less of a barrier than expected. In the Philippines poorly educated and low-income women successfully graduated from the Cisco Networking Academy Program (Walsh 2001); previous formal computer training proved not to be a factor for the success of women in the Carnegie Mellon University computer-science program (Margolis and Fisher 2002).

Women often take breaks in their professional careers and educational paths for personal and family reasons, including child rearing. This can make it difficult for them to re-enter or move up to higher-level educational programs.

Institutional barriers include the lack of female teachers and role models and the assumptions of male teachers mentioned above; inflexible admission, selection, and entry requirements that do not take into account women's varying educational backgrounds, approaches, and abilities; work conditions that do not consider women's life responsibilities; and heavy attendance requirements for practical skills and laboratory work that are more difficult for women to meet in view of their family responsibilities. Performance appraisals based on male life and research experience and difficulties in breaking into male professional networks also pose difficulties for women (NSF 2003).

Some general strategies to encourage women's participation in S&T education have proven to be effective in encouraging the continued participation of girls and women in education, such as scholarships based on merit, culturally appropriate facilities, actively seeking out and encouraging women candidates for fellowships and academic opportunities, women teachers and role models, alternative schools with flexible schedules, and vocational training. There is a substantial body of research on strategies and approaches to increase the participation and success rate of women and girls in S&T education. Some of these approaches include making changes in curricula to reflect a gender-neutral or gender-inclusive image of scientists and the practice of science. Promotion of science education and curricula that emphasizes hands-on activities and application to everyday life, society, and the environment has been proven to increase interest and success in science for both girls and boys, in addition to conscious efforts by teachers to ensure that girls and boys are treated as equals in the classroom.

Strategies to encourage continuing education and skills updating for women are especially important at higher levels of education and include the presence of female role models and mentors, bridging programs that allow re-entry for women already qualified in technical subjects, conversion programs that provide older women and school dropouts access to technical education, and community-based programs built around issues of direct relevance to the lives of women (Huyer 2004).

The experience of the Open University in the UK in attracting women into its computer program is a useful illustration of a bridging and conversion program. The university instituted an open-access policy in its technology courses in the 1980s in order to attract women into nontraditional subject areas. However this practice was insufficient in itself to attract more women students, who also experienced barriers of cost, confidence in their ability to handle the courses, and the burden of family commitments. A course for computer beginners helped to address one of these concerns. As at Carnegie Mellon, changes in the curriculum that placed technology in a larger context of real-world functionality proved to be more appealing to women. Pedagogical approaches that stressed skills development, reflective practice, and the teaching of technology ideas and concepts in a larger historical and social context also proved successful in attracting more women students. Other important strategies include encouraging peer networking and support and engaging in outreach programs with high schools (Bissell et al. 2003; Margolis and Fisher 2002).

ICTS TO PROMOTE LEARNING

While S&T studies, the prerequisite for the empowerment of women in IT-based professions, are often unattractive to women because little content is directed at their interests, ICTs can act as tools to promote the increased education of girls and women through both formal and non-formal educational approaches in all fields.

ICTs in Formal Education Systems

Computers and ICT-based education and teaching methods have been introduced at every level of formal education. In developed countries, students-per-computer ratios are decreasing rapidly, with accompanying increases in analysis of ICT use for educational, cultural, and social uses in classrooms. Hardware and software for education continue to expand and develop, with constant introduction of new products. While opinions on results and achievements vary, there is emerging consensus on some of the key elements of implementing successful ICT-based education programs.

In terms of educational or learning results, it appears that while the introduction of ICTs into a classroom will not automatically or immediately improve learning achievements to a dramatic extent, there can be good results in particular situations. Well-trained and motivated teachers can improve learning conditions with ICT and acquire ICT skills that will prepare them and their students for the knowledge society. Information-management processes can be improved through ICT; this allows teachers to spend more time on teaching, allows more efficient and transparent information flows in schools and the educational system, and provides policymakers with relevant and current data. ICTs also can provide access to high-quality curricula resources and expertise for both students and teachers. For developing countries, therefore, ICTs "are also an equity issue. . . . Low income and isolated rural schools may use them to dramatically enhance their learning tools and resources and connect students with other realities, peoples and educational projects around the world" (Hepp et al. 2004, iv).[7]

Current research indicates that the most consistent and effective contribution of ICT to education in developing countries is to teacher education, not only in training and certifying teachers, but also in providing opportunities for regular upgrading and, if necessary, retraining. A study by the Digital Education Enhancement Project of the Open University found that ICT-based teacher training enhanced teachers' professional knowledge and capability through the extension of subject knowledge, enabling planning and preparation for more efficient teaching and developing the range of teachers' pedagogic practices. It also facilitated new forms of cooperation and interaction among teachers and was flexible enough to adapt to the type of technology the teacher had access to, geographical location, local education and cultural practices, home language, and subject specializations (Leach 2004; see Capper 2002).[8]

In Guyana the Canadian International Development Agency has funded a project to train teachers in remote areas through distance education. The teachers are women aged sixteen to twenty-four with only primary education. They travel, often by foot, for two or three days to reach the training center, where they are taught using a combination of print materials and teacher support. Over three years, one thousand teachers have completed the three-year course in a region where there is no other form of teacher training or support.

The women often travel with their young children. Travel at any time of the year is difficult, and during the rainy season particularly so. To address this problem, the project planned to introduce audio and video cassettes to allow the women to learn at home (Sproule 2002).

Distance education carries risks and challenges for both teachers and students. These include supplying expert facilitation and training, which need to be based on an understanding of how to motivate learners and communicate the value of learners' contributions and perspectives from a distance. There is the additional risk of learners "not learning"—learners may focus on elements of a curriculum that they understand or are familiar with and are more able to master while overlooking aspects of a teaching approach or curriculum that they do not immediately comprehend. Finally, the need for feedback from trainers to teachers on the implications of new approaches and to confirm that they fully understand new concepts or approaches is an important part of distance teacher training (Capper n.d.).

In order to ensure that ICTs are implemented effectively for education of both teachers and students, a framework of policy, planning, and evaluation should be put in place to assess the feasibility and value of the ICT strategy implemented. ICTs should be implemented to support a pedagogical perspective; they should follow the learning approach, not determine it. A framework to ensure this should include a staff development plan (human capacity development) and support for hardware and software acquisition and development, repair, updates, and management. The existence and relevance of educational content on either the Internet or CD-ROMs should be taken into account, especially in terms of addressing learning needs, teaching practices, and models. A long-term commitment is required from various levels of governments, in terms of management, continuation, and program enhancement. All of these need to be accompanied by a consistent and sound evaluation strategy that includes achievement standards and performance indicators (Hepp et al. 2004). Additionally, the benefits of distance learning and technology-enabled training for women teachers should be assessed, as emerging research on it is inconclusive at this time.

Gender Equality and ICT-enabled Education

Computers in Schools: Will Girls Benefit?

Little research exists on the gender-differentiated effects and benefits of the use of technologies for education, especially the use of computers in schools in developing countries, although some studies on it have appeared.

Studies in developed countries indicate that

- boys often feel more confident in using technologies, which is likely partly due to the attitude of teachers;
- girls and boys have different learning styles, and boys' style of learning tends to be more accommodated to in the technology curriculum;
- girls are less interested in computers because of the stereotypes around computing and the violence of computer games;
- computer technologies are often considered the domain of boys, and video games and entertainment software tend to be geared toward boys' interests;
- both teachers and students tend to consider that boys are better at technology and more interested in technology subjects and accept the stereotype of the computer "geek" who is young and male (AAUW 2000; Derbyshire 2003; Margolis and Fisher 2002).

Some research is emerging in developing countries to support these conclusions and to provide some interesting examples of divergence as well. Research undertaken by SchoolNet Africa found that gender integration in programs to introduce computers to schools has been limited (Isaacs 2002; see also Chapter 5 herein). One of the few in-depth studies of gender patterns in use of computers in schools was done by World Links, which assessed the gendered effects of the introduction of computers in schools in four countries in Africa (Senegal, Mauritania, Uganda, and Ghana). One finding was that high student-to-computer ratios and first-come-first-serve computer policies disadvantage girls. In Uganda, seventeen hundred students and one hundred teachers competed for use of the seven functional computers. The computers were set up in a separate lab, away from the classroom. Because it was considered unsuitable for girls to run, the boys arrived first at the computers. As they were unwilling to limit their time at the computers, girls had less time to use them. Other sociocultural factors limiting girls' access included domestic chores, earlier curfews at boarding schools, and lack of confidence in using the computers.

A female student observed:

> Boys outnumber us and once they sit in front of the com-
> puter, they never get up. We always get discouraged and end
> up letting them have it all. . . . The boys are benefiting more
> but the girls make good use of the little they get. Some of the
> boys want us to think that as girls we do not need to know
> about computers. (in Gadio 2001, 2)

However, the value of computer use to the girls also should be noted. The study found that when girls did have access to computers, they tended to use them more for academic research and communication with friends and family, increasing their reasoning and communication skills. They also used Internet access to obtain information on issues such as reproduction and sexuality that was not available from their families or communities, and their self-confidence improved. One participant in Senegal said: "We are no longer dependent on boys. We feel capable of solving our problems with great autonomy" (Gadio 2001, 2).

Boys tended to use the computers for sports and music, with less academic benefit, a trend of concern in those regions where male enrollment in schools is decreasing. As we have seen, this can be for sociocultural reasons including lack of male role models, lack of male teachers, violence, and unemployment. In such situations computers may provide an opportunity to increase boys' interest in education. In the Caribbean, for example, the rate of education for boys decreases in comparison to girls at secondary and tertiary levels; this is so even at the primary level in some countries (see Barker 2005). The interest boys have in computers and their comfort and familiarity with computer and video games could be a means of enticing them back to the school environment. Further work needs to be done in this area.

Computers are not the only form of ICTs that can contribute to the education of girls (and boys). Radio, television, and video can be more appropriate educational technologies in certain situations. In Zimbabwe, interactive radio instruction (IRI) has been used successfully to improve access to primary education. Children from eight to ten years of age are organized into listening groups at IRI centers and follow lessons broadcast over the radio under the guidance of a mentor. Girls have a high participation rate—in 2001 they composed 48.7 percent of the total IRI enrollment, compared to 45.2 percent in other primary education programs during the same year. One incentive for parents to enroll their girls in IRI is that no user fees or uniforms are required (Green 2003).

Distance and E-learning

Distance education through ICT can provide a real opportunity for women and girls to overcome many educational obstacles. The flexibility of access and study times and the potential to reach women in rural areas can make this a very positive educational approach for women (Kramarae 2001; Maroba 2003). It is often difficult for women to travel to attend school for reasons of time, cost of transportation, safety, and perceptions of the appropriateness of traveling on their own (Evans 1995). The cost of education tends to be less for online courses as well, not only in direct fees, but also in travel, boarding, and related costs. (Of course, this assumes that women can bear the costs of online access and use of the computer or other ICT.) Interestingly, a study in Barbados indicates that participation in distance learning can inspire women to become more interested in and feel more confident about enrolling in S&T courses (Commonwealth of Learning 1999).

While both women and men experience problems in distance education, they become more acute for women for sociocultural and economic reasons, including irregular and unsystematic tutorial help and learner support, inadequate supply of reading material, and lack of study centers. The lack of affordable or dependable ICT infrastructure can also be a cost or barrier to distance learning in developing countries (Wolff 2002). Other challenges include access to (and language of) course content; content that tends to be aimed at more highly educated levels of the population; little content aimed at training and information needs of micro and small enterprises; need for maintenance and updating of technologies; and training for both teachers and students on how to use ICTs in support of education. Distance learning is sometimes viewed as providing a second-rate education, especially at higher education levels, suitable for those who have failed the "normal" system (Green 2003; Maroba 2003; Srivastava 2002; Capper 2002).

Interviews with women in Asia revealed that women take advantage of distance education to improve income generation, to enter a career that would enable them to support their families and send their children to the university, to improve performance in their current employment, to increase self-confidence, and to learn new skills. Most had to overcome strong opposition from family members, which often dissipated when the benefits to the family as a whole became evident (Kanwar and Taplin 2001).

E-learning[9] has been shown to be a useful educational strategy for women in the formal education system. In many countries in the developed world women's enrollment in e-learning courses is greater than men's, while in developing countries some numbers indicate women enroll in online education in greater numbers than in traditional courses. However, women are not equitably represented in e-learning in all countries, and there may be significant variations in their representation in distance learning between and within regions (Green and Trevor-Deutsch 2002).

In Kenya, men greatly outnumber women in ODL programs for which there was data available. Men tended to be represented in agricultural extension programs,[10] and programs for health-field workers, cooperative extension officers, and teachers. Women are found in adult literacy and traditional birth attendants' health programs.

The following data is for formal distance-learning programs in other African countries:

- At the University of Zambia during the period 1994–98, females made up 17 percent of distance-learning enrollment;
- At Zimbabwe Open University women make up about one-third of the student population;
- At the Kenyatta University campus of the African Virtual University, women make up 23 percent of students in the Faculty of Science;
- At Uganda Polytechnic in 2000, Kyambogo women made up 36 percent of students;
- Enrollment at the Botswana College of Distance and Open Learning, which offers secondary-level education, is 70 percent female (Green and Trevor-Deutsch 2002).

There appears to be more parity in enrollments in Asia, with the exception of India. According to reports received by the Commonwealth of Learning, this region sees little or no gender disparity in schools or in tertiary-level enrollment in either conventional or ODL schools. In Malaysia, the Institute for Distance Education at University Putra Malaysia has an enrollment of 46 percent women, while at the Pakistan Allama Iqbal Open University, 43 percent of students are women. At the Indira Gandhi National Open University, 27 percent of students were women in 2002.[11]

The South Pacific appears to have reached gender parity in distance-learning programming, where at the University of the South Pacific, the largest provider of distance education in the region, 48 percent of students in 2000 were women (Green and Trevor-Deutsch 2002).

In the Caribbean, as we have seen, the participation rate of females in education is equal to or greater than that of males at primary levels, and rates of male enrollment decline at secondary and tertiary levels. According to Green and Trevor-Deutsch (2002), "Where data is available, this includes the use of ICTs." In Jamaica, St. Kitts, and Nevis, available evidence indicates that more women than men use computer-based literacy programs (Huyer 2004).

For developed countries, the percentage of women in ODL programming also varies. In North America the participation of women in distance courses ranges from 61 to 78 percent in certain universities. A 1998 study found that women made up 27.4 percent of enrollments at the FernUniversitat in Germany, while at the National Distance Education University in Spain, the percentage was 54.7 percent. Enrollments at open universities in Europe vary as well, with women making up 50 percent of the student body in the UK, and 38 percent at the Open University in the Netherlands (Thompson 1998; Commonwealth of Learning 1999; Kanwar and Taplin 2001; Green and Trevor-Deutsch 2002).

Studies on gender differences in online education, peer support, discussion groups, and online tutorials indicate that females can benefit greatly from online or e-learning. Several studies indicate that there are clear gender differences in use of, comfort with, and benefits from online educational activities. Research on ICT-based lectures at the GH-Joanneum in Austria found that female students appreciate the privacy of virtual courses. They experience less pressure about their inputs and less fear of appearing "stupid" in front of male students. The Open University in the UK found that female students use computer conferences for contact with students, course directors, and tutors, and may feel better supported in an online teaching environment. A study of online education in North America found that compared to their male counterparts, female students seem to identify more with the process of learning and believe that IT improves their learning, while men think that IT has increased their academic productivity (Gferer and Pauschenwein 2002; Bissell et al. 2003; Rajagopal and Bojin 2003).

According to a US study of gender influences in online communication, gender influences online communication dynamics. Women appear to have different expectations concerning the frequency and nature of online communication than men and seek cooperative and supportive communication environments, while males tend to be more confrontational, autonomous, and abstract. Arbaugh (2000) found that women participated more in online class discussions and were more collaborative, while Herring (2000) found that female students tended to participate to a greater extent when the instructor promoted a civil and focused discourse. Other studies indicate that the anonymity and social distance of the Internet seem to encourage female participants to be more active (Im and Lee 2003).

An analysis of participation in an international online master's of adult education program among students from the University of Botswana and the University of Georgia (US) found that gender rather than nationality was the major variable influencing both quantity and quality of participation. Giannini-Gachago and Seleka (2005) found that female students were more active in posting and reading messages and also posted longer messages. Males tended to ask more questions and post more comments, while women replied to questions more often. The quality of messages also varied: males sent more "triggering" messages or messages meant to initiate discussion, while women's inputs were more explorative and integrative. Women dominated the discussions in terms of quantity and leadership.

Promoting Access to Vocational and Technical Education

Lifelong learning and vocational educational strategies are important to women. In general, they do not have the access to technical and skills training to move into more technical and cognitive employment. They continue to be concentrated in low or unskilled jobs and are not getting the training required for the more highly skilled jobs of the information society. For example, 42 percent of women in sub-Saharan Africa participate in the labor force, but few have access to skills development; illiteracy rates for women in many countries in the region are greater than 30 percent. Young women make up only 15–35 percent of formal training programs. Many other studies have found that women tend to lack access to technology and other resources much more than men (see Blackden and Banu 1999). In view of the rapidly changing set of skills required to participate in IT employment, this is a serious concern.

ICTs can facilitate access to technical and vocational training to address these concerns, through access to training and support in building and managing IT-based SMEs. ICTs can also facilitate technical education at varying levels, in varying formats and venues. The Cisco Systems

Networking Academy Program is one example of a technical training program that actively recruits female students and has the potential to reach large numbers of women in developing countries. It is a global training program that teaches students to design, build, and maintain computer networks, preparing them for industry-standard certification as networking professionals. To increase female enrollment it uses female role models in advertisements and promotional materials, and the curriculum includes a gender-equity training module. It has also formed partnerships with international organizations, nonprofit organizations, and NGOs to address the gender gap. It completed a project with the ECA that awarded scholarships to young women who traveled to ECA in Addis Ababa for training in Internet networking technology. At the same time as they received technical training, the trainees also received training in management, entrepreneurship, and gender issues. An evaluation of the project found that:

> The trainees gained increased knowledge in all four areas, as well as gaining enormously in self-confidence and self-esteem. It is highly likely that the project will have role model and multiplier effects on other young women in Africa: of twenty-seven young women surveyed from the first graduating class, 71 percent said that they intended to encourage other women to enter the IT field and to promote women in IT; 41 percent said that they intended to become IT entrepreneurs; and fully 82 percent said they intended to work in the IT field. (Hafkin 2002)

ICTs for Non-formal Education

ICTs have an important role to play in non-formal education. Considering the number of women and men who do not have access to formal education, and may not have received primary education, this could be one of the most important roles for ICTs. It is certainly an area where more attention is needed to assess and develop effective strategies and pedagogical approaches. Presented here is a range of examples of successful projects to provide education to women and girls on a range of subjects, including literacy, health, and rights.

Four community learning centers (CLCs) set up in remote rural areas of Iran focused on meeting education and development needs of women, minorities, and other rural poor groups. The CLCs focused on three main categories of activity: basic literacy, post literacy, and vocational training, including religious, health, and environmental education, animal husbandry, embroidery, sewing, knitting, making toys, and weaving carpets. Other activities included providing counseling services (such as family planning), providing day care, and organizing national and religious ceremonies, study visits, pilgrimages, and sightseeing. Activities were planned, designed, and implemented using a participatory approach, through group meetings attended by the learners as well as by representatives of local government organizations, the village council, and school and other local officials. Training modules and class schedules were flexible to adapt to learners' choices and time available, and local people were hired as teachers.

As a result of this participatory approach and focus, the CLCs played a very important role in providing learning opportunities for women in Islamic society. A large number of women and girls attended the CLC programs; 79 percent of participants were women. Men preferred that their wives and daughters used these centers because they were taught exclusively by women; even further, their husbands and fathers allowed them to go freely to CLC classes, since the environment was considered safe for women.

Results of the CLC programs included an increased level of literacy in the community; growing awareness among the women participants of their rights; greater participation of women in village council meetings and other community affairs; readiness to participate in elections; greater involvement in family decision making in matters related to the number of children, children's education, and marriage; increased earnings from selling handmade garments; greater self-confidence; and better knowledge of matters related to hygiene and sanitation. A major result of the programming was increased awareness on the part of the men of women's rights and changes in their views toward women's education. Other notable results were changes in the division of labor at home, improvement in family relations, and equal treatment of girls and boys in the family (Pant 2003).

In another example, the Commonwealth of Learning implemented literacy programs in several countries using radio-based learning in combination with print media and face-to-face training and discussion. Initiatives aimed at women included a project in Ghana that used radio to develop functional literacy as well as provide information in local languages on a wide range of topics, including AIDS, teenage pregnancy, nutrition, community empowerment, income-generating activities, food preservation, animal husbandry, child labor, and energy saving. In addition to providing information on locally relevant topics, radio was used to support literacy teaching with more detailed information that could not be provided in the classroom. Although there were some difficulties such as poor radio infrastructure and inadequate air time to offer literacy in fifteen languages, there were real benefits: use of the radio strengthened the coverage of the functional and development themes of the literacy program, changed people's attitudes toward issues such as family planning, and contributed to the establishment of income-generating ventures (Siacewena 2000).

The Tata Literacy project in India is a computer-based functional literacy program run by the Tata Consultancy Services in partnership with the Andhra Pradesh government. The project operates in Andhra Pradesh, Tamil Nadu, Madhya Pradesh, Maharashtra, Uttar Pradesh, and West Bengal. The program has helped more than twenty thousand people learn to read while also learning how to use computers. It uses animated graphics with voice-over to teach literacy and is tailored to fit different languages and dialects.[12]

Indira Soochna Shakti, a project in India, uses hand-held computers to provide girls in high schools with access to computer education. Volunteers, who share networked hand-held community computers in villages, find and locally disseminate information and information-enabled services. The project is intended both to educate the girls in IT in order to enable them to enter the information society and to support empowerment of the young women as they become respected technology resource persons and leaders in their communities.[13]

Radio remains an important educational technology, especially in rural areas and in the least developed countries. Radio Education for Afghan Children uses radio to broadcast education programs to children in Afghanistan who have few opportunities to attend school. While not a substitute for formal education, the radio programs offer informative, interesting, and thought-provoking material to children and adults on basic subjects such as science, social studies, mathematics, grammar, and spelling. Programs for adults concentrate on life skills, such as the dangers of landmines, adjustment after the civil war, and the role of women in Afghan society. The program is designed as a dynamic tool to respond to children's wider educational needs. Programs are developed based on participatory rural assessments with focus groups made up of men, women, girls, and boys. Program ideas from these meetings are further developed with experts in the topics covered and sent to the focus groups for feedback. The role of women and programs focusing on women's concerns are a major part of the Radio Education for Afghan Children programming, which includes sessions on family and children's health, home economics, and women's rights in the family and society (Siddiqi 2002).

CONCLUSION

The gender divide poses a threat to the ability of women and girls to participate actively in and benefit from the knowledge society. As global society becomes increasingly based on the exchange of knowledge and IT products, services, and processes, women and girls on the wrong side of the digital divide run the risk of becoming increasingly marginalized. However, we have also seen that ICTs, as carriers of the knowledge society, may help women to gain the education and knowledge that will enable them to become active contributors and to gain access to and use information that will contribute to their well-being.

Research, particularly in the following areas, is needed for us to understand more clearly how these trends may evolve:

- Gender-differentiated effects and benefits of the use of technologies for education.
- Feasibility, efficiency, and reach of various strategies for using ICTs for education, particularly on the benefits and degree of participation of women and girls.
- Costs, efficacy, and benefits of distance learning, including the use of computers and Internet, particularly related to the benefits for girls and women, at all levels of education.
- Collection of data and indicators on women's participation in computer sciences and IT in educational institutions and employment.
- Creative strategies to encourage the participation of women and girls in S&T education and training at school and in the work place, through a range of multi-stakeholder partnerships (see Morrell and Huyer 2005).

While recognizing the difficulties and challenges that girls and women have with ICTs and distance learning, we also know that ICTs and computers may present a means to overcome barriers to education experienced by a range of groups: girls and women, boys in violent societies, indigenous groups, and groups in areas where there are few or poorly financed schools.

Both the opportunities and the risks posed by the knowledge society and ICTs need to be understood clearly in order to devise strategies to overcome them and to allow students, teachers, and policymakers to engage in and develop ICT-based education systems that will promote greater equality and empowerment for all groups.

NOTES

[1] This chapter is based in part on work undertaken for the World Bank study on Engendering ICTs, June 2003. The views expressed here are those of the author and not those of the World Bank.

[2] This vulnerability affects girls' school attendance in several ways. Girls who are the victims of violence will attend school less, for fear of emotional or physical harm, while parents may also choose to keep them home for safety reasons. In some areas women and girls are recruited—on a volunteer or non-volunteer basis—into armies. It is estimated that approximately 100,000 girls directly participated in conflicts in at least thirty countries in the 1990s as fighters, cooks, porters, spies, servants, or sex slaves (UNESCO 2003). Armed conflict and violence also affect boys' enrollment when they leave school to join armies or gangs. Young men are also more likely to be killed by violent means (Barker 2005).

[3] In some cases dropout rates for boys account for increasing rates of girls' enrollments, but in other cases they are the result of public awareness, programs to encourage parents to send girls to schools, and increases in income levels (UNESCO 2003).

[4] Health sciences are not included in this category, which may account for the lower number in comparison with other regions.

[5] For a more detailed discussion of factors restricting female participation in S&T education, see Huyer 2004 and Huyer et al. 2005.

[6] Studies show that women scientists tend to have fathers and/or mothers who are scientists in greater proportion than their male colleagues (see Rathgeber 2002; National Research Council 2001).

[7] For a discussion of the experience of SNA, see Chapter 5 herein.

[8] The project also found that more women participated than men, since they made up the majority of teachers, while the majority of students were male.

[9] E-learning can be defined broadly to encompass all online or computer-assisted learning at all levels, both formal and informal. ODL (open and distance learning) is defined by the Commonwealth of Learning (2002) as "a way of providing learning opportunities that is characterized by the separation of teacher and learner in time or place, or both time and place"; it includes computer and other ICT media (see Tinio 2004). The definition of ODL in this

chapter accords to the Commonwealth of Learning definition, while e-learning in this chapter is restricted to online or computer-mediated learning.

[10] This is an interesting finding in view of women's overwhelming contribution to food production in Africa (up to 80 percent of all food production activities).

[11] This is a lower percentage than the approximately 30 percent participation in conventional tertiary education in the country. Additionally, students tend to be based in urban centers (Srivastava 2002).

[12] For more information, see www.tataliteracy.com/impact_people.htm.

[13] For more information, see http://iss.nic.in.

REFERENCES

Ajayi, Oolajire Bosede, and Ahbor Dolly A. Ighoroje. 1996. Female enrollment for IT training in Nigeria. Presentation at the Eighth International Conference of the Gender and Science and Technology Association. Ahmedabad, India. 5–10 January. http://www.wigsat.org/gasat/papers1/5.txt (accessed 5 December 2005).

AAUW (American Association of University Women). 1998. *The gender gap*. Washington, DC: AAUW Educational Foundation.

———. 2000. *Tech-savvy: Educating girls in the new computer age*. Washington, DC: AAUW Educational Foundation.

Arbaugh, J. B. 2000. Virtual classroom characteristics and student satisfaction with Internet-based MBA courses. *Journal of Management Education* 24: 32–54.

Barker, Gary T. 2005. *Dying to be men: Youth, masculinity and social exclusion*. London: Routledge.

Bissell, Chris, David Chapman, Clem Herman, and Ley Robinson. 2003. Still a gendered technology? Issues in teaching information and communication technologies at the UK Open University. *European Journal of Engineering Education* 28, no.1: 27–35.

Blackden, C. Mark, and Chitra Banu. 1999. Gender, growth and poverty reduction. World Bank Technical Paper no. 420. Washington, DC: World Bank.

CCWEST (Canadian Coalition of Women in Engineering, Trades and Technology). 2004. Women in SETT: Building Communities. Phase I Final Report. Toronto.

Capper, Joanne. n.d. International experience with e-learning.

———. 2002. Use of technology to support high quality teacher professional development. July. http://www.developmentgateway.org/node/133831/sdm/blob?pid=5736 (accessed 5 December 2005).

Commonwealth of Learning. 1999. Identifying barriers encountered by women in the use of information and communications technologies (ICTs) for open and distance learning in the Caribbean. Summary report of a workshop held in Bridgetown, Barbados.

Derbyshire, Helen. 2003. *Gender issues in the use of computers in education in Africa*. London: DFID.

European Commission. 2003. Directorate-General for Research. *She figures: Women and science statistics and indicators*. Luxembourg: European Communities.

Evans, Karen. 1995. Barriers to participation of women in technological education and the role of distance education. The Commonwealth of Learning. http://www.col.org/barriers.htm (accessed 5 December 2005).

Gadio, Coumba Mar. 2001. Exploring the gender impact of World Links. Washington, DC: World Links.

Gajjala, Radhika. 2002. Cyberfeminist technological practices: Exploring possibilities for a women-centered design of technological environments. Background paper prepared for the INSTRAW Virtual Seminar Series on Gender and ICTs. 1 June–18 September. http://www.un-instraw.org (accessed 5 December 2005).

Gferer, Margareth, and Jutta Pauschenwein. 2002. Is the change from traditional teaching methods to ICT-based methods going to attract more female students to study engineering? An analysis of ICT-based lectures at the Fh-Joanneum. Paper presented at the International Seminar on Improving the Gender Balance in Engineering Education Using ICT Methods and Contents. Oulu Polytechnic, Institute of Technology, and University of Oulu, Faculty of Technology, Oulu, Finland. 16–17 May.

Giannini-Gachago, Daniela, and Geoffrey Seleka. 2005. Experiences with international online discussions: Participation patterns of Botswana and American students in an adult education and development course at the University of Botswana. *International Journal of Education and Development Using ICT* 1, no. 2. http://ijedict.dec.uwi.edu/viewarticle.php?id=42&layout=html (accessed 5 December 2005).

Green, Lyndsay. 2003. Gender-based issues and trends in ICT applications in education in Asia and the Pacific. *UNESCO meta-survey on the use of technologies in education*. Bangkok: UNESCO. www.unescobkk.org/fileadmin/user_upload/ict/Metasurvey/2Regional29.pdf (accessed 5 December 2005).

Green, Lyndsay, and Lawry Trevor-Deutsch. 2002. Women and ICTs for open and distance learning: Some experiences and strategies from the Commonwealth. Vancouver, British Columbia: Commonwealth of Learning. September. http://www.col.org/wdd/Women%20and%20ICTs.pdf (accessed 5 December 2005).

Hafkin, Nancy. J. 2002. Is ICT gender neutral? A gender analysis of six case studies of multi-donor ICT projects. Background paper, INSTRAW Virtual Seminar on Gender and ICT. June-July 2002. http://www.un.instraw.org/docs.hafkin.doc (accessed 30 November).

Hepp, Pedro K., Enrique S. Hinostroza, Ernesto M. Laval, and Lucio F. Rehbein. 2004. Implementing ICT in schools requires evaluation and contextualised commitment. World Bank. www1.worldbank.org/education/pdf/ICT_report_oct04a.pdf.

Herring, S. C. 2000. Gender differences in CMC: Findings and implications. *The CPSR Newsletter* 18, no. 1:3–11.

Huyer, Sophia. 2004. Gender equality and science and technology policy knowledge and policy at the international level: S&T for gender equality and social development. Gender Advisory Board of the United Nations Commission of Science and Technology for Development, Canada/Office of Education, Science and Technology, Organization of American States. http://www.science.oas.org/english/ev_ini_e.htm (accessed 5 December 2005).

Huyer, Sophia, Nancy Hafkin, Heidi Ertl, and Heather Dryburgh. 2005. Women in the information society. In *From the digital divide to digital opportunities: Measuring infostates for development*, ed. G. Sciadis. Montreal: Orbicom.

Im, Y., and O. Lee. 2003. Pedagogical implications of online discussion for preservice teacher training. *Journal on Technology in Education* 36, no. 2.

Isaacs, Shafika. 2002. IT's hot for girls: ICTs as an instrument in advancing girls' and women's capabilities in school education in Africa. Paper presented at the UN Division for Advancement of Women Expert Meeting "Information and communication technologies. . . . "

Kanwar, Asha S., and Margaret Taplin, eds. 2001. *Brave new women of Asia: How distance education changed their lives*. Vancouver, British Columbia: Commonwealth of Learning.

Kramarae, Cheris. 2001. *The third shift: Women learning online*. Washington, DC: AAUW Educational Foundation.

Leach, J. 2004. An investigation of the use of information and communication technologies for teacher education in the global south: Researching the issues. Digital Education Enhancement Project. Open University, Milton Keynes, UK.

Margolis, Jane, and A. Fisher. 2002. *Unlocking the clubhouse: Women in computing*. Cambridge: MIT Press.

Maroba, Miriam B. 2003. RE: [CCEM Gender] Women in distance education. 1 October. http://hub.col.org/2003/ccemgender/0096.html (accessed 5 December 2005).

Morrell, Claudia, and Sophia Huyer. 2005. Engendering ICTs for education. In *Harnessing the potential of ICT for education—A multistakeholder approach*. Proceedings of the Dublin Global Forum of the UN ICT Task Force. New York: UN ICT Task Force.

National Research Council. 2001. Committee on Women in Science and Engineering. *Female engineering faculty at US institutions: A data profile*. Washington, DC: National Academy Press.

NSF (National Science Foundation). 2003. *Gender differences in the careers of academic scientists and engineers: A literature review*. Division of Science Resources Statistics, NSF 03–322. Arlington, VA.

———. 2004. *Women, minorities, and persons with disabilities in science and engineering*. NSF 04–317. Arlington, VA. http://www.nsf.gov/statistics/wmpd (accessed 5 December 2005).

Pant, Anita P. 2003. *Good practices: Gender equality in basic education and lifelong learning through CLCs: Experiences from 15 countries.* Bangkok: UNESCO Asia and the Pacific Regional Bureau for Education.

Rajagopal, Indu, and Nis Bojin. 2003. A gendered world: Students and instructional technologies. *First Monday* 8, no. 1 (January). http://firstmonday.org/issues/issue8_1/rajagopal/index.html (accessed 5 December 2005).

Rathgeber, Eva. 2002. Female and male CGIAR scientists in comparative perspective. October. Washington, DC: CGIAR.

Siaciwena, Richard. 2000. Introduction. In *Case studies of non-formal education by distance and open learning*, ed. R. Siaciwena. Vancouver, British Columbia: Commonwealth of Learning.

Siddiqi, Shirazuddin. 2002. Radio programming for life skills and child development. Afghan Education Projects, BBC World Service. Presentation at Delivering and Enhancing Basic Education Using Appropriate ICTs—Exploring Current Practice and Sharing Lessons Learned workshop. Ottawa: CIDA.

Sproule, S. 2002. *Training teachers in remote areas through distance education.* Presentation at workshop, Delivering and Enhancing Basic Education Using Appropriate ICTs—Exploring Current Practice and Sharing Lessons Learned. Ottawa. 17 October. CIDA.

Srivastava, Manjulika. 2002. A comparative study on current trends in distance education in Canada and India. *Turkish Online Journal of Distance Education* 3, no. 3 (October). http://tojde.anadolu.edu.tr/tojde8/articles/srivastava.htm (accessed 5 December 2005).

Thompson, Melody. 1998. Distance learners in higher education. In *Distance learners in higher education: Institutional responses for quality outcomes*, ed. C. Campbell Gibson. Madison, WI: Atwood Publishing. http://wbweb5.worldbank.org/disted/teaching/design/kn-02.html (accessed 5 December 2005).

Tinio, Victoria L. 2004. *ICT in education.* Asia-Pacific e-primers series. Bangkok: Asia-Pacific Development Information Programme.

Ufomata, T. T. 1996. Computer games and Nigerian children: The effect of socialization on girls' choice of careers in computerization. Presentation at eighth International Conference of the Gender and Science and Technology Association. Ahmedabad, India. 5–10 January.

UNESCO. 2003. *Gender and education for all: The leap to equality.* Summary report. Paris: UNESCO.

Walsh, Erin. 2001. *Creating opportunities for women in developing countries: Cisco Systems and partners work together to develop gender-sensitive ICT training programs.* World Bank Gender and the Digital Divide Seminar Series. http://www.worldbank.org/gender/digitaldivide.

Wolff, Laurence. The African virtual university: The challenge of higher education development in Sub-Saharan Africa. *TechKnowLogia* (April-June 2002): 23–25.

5

"We Have Womb"[1]— Engendering ICTs in Education

The SchoolNet Africa Experience

Shafika Isaacs

Where there is a sustained, conscious intervention in an organization to promote gender-equality perspectives by champions who lead, monitor, and innovate within their spheres of influence, an opportunity for gendered learning opens up for all. Spaces can even be created for women and girls to assume greater decision-making power. Because these spaces challenge gender power relations, critical questions arise that will consistently challenge or potentially derail the gender-equality project.

While SchoolNet Africa (SNA) does not have an official stated policy on the promotion of gender equality and women's empowerment in ICT-enabled education (ICT4E) in African schools, it is one example of such a sustained intervention. It has demonstrated ways to engage successfully with gender-equality issues in the African information society because its organizational goals, programmatic objectives, and implementation processes were formed in part according to the objectives of the international Education for All initiative, which recognizes the prevalence of gender disparities in education access and opportunities, both quantitatively and qualitatively (UNESCO 2004). The leadership of SNA based at the secretariat has the authority and the reputation for delivery to make decisions that accord with the broad objectives of the Education for All goals, including those relating to gender equality.[2] Mechanisms for the promotion of gender equality and women's empowerment have been implemented in programming and campaigns by its gender-responsive leadership, which, perhaps not coincidentally, is female.

SNA is an African- and female-led NGO that was set up to promote learning and teaching in schools through ICTs across Africa. It works with a network of communities of practice who coalesce around national schoolnet groups and organizations currently operating in thirty-five African countries. SNA's emergence in 2000 was strongly influenced by the African Information Society Initiative (AISI) of the UN Economic Commission for Africa, which was established to promote an African response to the evolving global information society. The AISI strategy called for the formation of an African Learning Network, of which SNA (along with a VarsityNet and an Out of School Youth Network) was seen as an integral part (James 2000).

SNA's goals are to promote access to quality learning in formal school systems in Africa by demonstrating the potential of ICTs to contribute to achieving these goals, particularly in areas where there are few schools. For these reasons SNA also has a social mandate: to promote social equity and development through interventions targeted mainly at African learners and teachers. The promotion of universal access to ICTs in African schools, capacity building in technical, managerial, and pedagogical competencies, and the development of Africanized, digital content and curriculum integration are its priority activities.

Since its formal inception in 2001, SNA has contributed to several initiatives addressing gender equality relating to ICT for education. One of these is the UN Division for the Advancement of Women (UNDAW) Expert Meeting and subsequent report on "Information and Communication Technologies and Their Impact on and Use of as an Instrument for the Advancement and Empowerment of Women," in early 2003 (UNDAW 2003).

This chapter focuses on SNA's experiences and lessons in engendering ICTs in education in Africa, set against a backdrop of existing research on the gendered digital divide in education. The focus is on the formal education system in Africa, although broader concerns relating to gender equality in education, and in S&T in general, are also considered. This chapter is based primarily on the experiences of the author as a practitioner based at SNA and as a researcher in the field of education and ICTs.

The chapter builds on Derbyshire's (2003) framework for gender equality in relation to ICTs and education. In her view gender equality in education is about critical *qualitative* dimensions, such as education content or *what* learners are learning, as well as about the abilities and opportunities open to girls and boys relating to their role and status in society. Gender equality is not about treating boys and girls in the same way; it is a recognition that girls and boys and women and men may face *different constraints* in accessing educational opportunities and in achieving their educational potential that will need to be addressed in different ways. Girls and boys and women and men may also have *different interests and priorities* when it comes to learning that need to be taken into account in order to enable students to reach their full potential.

ENGENDERING ICTS IN FORMAL EDUCATION

Discussions of technology-mediated education are often limited to discussions of computer-science courses, technical training based in schools, and incorporating teaching about computers, e-mail, and the Internet in the curriculum. The African schoolnet movement has demonstrated that technology-enhanced learning—also referred to as computer-mediated learning, computer-aided learning, blended learning, or e-learning—incorporates the integrated use of new ICTs to facilitate improved learning and teaching practice, support the production and consumption of education content and curriculum, streamline school administration and management, and contribute to related national policy and decision making.

A systemic approach to educational technologies in schools needs to encompass all components of the educational system from early childhood development to adult basic education, tertiary education, and further education and training, as well as the relations of the educational system to accompanying economic, labor market, social, cultural, and political contexts. These processes operate from the national level all the way down to the influences of education systems on schools, teachers, and learners.

Along with its partners, SNA has developed the concept of a "schoolnet value chain," shown in Figure 5–1.

The value-chain model sets the school as a unit of analysis within a national school-education system. It is an evolving concept that guides and is in turn updated from current practice. Related sets of issues and value chains branch off each of the chains of activity in themselves to catalyze a series of relationships (which Figure 5–1 cannot fully illustrate). For instance, the content, curriculum integration, and learning strategies chain will branch off into a sub-chain on language of instruction, quality of education content, intellectual property rights, and so

Figure 5–1. The SNA Value Chain

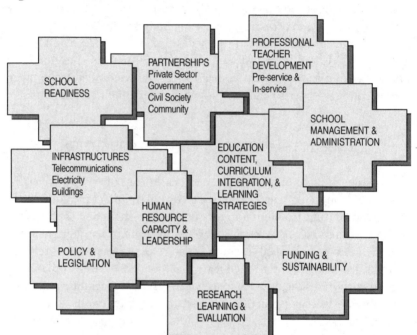

Source: *African SchoolNet Toolkit* 2005.

forth. In this way the schoolnet value chain attempts to encourage a system-wide approach and identify the broad areas, aspects, and activities that constitute a schoolnet.

The value-chain model provides an important conceptual stepping stone to understanding the gender dimensions of integrating ICTs in the formal education system. The existing literature on gender issues in education refers mainly to the position of women in science, the percentage of women enrolled in computer-science courses, and their participation in the S&T work force. The value-chain model raises issues beyond those addressing female representation in technology to identify the gendered nature of ICT access and application in pedagogy, learning and teaching, education content and curriculum, school management, administration, and national policy. It also encompasses gender issues in technology-enhanced learning relating to the qualitative and contextual sociocultural issues of values, attitudes, confidence levels, and beliefs of boys and men as well as girls and women.

SKEWED KNOWLEDGE PRODUCTION: CAN WE APPLY EXPERIENCE FROM DEVELOPED COUNTRIES TO THE AFRICAN SITUATION?

Research on the gendered digital divide in formal school systems is focused mainly on experiences in developed economies. Here, access and use of computers in schools is well documented, particularly in Europe and the United States (Derbyshire 2003; Sanders 2005). Research-based information on gender patterns in the educational digital divide in Africa—especially in the formal school system—remains extremely limited. The well-known evaluation of World Links projects in four African countries is one of the very few gender- and education-specific field research reports available (see Gadio 2001). Derbyshire's review of gender, ICTs, and education and a project by the Commonwealth of Learning (Green 2003) are desk reviews of African experiences, while the author has written about the experiences in the African schoolnet movement from the perspective of a practitioner (Isaacs 2002a; UNDAW 2003). Further, Sanders notes deficiencies and inconsistencies in the research methods on gender differences in computer-related areas in developed countries that make it difficult to make comparisons even within this larger body of research.

The lack of research-based knowledge on digital divide issues in education in general—and specifically on gender issues in Africa—reflects the large disparities in technology-mediated education between Africa and the rest of the world. It indicates the limited extent to which gendered experiences in this area are addressed. The literature that is available lists numerous examples of gender inequality or a lack of taking into account gender-equality concerns in the conceptualization, practice, and outcomes of ICT integration in formal education. These are present in the entire range of activities identified in the schoolnet value chain.

Given existing limitations in knowledge, there is a danger of comparing African situations with those of more developed economies, without making allowance for differing economic, political, and educational status. For example, Sanders makes the comment that concerns about computer access, the association of computer studies with mathematics as a disincentive for girls, and the physical safety of college women at computer labs are "now less relevant" (2005, 3). This statement will certainly not apply to the current situation in Africa, where high numbers of young people do not have access to even primary education, and is one example of ICT-enabled education issues that may be less urgent in North America but which remain of fundamental concern in less developed economies in Africa.

Elsewhere, the author has remarked on the importance of addressing technology related issues against the backdrop of a generalized education crisis in Africa. According to recent UNESCO reports, approximately 43 million youth of school age are excluded from formal school systems. Of these, approximately 50 percent are young women. This confluence of development trends with education- and ICT-related concerns highlights the complexity of the gender-equality challenge in Africa in ways that warrant its own Africa-specific research agenda (Isaacs 2002b).

Discussions around gender, ICTs, and education in Africa often tend to be characterized by a technology-centered approach that focuses mainly or exclusively on issues of access to ICTs. It is clear that access is an important issue in, for example, the average school in Mozambique, which sees a ratio of 680 students to each PC (compared to the 6:1 ratio in North America) (Isaacs 2002a). Within this skewed distribution we know that girls have less access than boys to computers in African schools, as confirmed by the World Links study. However, access to these technologies, an important starting point, is only one of the many issues that challenge the ability of girls to use and benefit from the use of computers equally with boys. Wider equality issues include confidence levels in working with new technologies, the role and gender of the teacher and his or her attempts to support girls to become more actively involved with technologies, the numbers of women and girls involved as technical co-coordinators and in help-desk and technical-support functions, and gender biases in education content and curriculum.

These issues are referred to by, among others, Derbyshire, who additionally argues that the behavior of teachers is a critical influence, since they act as role models for their students (2003). She notes that in European and North American schools, computer science originated in male-dominated math and technology departments, and that the number of male teachers of IT subjects continues to be substantially greater than that of female teachers. The experience in developed countries has been that even when computers are used in different parts of the curriculum, it is often men who are in charge of organizing access to hardware and networks, and male teachers outnumber female teachers in using computers as a learning tool.

Analysis of education content and software programs reveals a similar gendered pattern. In her review of the literature on educational software, Sanders (2005) suggests that sexist stereotypes and preconceptions are evident in characters, content, reward systems, and structure. She also finds that teachers, both male and female, promote gendered assumptions in use of software. Huff and Cooper (1987) and Rosenthal and Demetrulias (1988) found that teachers identified gender issues or messages portrayed in the software only when attention was called to them. When teachers from primary to college level were asked to design software for girls, they tended to design tool software; for boys, they tended to design game software featuring violence and competitiveness. The study was repeated fifteen years later with the same results, leading Huff (2002) to conclude that the expectations and stereotyping of teachers are at the root of the sex bias in software (Sanders 2005). This confirms that both gender sensitivity in the *design* of education content and software programs and gender-sensitive learning strategies of teachers in their *application* are important if gender biases are to be addressed in the ICT-enabled learning process. Derbyshire (2003) notes that the issues are complex and that subtle and unintended gender biases can also affect children's behavior and perceptions. While the use of androgynous figures is widespread in software and games, there is considerable evidence to show that children tend to attribute a gender—usually male—to non-gendered characters (Volman and van Eck 2002). In Africa, the Mindset Network and the Department of Education's Thutong Portal[3] in South Africa project positive images of girls and women, and they train teachers to use the content on these sites to promote sensitivity to gender differences.

Glaring gaps continue to exist in current research on these issues, in particular on the interrelations between the social systems within schools and how the ICT for education process relates to or is disconnected from them. This is arguably a function of the disconnect in practice between ICT-related interventions in African schools and broader social concerns such as food security, school safety, and the effects of the HIV/AIDS pandemic on social life within and around African schools (Isaacs 2005).

LIMITATIONS TO THE NUMBERS GAME

We have reached the objective of the MDGs in the Global Teenager Project (GTP) because we have more girls participating in the GTP Learning Circles than boys by far. So there isn't really a gender issue here.

What are you gender activists in SchoolNet saying about the attrition of boys from schools in Northern Namibia which correlates with the attrition also of male teachers? How's that for gender equality?

Gender and education in the digital divide are often referred to in terms of numbers: of girls compared to boys or men compared to women at various levels in S&T education and employment. Consistently, available data and indicators highlight stark gender disparities, with girls and women concentrated in the lower levels of participation and decision making, as well as in areas and disciplines that reflect women's accepted social role as nurturers and caregivers. For example, women make up the majority of teachers in Africa, while school principals and ministers of education are more likely to be men.

Numerous studies have called attention to the higher concentration of boys and men in technical and technology-centered activities in most regions in the world. Margolis (2001) notes that fewer than 20 percent of graduates of US computer-science departments are female, and fewer girls are enrolled in high school programming or advanced computer-science classes. She argues that women have lost ground in the world of computing, despite its historical coincidence with the rise of the women's movement. Huyer (2004) refers to gender imbalances in the S&T sector and in how S&T is applied for social development. Women's engagement with S&T for social development has been ignored as a policy and research area, and one result has been an actual decline in the overall position of women relative to men. Women have become disproportionately impoverished in comparison to men in their communities, according to the findings of the Gender Working Group of the UN Commission on Science and Technology for Development (UN Commission on Science and Technology for Development 1995). Derbyshire (2003) draws on the work of Volman and van Eck (2002) who note sharp gender differentials in choices to specialize in computing at school in

favor of males. The enrollment rates of African women in S&T education at all levels are the lowest in the world (Hafkin and Taggart 2001).

Statistics of the SNA network in July 2005 reflect some of these trends
(see Table 5–1).

Table 5–1. SNA Program Participants, Disaggregated by Sex

	Female	Male	Total
National schoolnet partner managers	10	20	30
Global Teenager Project (GTP) coordinators	9	11	20
African schoolnet technical coordinators	7	18	25
ThinkQuest Africa participants	363	671	1,034
GTP Learning Circle participants*	64	47	101

*Denotes figures made available in an evaluation report based on low response rate. GTP in 2005 had 7,225 learner participants while the figure reflects 101 learners.

Table 5–1 shows that slightly less than half of participants in the GTP
coordinators network are female, and more than one-third of learner
participants in the ThinkQuest Program are girls. In the learner-centered GTP Learning Circles Project, however, there is a substantially
higher participation of girls relative to boy learners overall (although
the data gathered reflects the responses of only nine of a possible thirty
country representatives). Girls' participation is not correlated with other
indicators, such as the gender of teachers. However, the higher participation of girls relative to boys did lead to conclusions that the project
"appeals more to girls," both according to anecdotal evidence of previous years and arguably because more female teachers were involved in
the program.

There are limited records of teachers trained in the application of
ICTs in learning and teaching through SNA's African Teachers Network, but a recent internal report on the training of 1,382 teachers from
ten African countries suggest that both trainers and trainees tend to be
male. The report identified the average teacher trainer in the course as
male, from twenty-six to thirty-five years of age, urban, possessing an
IT or computer-science background, and an ICT trainer by profession
with at least five years' experience. It was estimated that 30 percent of
the trainers were women, and an average of 40 percent of the teacher
trainee participants were women (Aranguren and Akinsanmi 2005).

These figures relate chiefly to SNA's regional and international programs and don't include activities of the national schoolnet organizations. A national-level example is that of SchoolNet Namibia, where of the two hundred technical practitioners sent on a Novell training program in Johannesburg, only four were women. This limited data confirms the trend articulated in the literature, that more girls and women tend to participate in learning-focused programs, but when it comes to technical training, the gender disparity tends to be substantial in both trainee and trainer groups.

In general, there appears to be a broad consensus in SNA regarding the importance of placing gender issues on its agenda in the first place. This can perhaps be attributed to an awareness within SNA's network of practitioners and policymakers of the need to consider differential effects on females and males. While it appears that progress has been made in both theory and practice toward gender parity in a few influential schoolnet organizations, perceptions of an inappropriate bias toward women and girls continue to exist. For example, participants at some SNA workshops have suggested that, in view of the attrition of male teachers and students (with accompanying increases in female enrollment and teaching staff) in some participating schools, a gender-equality perspective is becoming less relevant. Elsewhere, a comment by a leading female colleague that improving the situation of women and girls "all depends on the woman and the extent to which she promotes herself to be empowered" raised similar concerns. This comment was made in a conversation among SNA women staff who reported discomfort with the actions (inappropriate hugs and staring) of their male colleagues at a SNA workshop. Such perceptions prompt concern as to whether the gender equity project is fully understood and whether SNA's awareness-raising programs have been as successful as hoped.

Another question that is consistently raised is, "So what are you saying; that boys should be like girls and girls should be like boys for there to be gender equality?" At a meeting of GTP coordinators it was suggested that, given the high rate of girls' participation, gender is no longer an issue in the Learning Circles and that MDG Goal Number 2, gender parity in school enrollment, has been met. At the ICTs for African Schools workshop in Botswana (see discussion below), one successful two-hour breakaway session, "IT Is Hot for Girls," explored strategies for the integration of gender-equality perspectives and the empowerment of girls and women in education. It provided a venue for male participants to express concerns about a "gender" focus on girls and women: "What about the boys?" and "Why is there such a need for preferential treatment of women and girls?" The session was criticized for having only women speakers and for not recognizing or making allowance for a gender-sensitive male view.

These questions and comments do not necessarily reflect anti-gender-equality sentiments—and there are numerous examples of male teachers and coordinators supporting gender-equality goals and actions—but their existence indicates the extent to which the vision for the attainment of gender equality and women's empowerment in the ICT4E sector in Africa still needs to be clarified and understood. Where specific ICT4E policies have been adopted by African governments, references to the need to attain gender equality are made, usually in the vision sections of the policy statements. However, nowhere is it clearly outlined what that vision is and how it can be attained. As a result, there are few and limited references to gender-equality issues and strategies in ICT4E programming.

This explains why, in certain respects, the struggle for gender equality has been reduced to a numbers game. This is not to say that research into sex-disaggregated data is not important. Assumptions about lower female participation and enrollment in schools and higher dropout rates among girls based on limited data need to be tested against anecdotal evidence that the contrary appears to be the case in a few countries. Similarly, assumptions about the greater participation of girls in ICT4E projects need to be tested.

Derbyshire summarizes the importance of recognizing the disproportionate representation of women and girls in the ICT4E sector in terms that go beyond numbers to address fairness and justice in girls' and boys' access to and benefits from education:

> If women are to participate as shapers of the information revolution in Africa as well as users, it is critical to ensure that more girls have access to, and are encouraged to pursue, the kind of specialist education that will lead on to jobs in the ICT sector. Tackling the problem of the limited number of girls taking science and technology based courses, including computer-related courses, requires clear understanding of the reasons for girls' choices. (Derbyshire 2003,7)

Gender—like race, class, HIV status, educational levels, and the digital divide—is a systemic issue. Gender inequality is interwoven into a larger fabric of generalized social inequality, particularly in Africa. Taking a gender-equality perspective in ICT-enabled education involves taking into account the complex social influences that perpetuate gender inequality within the larger educational digital divide. Addressing gender equality and women's empowerment, whether in the ICT4D sector or in the development sector as a whole, requires an approach that aims for a transformation in the relationship between men and women in a way that challenges prevailing norms and attitudes, the very fabric of the society that perpetuates gender discrimination.

STRATEGIES TOWARD GENDER EQUALITY: THE EXPERIENCE OF SNA

The role of a regional, continent-wide networking organization is mainly to mobilize support for groups at the local level and to facilitate virtual and face-to-face collaboration. Online discussions, face-to-face workshops, and conferences are some of the mechanisms through which SNA expands and supports its networks of practitioners, policymakers, "techies," learners, and teachers. The SNA experience demonstrates that opening up opportunities for practitioners and policymakers to integrate gender dimensions within the education system has encouraged creative strategies in the continuing struggle to promote gender equality and women's empowerment in ways that go beyond the numbers game.

The gender-equality project is often premised on redressing imbalances. However, treating people the same does not necessarily lead to equal opportunity or equal outcome. Targeted interventions are often necessary—directed at girls or boys, women or men—to address particular aspects of inequality. Often this requires a perspective that is transformative of gendered roles. Such a transformative perspective requires an integrated approach in tackling a range of societal, cultural, political, and economic influences that perpetuate unequal gender relations. Here the potential that ICTs in particular have to challenge unequal gender relations and advance the interests of girls and women has to be underscored. The UNDAW report (2003) highlights a number of strategies that have worked successfully, as do other chapters in this book. Similarly, the WSIS Declaration of Principles and Plan of Action adopted in December 2003 highlights the importance, albeit in a limited way, of a gender-equality and women's empowerment perspective in the information society in general and in tackling the gendered digital divide in education in particular.

Gender Mainstreaming

Gender mainstreaming as a successful strategy to address imbalances in gender power relations is highlighted consistently in the literature (Green 2003; Bisnath 2005; Derbyshire 2003; UNDAW 2003). The term refers to the systematic integration of gender concerns into any planning, policy, or program process from conception through to execution, based on the understanding that unequal gender relations are part of a larger pattern of social inequality that translates into these processes as well. Bisnath (2005), drawing on the decision of ECOSOC in July 1997, defines gender mainstreaming as the process of assessing the implications for women and men of any planned action, including legislation, policies, and programs in any area at all levels. It is a strategy for making the concerns of women and men an integral part of the design, implementation, monitoring, and evaluation of policies and programs in all political, economic, and societal spheres so that women and men benefit equally and inequality is not perpetuated. The ultimate goal is the achievement of gender equality. Gender mainstreaming acknowledges that there are no gender-neutral decisions (Green 2003).

SNA's gender mainstreaming approach, or the active integration of gender considerations into all aspects of its networking, appears to have been a successful strategy. The ICTs for African Schools Workshop,[4] which was held in Botswana in April 2003, is perhaps the most visible example of how an opportunity was seized to promote awareness of gender-equality issues relating to ICT-enabled education in the schoolnet network. The workshop concept and program highlighted the relevance of gendered concepts, gendered characterization, and gendered effects, both quantitative and qualitative, to every topic under discussion among the estimated three hundred policymakers and practitioners from twenty-five African countries who participated.

But how do you make open source a gender issue when it is a non-gender topic? Questions of this kind were posed by several speakers on "non-gendered" topics. The open-source presenter was provided with several suggestions for identifying gender trends:

- Of the schools that have access to computers with open-source software, how many girls relative to boys have access to the PCs and how many are using them?
- How do open-source software interfaces demonstrate sensitivity to the conditions of both women and men, girls and boys in African schools?

- Can you provide information on the numbers of men and women who are open-source programmers or developers and open-source users, and what can you infer from these statistics?
- What about content on open-source platforms? Does it display sensitivity and responsiveness to varying and differing content needs of men and women?
- What about policies on the promotion of open source? Do these policies consciously promote the growth of women developers and technical expertise among women?
- Are there cases and models of women open-source programmers that can be highlighted?

Presenters on all topics—technology access, intellectual property rights, teacher training, capacity building, content development, policy or resourcing strategies—were guided on how to integrate gendered perspectives in their areas of expertise, both during the eight-week online discussion before the workshop and at the workshop itself. Gender balance was achieved for participants in online facilitation, speaker panels and rapporteurs, and rapporteurs were briefed to include in their reports the gender aspects of issues under discussion.

The program of action adopted at the workshop incorporated this gender integration approach, and the Campaign for One Million PCs for African Schools, an immediate outcome of the Botswana workshop, also incorporated gender-equality elements. The campaign was launched to increase awareness of the importance of universal access to ICTs in African schools as a way to promote greater access to e-learning. A media campaign to present this issue from the perspective of the African practitioner highlighted, among other issues, gender disparities and the need for targeted actions to address these disparities. Related strategies agreed upon include addressing barriers to access in schools where girls use PC labs less than boys, the placement of women "techies" at technical service centers (TSCs), ensuring that local training programs at TSCs include proportional representation of male and female participants, and women-only training sessions. The gender-equality component of the campaign was implemented by program leaders based at the SNA secretariat in Johannesburg, in consultation with the schoolnet practitioners involved in the campaign. In addition to accepting that only schoolnets with demonstrated established infrastructure to distribute and support the educational use of PCs in large volumes would be considered, criteria such as demonstrated support for gender equality and women's empowerment were also agreed on. Here the active presence of women practitioners in the leadership of the schoolnet organizations concerned and programs targeted to women and girls in the schoolnet programs, with reference to ICT access in particular, were made important criteria for consideration. In April 2005, SNA signed an agreement to receive the first large-scale donation of ten thousand PCs with Dutch telecom company KPN. These PCs will go to the Schoolnets in Namibia, Kenya, Nigeria, and Uganda, which have dedicated women leaders, target the training of women practitioners, and incorporate gender-equality approaches in their work.

In another activity a comprehensive course to train schoolnet practitioners to set up and manage TSCs incorporates materials on gender equality and fair-use policies. Twenty African practitioners were trained, 30 percent of whom were women. TSCs are currently being set up in a number of African countries modeled on the experiences of SNA partners in Namibia, Kenya, and Uganda, and a monitoring-and-evaluation system has been developed that specifically identifies indicators of gender integration and women's empowerment in the TSCs.[5]

In addition to the activities outlined above, individual national schoolnet organizations have developed local approaches to gender mainstreaming. SchoolNet Nigeria's print-media project distributes education inserts in local newspapers that regularly feature gender issues. Similarly SchoolNet Uganda adopted a program of gender responsiveness that it applies to all the schools in its network, and SchoolNet Namibia recently launched the first comic strip in Africa *(Hai Ti)* that features positive images of women and raises gender-equality issues.

Fair-use Policies

Fair-use policies involve guidelines established and accepted by school management that encourage gender-equitable access and use of ICTs in schools. In her study of the World Links projects in Africa, Gadio makes a case for the adoption of "fair use policies in schools which promote equitable access to the PC labs" (Gadio 2001, 19). While a number of African schools that belong to national schoolnet networks have adopted use policies for their computer labs that offer general guidelines, the adoption of gender-responsive fair-use policies exist mainly in theory at this stage, remaining an important goal for African education practitioners. The SNA *African SchoolNet Toolkit* takes an important step in moving this idea along by incorporating these policies in training programs of African schoolnet practitioners and policymakers.

Targeted Women's Empowerment Programs

Gender mainstreaming strategies should not entirely replace strategies that target women and girls separately from men and boys. Rather, they can be implemented as an additional strategy to gender mainstreaming and may in certain situations be more appropriate. Margolis (2001) reviews specific strategies to recruit and retain girls in separate computer science classes, while Derbyshire (2003) refers to the range of school-based initiatives in Europe and North America that are specifically designed to promote girls' confidence, interest, and skills. Common activities include all-girl computer clubs, mentoring programs, interaction with women working in the computer industry, and attention to gender issues in curriculum and software. Sanders (2005) also reviews programs that are targeted specifically at girls but suggests that many are extracurricular in approach, focusing mainly on attitudes instead of academics. She also found that there was a strong focus on teachers at in-service level but significantly less on teachers at pre-service level.

In relation to these discussions, SNA has approached a number of prospective partners to support programs that target access to ICTs and training for women practitioners and policymakers. One proposed project will provide women teachers in Namibia (who constitute 75 percent of teachers in the country) with individual access to PCs in their homes. Another will set up a female-run TSC that targets the training of women practitioners by SchoolNet Nigeria, while a program to train a network of women practitioners across Africa through the SNA TSC course is also being considered. These ideas draw on the success of SchoolNet Uganda, which has trained women teachers in PC refurbishment.

Behavioral Changes in the Industry

Derbyshire (2003) notes that recently, definition of the "problem" has begun to shift away from girls (and, implicitly, their need to be more like boys) to computing and the computer industry itself. Concern in Europe and North America about low and declining numbers of female enrollments in IT at the tertiary level, and the overall skills shortage in this area, has focused attention on the ways in which the masculine culture of computing discourages girls and young women from entering the profession. In this context the solution becomes less about behavior change on the part of girls and women, and more about change in the computer industry itself. How can the image and reality of computing be changed to appeal to girls' interests and strengths? How can computer innovation and the design of hardware and software benefit from the contribution and perspective of women? African networks have much to learn from attempts at changing behavioral patterns at an industry level, as there are few documented examples to date.

Positive Role Models

A week before writing this chapter, I facilitated an ICTs and virtual collaborative learning program for grade ten learners at a high school in the Alexandra township of Johannesburg. Fifteen participants attended, eight of whom were girls. During discussions on learning expectations, two of the seven boys expressed surprise that the trainers were women. Activities like this can encourage a shift in perceptions that technical training is an exclusively male domain. In another activity to present women as positive role models in ICT—Schoolnets in Africa: The FeMail Face—African women practitioners talked to students about how they came to be digital pioneers.[6]

A number of national schoolnet managers in the pan-African network, some of whom are male, are gender-equality champions. Gender-sensitive male schoolnet practitioners supported the adoption of gender mainstreaming practices in partner schoolnets.

Gender-equality Partners

SNA has also contributed to the promotion of gender equality in the information society through international partnerships with gender-equality programs and organizations, particularly in acting as secretariat for the WSIS Gender Caucus in the lead up to the first summit in Geneva in December 2003. This gave SNA the opportunity to participate in a global network of practitioners, academics, and gender-equality advocates.

IMPACT

Assessment of the impact of ICT-enabled education on targeted communities in Africa would normally be based on the assumption that there has been a sustained intervention over a prolonged period of time to a sufficiently large scale. ICT-enabled education programs in Africa, particularly schoolnets, generally date back only to 1999–2000. The scale of these kinds of interventions has also tended to be small, as many were initially set up as donor-led pilot projects. It is therefore difficult to measure the impact of school networking in a significant way at this time. However, one can speak of the effects of the schoolnet programs on their target communities and their spheres of influence, based on the limited monitoring and evaluation studies generated so far. An IDRC study published in 2004 represents one of the most extensive, covering the experiences of nine African schoolnet organizations (James 2004). However, references to gendered concerns are limited. Similarly, an evaluation of the experiences in the World Links Program (Hawkins 2002), SchoolNet Namibia (SIDA 2004), The Computer Education Trust in Swaziland (James et al. 2002), as well as programmatic evaluations of ThinkQuest Africa (Broekman 2002), the African Teachers Network (Roberts 2004), and the Global Teenager Project (Blommenstein 2005) all pay limited attention to gender considerations, reflecting once again the dearth of gender specific knowledge in Africa.

Nevertheless, based on the limited existing literature and anecdotal evidence, the following conclusions can be drawn:

- There is a general awareness among male and female practitioners in the African schoolnet movement that gender equality is a critical issue to be addressed in school networking.
- Access to schoolnet programs increased the confidence of women participants in encouraging exposure to new technologies and (also important) to international communities. This is evident from the experiences of four African women staff members of SNA, from comments made by the female technical coordinators of SchoolNet Uganda, SchoolNet Namibia, and SchoolNet Nigeria, and the women teachers involved in the African Teachers Network and ThinkQuest Africa.
- The participants in the learner-centered programs of SNA have gained confidence, have learned from cultures around the world, and have learned more about their own cultures. The ThinkQuest Africa program in particular provides examples of this, as interviews conducted by the author with female Egyptian learners revealed that

exposure to the program encouraged them to pursue careers in computer-related fields at the University of Cairo.

These preliminary findings highlight the need for more gendered research into the African experience of ICT-enabled education. There is also a major knowledge gap on research methodologies that are appropriate to gender relations in education in developing-economy contexts. Here the work of the APC's gender evaluation methodology (GEM) offers a worthwhile contribution that may be considered for the African education context as well.

CONCLUSION

This chapter has drawn both on existing literature and practical experience to assess gender-equality and empowerment issues around the integration of ICTs in formal education in Africa. It highlights the need for greater conceptual clarity in considering gender relations in the African education context and presents the schoolnet value chain as a framework for understanding these issues. It also expresses the highly skewed nature of existing knowledge in the area and the limitations of current research methodologies. These issues form part of a new action research agenda of SNA, which we hope will contribute to further knowledge and improvement in the lives of African women and girls.

NOTES

[1] A male participant, impressed by the launch of SNA, remarked to an SNA representative, "My goodness, woman, you have balls," to which she replied, "No, we have womb."

[2] This also speaks to the nature of school networking in Africa, which is largely driven by the work of individual champions (see James 2004).

[3] http://www.mindset.co.za and http://www.thutong.org.za.

[4] The workshop report is available from http://www.schoolnetafrica.net/fileadmin/resources/Workshop_Report.zip.

[5] See http://www.schoolnetafrica.net/fileadmin/1MillionPCsTraining/Index.htm.

[6] See the SNA website, http://www.schoolnetafrica.net.

REFERENCES

Aranguren, A., and Akinsanmi T. 2005. Towards more ICT-enabled African teachers. SNA internal report.

Bisnath S. 2005. Women take the ICT leap. Gaining entry into service sector employment. Geneva: ITU.

Blommenstein, N. 2005. Monitoring and evaluation results of students participating in the global teenager project. The Hague: International Institute for Communication and Development.

Broekman, I. 2002. Learning possibilities of ThinkQuest in the African context. Johannesburg, South Africa: SNA.

Derbyshire, Helen. 2003. Gender issues in the use of computers in education in Africa, Imfundo. London: DFID. http://www.schoolnetafrica.net/fileadmin/resources/Gender_Report.pdf (accessed 21 September 2005).

Gadio, Coumba Mar. 2001. Exploring the gender impacts of World Links. Washington, DC: World Links.

Green, Lyndsay. 2003. Gender-based issues and trends in ICT application in education in Asia and the Pacific. In *UNESCO meta survey on the use of technologies in education*, ed. C. Farrell. Bangkok: UNESCO. http://www.unescobkk.org/fileadmin/user_upload/ict/Metasurvey/2Regional29.pdf (accessed 7 October 2005).

Hafkin, Nancy, and Nancy Taggart. 2001. *Gender, information technology and developing countries: An analytic study*. Washington, DC: USAID, Office of Women in Development. http://learnlink.aed.org/Publications/Gender_Book/Home.htm (accessed 30 November 2005).

Hawkins, Robert J. 2002. Ten lessons for ICT and education in the developing world. In *The global information technology report 2001–2002: Readiness for the networked world*. Oxford: Oxford Univ. Press. http://www.cid.harvard.edu/cr/gitrr_030202.html (accessed 30 November 2005).

Huff, Chuck. 2002. Gender, software design, and occupational equity. *SIGCSE Bulletin* 34, no. 2: 112–15.

Huff, Charles, and Joel Cooper. 1987. Sex bias in educational software: The effect of designers' stereotypes on the software they design. *Journal of Applied Social Psychology* 17, no. 6: 519–32.

Huyer, Sophia. 2004. Gender equality and science and technology policy knowledge and policy at the international level: S&T for gender equality and social development. Gender Advisory Board of the United Nations Commission of Science and Technology for Development, Canada. Office of Education, Science, and Technology. OAS. http://www.science.oas.org/english/ev_ini_e.htm (accessed 22 March 2005).

Isaacs, Shafika. 2002a. ICTs in African schools: A multi-media approach for enhancing learning and teaching. *TechKnowLogia* 4, no. 1: 32–34. http://www.techknowlogia.org (accessed 15 November 2005).

————. 2002b. IT's hot for girls: ICTs as an instrument in advancing girls' and women's capabilities in school education in Africa. Presented at the UN Division for the Advancement of Women Expert Group Meeting on ICTs and Their Impact on and Use as an Instrument for the Advancement and Empowerment of Women. Seoul, Korea, 11–14 November. http://www.un.org/womenwatch/daw/egm/ict2002 (accessed 30 November 2005).

————. 2005. Against all odds: Critical reflections on SchoolNet Africa. In *Harnessing the potential of ICT for education—A multistakeholder approach.* Proceedings of the Dublin Global Forum of the UN ICT Task Force. New York: United Nations ICT Task Force.

James, T. 2000. The African learning network: Emerging from behind the knowledge curtain—An agenda for youth and education in Africa. Addis Ababa: UN Economic Commission for Africa.

James T., ed. 2004. The role of ICTs in networking institutions of learning—SchoolNet. *Information and communication technologies for development in Africa.* Vol. 3. IDRC and CODESRIA, Senegal Information and Communication.

James, T., O. Hesselmark, and T. Sibiya. 2002. An evaluation of the Computer Education Trust (CET). In *Swaziland: Implications for the development of a national computers-in-schools initiative.* London: The Imfundo Initiative, Partnership for IT in Education, DFID.

Margolis, J. 2001. Unlocking the clubhouse: Women in computing. In *The Digital Divide* 1, no. 2. Graduate School of Education and Information Studies, UCLA.

Roberts, J. 2004. Interim evaluation of SchoolNet Africa. Johannesburg, South Africa: SNA.

Rosenthal, Nina Ribak, and Diana Mayer Demetrulias. 1988. Assessing gender bias in computer software. *Computers in the Schools* 5, nos. 1/2, 153-63.

Sanders, Jo. 2005. Gender and technology in education: A research review. In *Handbook of gender in education,* ed. C. Skelton, B. Francis, and L. Smulyan. London: Sage Publications, 2006. http://www.josanders.com/pdf/gendertech0705.pdf (accessed 30 November 2005).

SchoolNet Africa and The Commonwealth of Learning. 2005. *African SchoolNet toolkit.* http://www.schoolnetafrica.net/1500.0.html (accessed 15 November 2005).

SIDA. 2004. Using the Internet in Namibian schools: Evaluation of Swedish support to SchoolNet Namibia. http://www.schoolnetafrica.net/fileadmin/resources/Using_the_internet_in_Namibian_schools.pdf (accessed 1 December 2005).

UN Commission on Science and Technology for Development. 1995. Gender Working Group. Introduction. In *Missing links: Gender equity in science and technology for development.* Ottawa: IDRC and Intermediate Technology Publications.

UNDAW (United Nations Division for the Advancement of Women). 2003. Information and communication technologies and their impact on and use as an instrument for the advancement and empowerment of women. New York: UNDAW. http://www.un.org/womenwatch/daw/egm/ict2002/index.html (accessed 30 November 2005).

UNESCO. 2004. Education for all: The quality imperative: Summary. EFA global monitoring report. Paris: UNESCO. http://www.unesco.org/education/efa/index.shtml (accessed 30 November 2005).

Volman, M., and E. van Eck. 2002. Gender equity and information technology in education: The second decade. *Journal of Educational Research* 71, no. 4.

6

Improved Livelihoods and Empowerment for Poor Women through IT-Sector Intervention

Shoba Arun, Richard Heeks, and Sharon Morgan

INTRODUCTION

There is a growing and compelling body of evidence that suggests that persistent gender inequalities have a negative impact on both economic and social development (Narayan et al. 2000; World Bank 2001). Since developing countries are beset by such inequalities, it is no surprise that one of the MDGs is to increase gender equality and empower women. What role can be played by ICTs, which are already seen to have the potential to contribute to other MDGs, such as economic development and poverty alleviation (Cecchini 2002; Kenny 2002)?

We have some evidence that, with an enabling environment, ICTs can facilitate women's economic development and their empowerment (Hafkin and Taggart 2001; Huyer and Mitter 2003). Nevertheless, feminist scholarship points to a complex relationship between gender and technology in which ICTs, as a new technology, should be viewed as socially contextualized and gendered (UNDP 1999; Huyer and Sikoska 2002; Marcelle 2002). This insight, in turn, has led to the identification of a gender dimension to the digital divide and to concerns that ICTs can be applied in ways that maintain or even exacerbate existing gender inequalities rather than guaranteeing equitable growth (Jorge 2002). There is a sizable body of work that studies the relation between ICT and gender in industrialized countries. But there is relatively little empirical material to help us understand the role ICTs will take vis-à-vis women in developing countries. In particular, there is a significant dearth of evidence about ICTs and the true global Cinderellas: poor women from developing countries.

This chapter makes an initial, exploratory contribution to filling this gap in our knowledge on the role of ICTs in promoting economic empowerment for women. It draws primary data from one of the very few significant-scale initiatives that attempts to make direct use of ICTs to deliver livelihood benefits to poor women—in this case, in Southern India. The following section reviews key issues arising from evidence to date and presents a preliminary framework for understanding the relation between ICTs and livelihoods of poor women. Subsequent sections present the background to the initiative studied—Kudumbashree, based in Kerala State, India—and the resulting data and analysis. The final section draws some conclusions and broader lessons.

UNDERSTANDING ICTS, GENDER, AND DEVELOPMENT

Reflecting the tensions in the relation between ICTs and gender, we know that use of ICTs has resulted in mixed patterns of benefit for women in terms of access to markets and services, as well as employment and income generation. For example, in situations where women appear to have relatively good access to ICTs, or where there is a substantial representation of women in IT-sector employment, one may also find no clear relation to higher indicators of female social development (Hafkin and Taggart 2001; Huyer and Mitter 2003).

One reason for this is the market-driven nature of growth in IT employment opportunities for women, such as the growth in "offshoring" of software development, call centers, and other business activities. Such growth has benefited some groups of women, generally those from the urban middle class who already possess knowledge and skills of value in this sector (Arun and Arun 2002). Research nevertheless indicates that despite its relatively recent emergence, this is a strongly gendered sector that reproduces gender inequalities, ideologies, and insecurities that are present in the broader society (Elmoudden 2004). As a result, a "genderization" of this work has developed: women are over-represented in unskilled and routine jobs that are in turn under threat as a result of automation and commodification. They are also significantly under-represented in higher-level design and managerial positions (Wajcman 2004). A supposedly gender-blind neo-liberal agenda of market forces and flexibility in fact is seen to reinforce gender inequities, which in many contexts may be exacerbated by interactions with other identities of class, ethnicity, caste, race, and age (Bonder 2002; Gurumurthy 2004).

If market-driven ICT initiatives run the risk of reinforcing gender inequities and of excluding poor women, what can we say about intervention-driven ICT initiatives, put in place by government or NGOs? One can certainly see instances in which such initiatives have enabled vulnerable groups to benefit from ICTs in health, education, governance, and economic livelihoods (Gurumurthy 2004). Examples of ICTs improving livelihoods of poor women through improved access to markets and productive activities have been documented in examples such as e-commerce in the Balkan regions, use of mobile phones for women's community-based organizations in India, and improved information systems for women dairy producers in India (GKP 2003; Gurumurthy 2004).

However, two limitations of intervention-driven ICT initiatives can be noted. First, almost all to date have been "intensive," or what Narasimhan (1983) refers to as applications of ICTs to preexisting processes and outcomes. Yet there is evidence that the greater benefits from ICTs may derive from "extensive" application, where ICTs are used to do something new, that is, through ICT-based enterprises (Heeks 2002). The IT sector constitutes a major segment of the extensive ICT application category, in the form of a set of economic activities that did not exist before the introduction of ICTs. This category consists of three types of enterprise:

- Those producing ICTs as an enterprise output: enterprises that produce hardware, software, and telecommunications products.
- Those using ICTs as a primary, processing technology: enterprises that provide data-entry services, ICT-based business services, software customization, ICT-based distance learning, and similar services.
- Those providing other ICT-related support activities: enterprises that provide computer training, consultancy, and other services.

This sector provides a much clearer link between ICTs and the creation of jobs, incomes, and skills than is the case for intensive uses of the new technologies (Heeks 2005). However, a practical difficulty has emerged in that most intervention-driven projects ignore the IT sector, while market-driven activity often fails to address gender inequities.

Hence, this chapter examines a project that is an extensive application of ICTs, based around the creation of women's ICT-based enterprises. Since it is also an intervention-driven initiative, it may also pose greater potential to address gender equality issues.

Another typical limitation of intervention-driven ICT initiatives concerns their conceptual framework. They have tended to take a technology focus, with little attention paid to the social context in which women operate (Thioune 2003). They have therefore been limited in their ability to deliver developmental benefits to women. Before looking at our intervention-driven IT-sector initiative, we will therefore first discuss conceptualization of the impacts of such initiatives.

A Framework for Analysis of ICTs, Gender, and Development

In thinking about the impact of ICT initiatives on poor women, a natural point of departure will be poverty. Recently, discussions on poverty have moved from understanding it solely in terms of income to understanding the *multi-dimensionality* of poverty. Sen (1999), for example, conceives poverty and livelihoods in terms of the expansion of substantive freedoms based on development of capabilities and entitlements. Such a perspective provides a much richer understanding of gender and development. It has, for example, called attention to the nexus between gender and poverty by showing that gender inequalities in relation to economic resources and gender biases in institutions and policies will often make it *harder* for women to transform their capabilities into incomes or well-being (Cagatay 1998).

Perhaps the most well-known conceptual model drawing from the new perspective of multi-dimensionality is the sustainable livelihoods (SL) framework (DFID 1999). In the work reported here we focus on a subset of components within the SL model, taking an assets-vulnerability approach that has been used previously for work on women and antipoverty initiatives (Moser 1998). This approach begins with an identification of what the poor *have* (in terms of a multi-dimensional view of assets that can be deployed to reduce poverty and vulnerability) rather than what they *do not* have (such as baseline monetary indicators). In this way it "contributes to the development of analytical tools to facilitate those interventions which promote opportunities, as well as removing key obstacles" (Moser 1998, 1). It also incorporates the notion of vulnerability as a dynamic, contextual concept that captures change processes and can be linked to the ability of poor women to own and manage assets to promote livelihoods.

Assets are considered to be both tangible and intangible. Tangible assets include physical tools, while intangible assets involve assets like social relations. In all, five main classes of assets will be considered here, as drawn from the SL framework:

1. *Human capital* represents the skills, knowledge, ability to work, and good health that combined enable women to pursue different live-lihood strategies and achieve their livelihood objectives.
2. *Natural capital* is the term used for the natural resource stocks from which resource flows and services useful for livelihoods are de-rived.
3. *Financial capital* denotes the financial resources that women use to achieve their livelihood, including available stocks that can be held in several forms, including cash, bank deposits, liquid assets such as livestock and jewelry, or resources obtained through credit-pro-viding institutions; and regular inflows of money, including earned income, pensions, other transfers from the state, and remittances.
4. *Physical capital* comprises the basic infrastructure and producer goods needed to support livelihoods.
5. *Social capital* is the genre of social resources that women draw upon in pursuit of their livelihood objectives; mainly conceived as net-works and relationships based on trust, reciprocity, and exchanges.

As will be seen later, when we consider the impact of involvement in a women's IT-sector enterprise, this five-asset framework has limitations in relation to power and power relations. It is therefore necessary to consider separately a sixth aspect: empowerment.

IT-SECTOR ENTERPRISES FOR POOR WOMEN: THE CASE OF KUDUMBASHREE

The intervention-driven initiative reported on here is based in Kerala State in South India. At the national level India has set great store by ICTs, with an operational policy in the sector for nearly four decades. The policy has combined a growing role for the market and the pri-vate sector with continuous state intervention, with an approach that combines both intensive and extensive application of ICTs (Heeks 1996). Its IT sector in particular has shown very strong growth, especially the heavily globalized software and services segment (Heeks and Nicholson 2004).

Policies and initiatives at the national level have been replicated at the state level. The government of Kerala State has developed a three-part ICT strategy that aims to (1) establish a vibrant IT sector; (2) build up a robust ICT infrastructure; and (3) upgrade the quality of ICT-related human resources through training (Government of Kerala 2003).

In addition to policies to promote ICTs, the Government of Kerala has made a strong commitment to reduce poverty. Strategies developed from livelihoods concepts address the multi-dimensional nature of poverty faced by poor families that fall below a minimum threshold of capabilities, as defined by a set of financial and nonmonetary asset indicators. A central theme of these strategies has been a focus on economic empowerment through increased economic opportunities and assets. One of the initiatives resulting from these strategies is Kudumbashree (the term means "prosperity of the family"). This is an initiative of Kerala's State Poverty Eradication Mission (SPEM) with support from the central government (Government of Kerala 2003). It was launched in 1999 as a women-oriented, participatory, and integrated approach to fighting poverty based on the experiences of two pilot initiatives of the mid-1990s.

Under the Kudumbashree scheme, ten women from a neighborhood *ayalkootam*—a type of self-help group for women from poor families—are brought together as a core group of the Kudumbashree unit. These self-help groups operate in a multi-functional mode, partly as a microenterprise aiming to increase employment and to ensure a stable income for members, but also as a communal body with savings, credit, self-education, and advocacy functions.

The enterprise side of the Kudumbashree units is based on four criteria for establishment/creation: (1) full cooperative ownership, management, and operation of the enterprise by women from families living below the poverty line; (2) a group investment ranging from US$111 to US$5,550; (3) potential to return two to ten times the initial capital investment; and (4) potential to raise a minimum of US$33 monthly per member, in the form of wage or profit (Kudumbashree 2004). The enterprises have been formed in many different areas of activity, for example, clothing production or processing of agricultural produce. However, one of Kudumbashree's most innovative aspects has been its use of ICTs as the basis of some of its enterprises. Of the 1,206 Kudumbashree units operational at the time of writing:

- Fifty-six are data entry and digitization units that mainly create digital content for local organizations (although they may also engage in other IT work, such as training, to a limited extent);
- Forty-five are IT-training units that provide training mainly to local schools; and
- Five are hardware assembly units that build, sell, and maintain personal computers.

Government intervention played a direct role in creating these units, but it has also played—and continues to play—a direct role in creating a market for their goods and services. Requirements within all levels of government in the state—from the main state government down to local councils (*panchayats*)—have created a need for digitization of public records, which forms the bulk of work for the Kudumbashree data-entry units. The state decision to introduce IT training into public secondary schools in Kerala provides the main market for the training units. Likewise, the hardware units earn most of their money from public-sector contracts. While specific decisions have played a role—including the 1999 court ruling ordering computerization of the *panchayats*—overall the state ICT strategy has been the underlying impetus behind creation of *all* of the Kudumbashree IT markets.

In other ways contextual factors have shaped—and sometimes supported—this ICT initiative. Kerala rates highly in comparison with other Indian states on social development indicators such as literacy levels, female-male sex ratios, and life expectancy (Franke and Chasin 1994; Parayil 2000). More generally, levels of education and civil society activity are also relatively high, so that favorable conditions exist for social initiatives based on women's human capital.

However, while recognizing the unique nature of the local context and the importance of enabling environmental factors, we should not see Kerala as fundamentally different from other developing-country locations. As one example, while the female participation rate in employment in India increased from 19.7 percent to 22.7 percent between 1981 and 2001, in Kerala the rate declined from 16.6 percent to 15.8 percent (Government of Kerala 2003). This economic marginalization of women in Kerala is an impediment to women's development as well as the development of society as a whole (Arun and Arun 2001).

EMPIRICAL EVIDENCE OF IMPACT
ON WOMEN'S LIVELIHOODS

Having presented the background to the Kudumbashree initiative and its women's ICT units, we can now look in more detail at these enterprises and their impact on women's livelihoods. The empirical evidence presented here was gathered during the period from July 2004 to July 2005 as part of a project on ICT-sector enterprises for poor women funded by DFID. Data was drawn from a variety of sources:

- group interviews with members of twenty-four Kudumbashree ICT units, used mainly to build up detailed case studies;
- structured interviews conducted with eighty-one individual women working in ICT units, focused particularly on the livelihood effects of their work;
- unstructured life-story sessions completed by six women from the ICT units, used as a source of broader background and context; and
- semi-structured interviews with officials of SPEM.

Observational data and documentary evidence, such as annual audit figures, were gathered during visits to the units.

Examples of each of the three types of Kudumbashree IT unit are provided in Table 6–1. These cases are typical and indicate the particular groups involved. Women in this study fall below the poverty line but are not without assets. Almost all possess degree or pre-degree (ten years' education equivalent) qualifications. Each is required to contribute approximately US$30 for investment. The total group investment is matched with a subsidy from the government of around ten times the group investment as well as an equivalent amount in the form of a bank loan. In total, then, a typical unit might start with an investment of US$6,000, of which about one-half would be a repayable loan.

Beyond this, it can be seen that the fortunes of the units vary, with some losing their core membership while others expand to employ additional workers, including men. Virtually every unit has been able to provide members with the targeted income of at least US$33 per month. A majority (75 percent) of the units studied were able to repay their initial loans, some within two or three years of start up.

Table 6–1. Profile of Typical Women's IT Units

	Type of Women's IT Unit		
Variable	Data Entry	Hardware Assembly	IT Training
Name	Technoworld, Kumarapuram	InfoShree Systems and Peripherals, Kasargod	Divine Computers, Vadakara
Date of formation	1999	2003	2002
Main activities	Digitization of records for state and local government; some work for private clients	Assembly of computers and sales of peripherals to state government, schools, and a few private clients	IT training to secondary-level students in state schools
Core cooperative membership	10 members with bachelor degrees	10 members with predegree qualifications	6 members with predegree qualifications
Additional employees	52 casual workers and one male supervisor	Four male assembly assistants	None
Source of original finance	Group contribution, subsidy, loan	Group contribution, subsidy, loan	Group contribution, subsidy, loan
Turnover in 2004	US$15,600	US$8,440(160 PCs sold)	US$2,380 (485 students trained)
Average earnings per member per month	US$55	US$50	US$33

Using the conceptual framework discussed earlier, we can now look in greater detail at the effects on women's livelihoods of working in the IT units, drawing on data from both group and individual interviews. We will consider this in terms of the five asset categories and related vulnerabilities drawn from the SL framework. (A summary is in Table 6–2.) It should be noted that this analysis relates only to the core female members of each IT cooperative (there are approximately 750 in total). However, these IT units also significantly affect other poor women indirectly: those employed by the units for additional work (an estimated 750 persons); those whose goods and services are purchased through the earned income of core women members; and female members of the core-group families.

Human Capital

Human capital—reflected in educational and training qualifications and embodied in the skills and knowledge of the work force—is often cited as a key asset for IT sector enterprises (see, e.g., Heeks 2005). It should be reiterated that the Keralan population has higher skill qualification levels than those found in areas with equivalent income levels, a result of its particular institutional history, although opportunities for employment for qualified workers are limited. State education-access policies mean that this pattern is found among a range of groups, including the women involved in the Kudumbashree initiative; those working in the IT units typically possessed at least ten years of education prior to joining, while many also had basic typing skills.

Employment in the Kudumbashree IT units has increased this comparatively high level of human capital, most noticeably in relation to technical skills. All of the roughly 750 female core members of IT units have developed abilities in computer operation, while a number of specializations have been developed around troubleshooting the software and hardware problems that develop when computers are used intensively in tropical environments; networking; computer assembly; and IT training. Some members have reinforced these specializations with formal qualifications.

Those women who have taken on roles within each unit of group leader, deputy leader, or secretary have developed managerial and supervisory skills. Rather harder to ascertain was the effect on entrepreneurship skills. About half of those interviewed did not consider themselves to have developed such skills, but others recognized that they had gained a better understanding of basic business elements such as balance sheets, cash flow, and customer service.

The Performance Improvement Programme, a government-subsidized training program for technical, entrepreneurial, and managerial skills, provided a base for this strengthening of human-capital assets, but the experience of working in the IT units contributed to a much greater extent.

Ongoing technical change means that some of the technical skills developed will need to be continuously updated. However, these skills represent only a small fraction of the total assets gained, and, further, any future training will likely consist of an incremental upgrading of the women's skills rather than an entire relearning process. In the context of the overall IT sector it would be fair to say that the human capital developed in this initiative lies at the relatively low-skill end of the spectrum. This is typical of developing countries, given the international divisions of labor within the IT sector (Heeks 1996), but nevertheless represents a vital "foot on the ladder" for workers who were previously poor, unemployed, and semi-skilled. A small number of the IT units surveyed made some attempt to shift their products and skills base higher up in the value chain, for example by adding basic Web and software development to their portfolio. In general, though, this kind of action was an exception. More typical were attempts at diversification into equivalent-level activities, as seen in data-entry units that expanded into IT training.

Natural Capital

While this may be an important asset for poor women, particularly in rural areas, it is not a factor directly associated with work in an IT-sector enterprise.

Financial Capital

As already noted, almost every unit achieved the goal of providing core members with an income of at least US$1 per day. Although a relatively small amount, this income made a significant difference to the lives of the women interviewed. In just over half of cases it represented 50 percent or more of total household income, and in a few cases, it was the sole source of household income (for example, for single women living with elderly parents).

Some of the money was spent on everyday household expenditures, but its value was more often reported in relation to exceptional items, such as health-care expenditures for family members; education expenses; land purchase or house construction; redeeming loans or pawned items such as gold jewelry; and marriages of family members. In the case of almost every woman interviewed, this income was considered to be the

main benefit of employment in the IT unit and the main factor in reducing the vulnerabilities they experienced.

The presence of an income allowed some members to join savings
schemes or take out individual loans. As mentioned above, the group
itself took out an institutional loan that formed the main source of financial capital for the unit. The degree of financial asset strengthening
can be seen from the high proportion of units that were able to repay
this initial loan. Some had even taken out a second group loan to purchase new or additional technologies. This kind of action would have
been inconceivable prior to joining the Kudumbashree scheme.

Income from the IT units may be the main source of vulnerability
reduction, but it introduced its own set of vulnerabilities related to
outsourcing and public-sector contracts. A major difficulty cited by every unit was irregularity of payment for work completed. At times units
were required to wait three, six, or in some cases even twelve months to
receive payment for services or goods provided. The resulting cash-
flow problems forced some units to pawn personal items of members in
order to make loan payments. A second issue, discussed further below, is
the sustainability of this income source over time.

Physical Capital

Investment in physical capital varies, but a typical pattern involves an
initial investment of around US$5,000 for five computers, a printer, and
software. This is subsequently doubled after two to three years to bring
the assets to ten computers. These assets are cooperatively owned but
provide each woman with a work-related asset worth the equivalent of
almost two years' income—useful collateral for additional loans.

A very significant associated vulnerability not found in most of
Kudumbashree's non-IT units is the pace of technical change. All IT
assets, whether hardware or software, will lose their value rapidly, de-
preciating to a value close to zero within about five years. Continuous
investment to replenish these assets is therefore required. More threat-
ening still, though perhaps some distance in the future, are technical
innovations that will automate the work that employs the women in the
IT units: scanning and voice recognition technologies will replace data
entry, while DVD and Web-based packages are likely to replace face-
to-face IT training.

Reliance on IT as a main physical asset and the inability of units to
purchase more secure assets, such as their own premises, therefore has
its limitations.

Social Capital

Because of its intangible nature, changes in social capital were not well understood by the women participants. The majority did not identify significant changes in any of the three main sets of linkages for businesses: linkages to suppliers and customers; social and community networks and links; and other institutional connections, such as those to supporting or regulatory institutions (Duncombe and Heeks 2002). However, when asked directly and collectively, interviewees identified a range of related changes and connections.

All groups identified as important the new linkages with public officials, particularly those in SPEM and local government offices. These were typically a combination of business and institutional linkages, since SPEM itself often acted as an intermediary between the IT units and their suppliers (of hardware, software, training, and even some loans) as well as their public-sector customers.[1] An identified lack of private-sector contacts reflected the predominance of public sector connections.

There was little recognition of change in social and community linkages, although perhaps the strongest source of social capital derived from the relations that each woman formed with other core members in her cooperative. Cooperation, mutual support, and team spirit among the members were identified as critical success factors by almost all interviewees. As described below, there were also changes in relation to the community, although these were characterized more in terms of status and identity than as new social networks that might increase social capital.

The actions of SPEM have obviously been integral to the creation and operation of the women's IT units, but they also introduce a vulnerability. Because SPEM has acted as an intermediary between the IT units and, in particular, key business partners, opportunities for the women entrepreneurs to create their own business connections are decreased.

Empowerment

The issue of empowerment sits somewhat awkwardly in the five-asset approach to livelihoods. In one respect it can be seen as a combination of human capital, related to the attitudes women have, and social capital, related to the access to power that particular social relations make possible. In another respect, empowerment transcends or overarches the assets framework as the component that determines whether women feel able or are able to make use of their assets. Empowerment therefore merits separate treatment for conceptual reasons. It also merits separate treatment in practice, since it was a theme consistently raised by those involved with Kudumbashree's IT units. An example is seen in Box 6–1.

Box 6–1. Preetha's Story

The life of Preetha, twenty-six, is the story of a woman born into a scheduled caste (one of the deprived and excluded caste groups in India) to illiterate parents in a community housing project. Her father encouraged Preetha and her five sisters to go to school, although she had to work from the age of eleven in order to support her education. She began a degree course but could not afford to continue it. Preetha then entered state-subsidized training courses for scheduled caste members on Microsoft Office and desk-top publishing. She was unable to find employment until she helped to establish an IT training unit under the Kudumbashree initiative.

Life for Preetha is now very different. She is both group leader and accountant for the IT training enterprise. She states: "People like me, poor scheduled castes, cannot expect to get a job. Now I have a job and my family has benefited." She is able to support the household financially, including assisting her younger sisters. She also feels her personality has changed, partly as a result of the training she received, which increased her self-confidence and helped her face social barriers. Previously shy, she is now confident and able to interact with other people, even government officials. As well as providing IT training to students in the school where she previously studied, she has found work with the local council (*grama panchayat*). She now feels free to travel on her own without restrictions on time or distance. Her success is such that animosity is expressed by some neighbors, but this cannot detract from her increased status as a teacher in her alma mater, which counts for even more than the income gained from working in the IT unit.

When asked about human capital, for example, respondents tended to talk about confidence in applying specific skills rather than the skills themselves—such as the confidence to tackle a computing problem; the confidence to deal with other businesses and institutions ("I can walk into any office now and talk confidently"); the confidence to supervise other staff; and more generally, a greater sense of self-confidence and self-esteem.

The same was true of social capital within the community. Women talked not about new linkages or networks within their community but about respect, recognition, and acceptance, and about a new confidence allowing them to attend community social functions such as marriage celebrations. In part this arose from the simple fact of employment and income, but it also resulted from working in an IT unit, given the association of the technology with modernism and progress.

In this way both identity and status change as part of the empowerment process. Tangible signs of this are seen in the women's active role in their *ayalkootams*—neighborhood self-help groups—and in their participation in neighborhood projects or as community resource persons helping others to access government services.

There is a perception that this empowerment extends to some of the deepest sources of inequality. Preetha, for example, stated, "Women like me have not only attained increased levels of both personal and professional skills but also confidence to tackle gender and social [caste] barriers." The extent to which the women have truly achieved a break from preexisting gender relations is not completely clear. Certainly there are positive signs in the capacity of women to take on the managerial roles required in an IT-sector enterprise, something traditionally seen as the preserve of men; in the actions of these women to hire and manage men as employees; and in the ability of some to break away from traditional female goals of security and stasis to push for growth in their enterprises. There were also signs of change in household roles that resulted from the new income and status of these women.

Nevertheless, there are also signs of continuing inequity:

- Men continue to fill pivotal roles as public officials in SPEM and the local government, and continue to exert significant control over the working lives and futures of the IT units (and the women who work in them).
- There remains a tendency to hire men in traditional male roles in the IT units, such as in positions that involve travel and night-shift work, as technical staff, and even in some cases as supervisors.
- There remains a degree of deference to fathers or husbands as ultimate decision makers within the household.

The ground, then, has certainly shifted. These women have been empowered and possess greater opportunities to negotiate traditional roles and assumptions, but—not surprisingly for one initiative within a much broader context—this is not yet equality. There are still too many undercurrents based on an image of men as the stars around which the women orbit.

Table 6–2. Summary of Changes in Asset–Vulnerability Portfolio Due to Involvement in Women's IT Units

	Changes in Asset Base	**Vulnerabilities/Obstacles**
Human Capital	Computer operational skills Technical skills in troubleshooting and networking Some managerial/supervisory skills Some entrepreneurial skills	Technical change Skills at low-end of value chain
Natural Capital	Not applicable	Not applicable
Financial Capital	Personal income	Irregularity of payment Sustainability
Physical Capital	Access to institutional loans	Technical obsolescence Technical innovation Lack of other physical assets
Social Capital	Acquisition of hardware and software	Intermediation of government department
Empowerment	New social and institutional contacts	Continuing gender norms, barriers and inequities

Impacts on Women's Livelihoods

In addition to the points already discussed, a number of other issues were raised in our fieldwork with the women of the Kudumbashree IT units.

Other Impacts

The scope of impacts considered in this study has been limited to the livelihoods of core members of the IT units. There have been other effects. The families of core members have benefited, such as the children whose education has been paid for, the sisters whose marriages have been paid for, the parents who live in new homes, and so on. The IT units also employ other women (and some men): the twenty-four units surveyed employed an additional 185 staff, suggesting that the units overall may employ an additional 750 or so staff. Nearly one-third of these are quasi-replacements for departed core members, and many of the other positions are temporary and/or part-time posts used to cope with additional demand, but they will nevertheless provide a number of the benefits to these workers.

There are broader impacts as well. The work itself—digitizing government records or training students and citizens in IT skills—provides some benefits. Interactions with public institutions such as SPEM, the local government, banks and schools have helped the women's enterprises develop, but those institutions at the same time have developed and learned. Staff in these institutions now have a better understanding of the livelihoods and needs of women in poor communities. As one official commented, "This initiative facilitated not only economic empowerment of women but also enabled a network of new information across various levels."

Sustainability

The women's IT units have produced a range of benefits and have endured, at least in the short-to-medium term. Some units have been in existence for more than five years. A key question, however, for an intervention-driven initiative like this is whether or not these enterprises are sustainable. There are many factors affecting sustainability, of which three will be addressed here:

- *Membership.* The average number of core members in the units surveyed was seven, that is, less than ten, since women drop out for various reasons. Some move away from the area for marriage or new employment. In other cases, such as maternity, further education, or marriage in the local area, it is unclear if the members will return. In only one or two cases has this loss of members potentially jeopardized the unit, as most units simply hire new employees.

- *Support.* Development of the Kudumbashree IT units has required a significant degree of institutional support from government departments, banks, other financial intermediaries, and other local organizations. This is a reminder of the downside of intervention-driven ICT projects: they may not continue without ongoing intervention and support. Having said this, the units in this study have moved beyond the start-up phase with access to a solid network of support institutions that provide finance, training, and other services when necessary.

- *Markets.* The intervention of a single institution—SPEM—has been critical in providing access to markets. SPEM has been the key intermediary in the location of and interaction with data-entry customers. Efforts are being made to diversify clients and products; more public-sector work is obtained through open and competitive tendering, while more private-sector customers are being taken on. However, at the time of writing the units continued to rely on public-sector clients. In this they face two main threats: "insourcing," as schools are beginning to set up their own computer laboratories and training resources; and loss of market, which will be a problem for the data-entry units once the vast number of paper records in the public sector has been digitized.

In all, concerns about sustainability exist, but they are not yet an overriding issue and must be balanced against the outcomes already achieved. Even in the inconceivable event that all the ICT units were to cease operation tomorrow, household assets already purchased would remain: land, housing, gold, education for children, health care for family members, and marriage, among others. In addition, the women possess assets they can take with them into future employment—computers and software as well as computing knowledge and skills. Almost all participants mentioned two additional factors: team spirit, with a widespread assumption that the cooperative group would continue to work together in any new venture; and, most frequently mentioned, empowerment, particularly the self-esteem and self-confidence that are central to the success of new business ventures (Heeks, Arun, and Morgan 2004).

Alternatives

Finally, we must remember that there may be alternatives to intervention-driven IT unit employment that can also contribute to women's livelihoods. These include employment outside the IT sector in a different type of Kudumbashree unit such as soap making, catering services, coconut processing, or employment in a private-sector IT firm.

When asked about the first alternative, some of the women pointed out that the notion of choice and alternative was potentially misguided, as their typing skills background, interest in IT, and the lack of available opportunities in non-IT enterprises meant they should not be seen as having a range of options. Likewise, most would not have been readily employable by private-sector IT firms earlier, although this option may be more likely as a result of the Kudumbashree initiative.

We lack objective evidence about the differing benefits of alternative employment paths, even assuming these had been open. However, the subjective perceptions of the women on this issue were fairly clear. Only one group felt it would be better to work in a different sector, while others perceived the benefits of the IT sector to include its continuous growth, the relatively secure income it provided, working conditions, status in the community and household, and interaction with customers at professional and managerial levels.

Perhaps a half-dozen members in the units left to take up other IT-sector jobs, but there seemed to be a general understanding of the difference in intervention-driven as opposed to market-driven IT work for women. One interviewee, Janu, reflected:

> Initially my family was concerned about the financial sustainability of the project, compared to a secure paid employment in related computer firm. . . . They preferred that I work in the paid sector such as IT firms, but with the recent slump in the IT industry . . . most probably the thriving nature of our project has instilled confidence in self-employment as a viable livelihood.

CONCLUSIONS

The Kudumbashree initiative demonstrates that ICTs can be used to provide direct benefits to women in poor communities. The participants in this initiative are not the most excluded or the absolute poorest of the poor, and they have a certain level of education, but there is no sleight of hand here: they were unemployed and lived in below-poverty-line households, most scraping by on US$1 per day or less. These Cinderellas have transformed into Cyberellas and become active participants in the information society with an experience of change that is integrally empowering. In part, this has been the empowerment of accessing new assets: new skills, new income, new physical assets, new contacts. But to the same extent this has been a story of psychosocial empowerment, involving new attitudes, new confidence, new status, new roles, and new identity.

Of course, the Kudumbashree project carries some risks: ongoing vulnerabilities, introduced vulnerabilities, questions of sustainability, and some uncertainties about comparative benefits of alternative livelihood pathways. But these should be seen as questions rather than fatal flaws. This is not a study in perfection but a demonstration that the "holy grail" of e-development, or development that directly touches and improves the lives of poor women with new technology, is possible over a sustained period.

In looking to broader conclusions, some care must be taken to recognize the importance of contextual factors such as culture and history in shaping relations between gender and technology (Gajjala 2002). Kerala is characterized by a particular institutional history of government, civil society, and culture; the women participants were poor and unemployed but educated. A strong public-sector market for digitization and training created a window of opportunity, and individual champions such as T. K. Jose, the executive director of Kudumbashree, were pivotal in creating and sustaining the initiative. We would certainly recommend that other organizations working in ICTs, gender, and development investigate pilot schemes supporting the creation of women's IT-sector enterprises. But this must be done in a way that is sensitive to context rather than simply duplicating existing blueprints.

Beyond this specific recommendation for action, we reflect on two broader lessons. Decisions and actions for women, ICTs, and development have tended to center around intensive ICT applications, that is, around the application of ICTs in spheres such as e-governance, e-health, and existing microenterprises and small enterprises. The experience here suggests that equal weight should be placed on extensive ICT applications, particularly the production by women of ICT-related goods and services through IT-sector activity. Indeed, perhaps greater emphasis should be given to the latter. How many intensive, consumption-related projects can demonstrate the type of socioeconomic empowerment benefits of Kudumbashree in terms of skills, income, status, and self-worth, sustained over four, five, or even six years?

We also need a more nuanced view of business as part of the development process. The market and the private sector are seen as key actors in the creation of an information society, for example, in stimulating the conditions for spread of ICT infrastructure. The most successful holistic approach, however, may consist of entering into partnerships with other actors such as the state and civil society, to support the "soft" infrastructure of skills and sociopolitical capacities (Pigato 2001).

More directly, though, we began this chapter by questioning the efficacy of market-driven initiatives in addressing gender inequalities. Kerala's experiences do little to dispel this concern: the gender-unaware, market-driven jobs of the private IT sector in the state are seen to bring stresses and insecurities not found in Kudumbashree; nor have they done anything much other than reproduce existing gender roles and attitudes (Arun et al. 2004). In contrast, Kudumbashree's quite different intervention-driven initiative—gender focused, locally owned, participative, and cooperative—has provided sustainable jobs that break down some of the traditional stereotypes of "women's work" and "men's work," and begin to break down the economic, social, and psychological power bases and attitudes that sustain gender inequality.

This was done not by rejecting business but by embracing it: by creating IT enterprises, by seeking to create IT entrepreneurs, and by demonstrating how IT in business can support gender and development goals.[2]

NOTES

[1] In other cases the women were in direct contact with their customers.

[2] This chapter was written from data collected in a research project on women's ICT-based enterprises funded by DFID. The views expressed here are those of the authors and not those of DFID. Data was collected through the support of SPEM in Kerala State, and through the research activity of

consultants Planet Kerala. Thanks are due to all those who have given of their time and data.

REFERENCES

Arun, S., and T. Arun. 2001. Gender at work within the software industry: An Indian perspective. *Journal of Women and Minorities in Science and Engineering* 7, no. 3: 217–31.

———. 2002. Gender, ICTs and development: The case of Kerala, India. *Journal of International Development* 14, no. 1: 39–50.

Arun, S., R. B. Heeks, and S. Morgan. 2004. ICT initiatives, women and work in developing countries: Reinforcing or changing gender inequalities in South India? IDPM Development Informatics Working Paper. University of Manchester, UK.

Bonder, Gloria. 2002. From access to appropriation: Women and ICT policies in Latin America and the Caribbean. Paper presented at the UN Division for the Advancement of Women Expert Group Meeting on ICTs and Their Impact on and Use as an Instrument for the Advancement and Empowerment of Women. Seoul, Korea. 11–14 November. http://www.un.org/womenwatch/daw/egm/ict2002/index.html (accessed 30 November 2005).

Cagatay, N. 1998. Gender and poverty. Social Development and Poverty Elimination Division Working Paper. New York: UNDP.

Cecchini, S. 2002. Can ICT applications contribute to poverty reduction? World Bank Working Paper. Washington, DC: World Bank.

DFID (Department for International Development). 1999. Sustainable livelihood guidance sheets. London: DFID.

Duncombe, R., and R. B. Heeks. 2002. Enterprise across the digital divide: Information systems and rural microenterprise in Botswana. *Journal of International Development* 14, no. 1: 61–74.

Elmoudden, S. 2004. A review of global gendering in offshore call centres: The case of India and the Philippines. Paper presented at Work, Employment and Society Conference. Manchester, UK. 1–3 September.

Franke, R., and B. Chasin. 1994. *Kerala: Radical reform as development in an Indian state.* Oakland, CA: Food First and Promilla.

Gajjala, R. 2002. Cyberfeminist technological practices: Exploring possibilities for a women-centered design of technological environments. Background paper prepared for the INSTRAW Virtual Seminar Series on Gender and ICTs. 15–26 July. http://www.un-instraw.org/docs/gender_and_ict/Gajjala.pdf (accessed 5 July 2005).

GKP (Global Knowledge Partnership). 2003. Youth, poverty, gender: ICT for development success stories. Knowledge for Development series. Kuala Lumpur: GKP Secretariat.

Government of Kerala. 2003. Economic review. State Planning Board, Government of Kerala, Thiruvananthapuram.

Gurumurthy, Anita. 2004. Bridging the digital gender divide: Issues and insights on ICT for women's economic empowerment. New Delhi: UNIFEM.

Hafkin, Nancy, and Nancy Taggart. 2001. *Gender, information technology, and developing countries: An analytic study*. Washington, DC: USAID.

Heeks, R. B. 1996. *India's software industry*. New Delhi: Sage Publications.

———. 2002. I-development not e-development. *Journal of International Development* 14, no. 1: 1–12.

———. 2005. Analysing the software sector in developing countries using competitive advantage theory. Paper presented at Theorising Development Informatics seminar, Manchester, UK. 20 January.

Heeks, R. B., and B. Nicholson. 2004. Software export success factors and strategies in "follower" nations. *Competition & Change* 8, no. 3: 267–303.

Heeks, R. B., S. Arun, and S. Morgan. 2004. Researching ICT-based enterprise for women in developing countries: An enterprise perspective. University of Manchester, UK: IDPM.

Huyer, Sophia, and Swasti Mitter. 2003. ICTs, globalisation and poverty reduction: Gender dimensions of the knowledge society. Gender Advisory Board. UN Commission on Science and Technology for Development. http://gab.wigsat.org/policy.htm (accessed 10 November 2005).

Huyer, Sophia, and Tatiana Sikoska. 2002. INSTRAW virtual seminar series on gender and information and communication technologies. Presented at the UN Division for the Advancement of Women Expert Group Meeting on ICTs and Their Impact on and Use as an Instrument for the Advancement and Empowerment of Women. Seoul, Korea, 11–14 November. http://www.un-instraw.org/en/docs/gender_and_ict/Synthesis_paper.pdf (accessed 10 November 2005).

Jorge, Sonia N. 2002. The economics of ICT: Challenges and practical strategies of ICT use for women's economic empowerment. Presented at the UN Division for the Advancement of Women Expert Group Meeting on ICTs and Their Impact on and Use as an Instrument for the Advancement and Empowerment of Women. Seoul, Korea, 11–14 November. http://www.un.org/womenwatch/daw/egm/ict2002/index.html (accessed 30 November 2005).

Kenny, C. 2002. ICT for direct poverty alleviation: Cost and benefit. *Development Policy Review* 20, no. 2: 20–30.

Kudumbashree. 2004. Concept, organisation, and activities. Kudumbashree, State Poverty Eradication Mission, Thiruvananthapuram.

Marcelle, G. M. 2002. Report from the online conference conducted by the Division for the Advancement of Women. Presented at the UN Division for the Advancement of Women Expert Group Meeting on ICTs and Their Impact on and Use as an Instrument for the Advancement and Empowerment of Women. Seoul, Korea, 11–14 November. http://

www.un.org/womenwatch/daw/egm/ict2002/index.html (accessed 30 November 2005).

Moser, C. 1998. The asset-vulnerability framework: Reassessing urban poverty reduction strategies. *World Development* 26, no. 1: 1–19.

Narasimhan, R. 1983. The socioeconomic significance of information technology to developing countries. *The Information Society* 2, no. 1: 65–79.

Narayan, D., R. Chambers, M. K. Shah, and P. Petesch. 2000. *Crying out for change*. Oxford: Oxford Univ. Press.

Parayil, G. 2000. Is Kerala's development experience a "model"? *The development experience: Reflections on sustainability and replicability*, ed. G. Parayil, 1–15. London: Zed Books.

Pigato, M. 2001. Information and communication technology, poverty and development in Sub-Saharan Africa and South Asia. Africa Region Working Paper Series. Washington, DC: World Bank. http://www.worldbank .org/afr/wps/wp20.htm (accessed 30 November 2005).

Sen, A. 1999. *Development as freedom*. Oxford: Oxford Univ. Press.

Thioune, R. M., ed. 2003. *Information and communication technologies for development in Africa*. Vol. 1, *Opportunities and challenges for community development*. Ottawa: IDRC.

UNDP (United Nations Development Programme). 1999. *Human development report 1999*. New York: UNDP.

Wajcman, J. 2004. *Techno-feminism*. Cambridge: Polity Press.

World Bank. 2001. *Engendering development*. New York: Oxford Univ. Press.

7

Women in Latin America
Appropriating ICTs for Social Change

Maria Garrido and Raul Roman

> Development can be seen as a process of expanding the real free-
> doms that people enjoy. . . . Development requires the removal
> of major sources of economic unfreedom: poverty as well as tyr-
> anny, poor economic opportunities as well as systematic social
> deprivation, neglect of public facilities as well as intolerance or
> overactivity of repressive states.
>
> —AMARTYA SEN

WORKING TOWARD GENDER EQUALITY
AND SOCIAL CHANGE IN LATIN AMERICA

Ever since women were granted the right to vote in most Latin American countries between the 1930s and 1940s (Sivard et al. 1995), significant progress has been made to improve the situation of women in the
region.[1] Today, we see an increasing number of women in Latin America
represented in government, as researchers in S&T areas, participating
in civil society organizations to secure their rights, and generating and
disseminating knowledge through channels of communication respon-
sive to their needs. Despite this progress the situation of women in Latin
America is still a difficult one. Unequal access to education, increasing
feminization of poverty, labor discrimination and exploitation, gender-
related differences in wages and skills, domestic and sexual violence, the
denial of reproductive rights, and a pervasive culture of *machismo* remain barriers preventing the empowerment of women. In this context

two interrelated phenomena are opening new opportunities—and posing new challenges—for women and other groups to further their quest for social justice, cultural recognition, and economic empowerment in Latin America: the process of economic globalization, and the development and use of ICTs.

On the one hand, neo-liberal policies are paving the way for Latin American markets to enter the global economy. These trends toward economic globalization have redefined the way people in the region work, interact across cultures, communicate, and relate to their environment, their community, and the state (Chase 2003). Although the process toward globalization has had some positive effects—for example, an increase in democratization of the region—it has also carried some negative consequences (for examples, see Stiglitz 2003). In the last decade Latin America has experienced a widening gap between the poor and the rich, a steady decline in the quality and availability of social services, the severe exploitation of natural resources, and the deterioration of living standards, especially among the working class and poorer segments of the population (see, for example, Zermeño 1996; Veltemeyer and Petras 2000; Chase 2003; Gwyne and Cristobal 2004; Hall and Patrinos 2005).

On the other hand, the development of IT in the last decade has challenged the commonly held assumption that communication among people in different countries is channeled through a hierarchy of institutions, leaving little or no power for grassroots organizations to seek alternative routes for intercultural interaction. The Internet has opened new opportunities for unrepresented voices or "resource-poor organizations," as defined by Bennett (2003), to bypass traditional centers of power—such as governments, corporations, and international organizations—in their quest for social justice and enhanced democracy. Furthermore, the effective use of communication networks has broadened the scale and scope of action for civil society groups in Latin America working for social change. Communication networks have empowered their struggle internationally by opening new spaces that allow better information exchange and coordination (Diani 1992; Cleaver 1998). In addition, ICTs are being used at the grassroots level to enhance educational and health systems, improve policy formulation and execution, and increase the range of strategies to alleviate poverty in marginalized communities (see, for example, Mansell and Wehn 1998; Kirkman et al. 2001; Badshah, Khan, and Garrido 2003; Warschauer 2003).

WOMEN USING ICTS IN LATIN AMERICA

This chapter analyzes the ways in which women in Latin America are appropriating ICTs in their quest for gender equality and social change in the context of economic globalization. As Hafkin and Taggart point out, "women within developing countries are in the deepest part of the [digital] divide further removed from the information age than the men whose poverty they share" (2001, 1). If we recognize that knowledge and information exchange is becoming an increasingly determinant competitive factor for developing economies and an engine for socioeconomic development in marginalized communities, it becomes imperative to harness its potential to serve the goals of equality and social justice. Among other aspects, these goals need to address the "issues of gender and women's equal right to access, use and shape ICTs" (Gurumurthy 2004, 1). ICTs have the potential to become a catalyst for social change (see Gumucio-Dagrón 2001, for example). However, without specific efforts to enable women's appropriation of these technologies to further their rights, existing patterns of gender inequality in Latin American will not change; in fact, they may worsen.

Our analysis is founded primarily on a gender perspective but integrates into the discussion the relationship between women's rights and other social justice movements in the region, such as those seeking human rights, fair trade, and alternative development. Women in the region are becoming key participants in these struggles, advancing their rights while addressing broader social issues that concern their livelihoods and the welfare of their families, their communities, their countries, and the region in general. We argue that by establishing the links between women's political activities and social justice movements, we can broaden our understanding of the role of women in reweaving the social, political, and economic fabric of Latin America. The opportunities for women to harness the potential of ICTs to advance their rights must be analyzed within the context of these diverse social justice movements taking place in Latin America.

The information presented in this chapter was gathered from a review of the literature on gender and ICTs, phone and e-mail interviews with women activists and community leaders in Latin America, an online consultation entitled Cenicienta o Cibercienta: Las Mujeres y las TICs en America Latina distributed to the members of Somos@Telecentros online network, and the authors' research on ICT for development, telecenters, and social movements in the region.

WOMEN, ICTS, AND COLLECTIVE ACTION

The chapter incorporates the experiences of women—and men working on their behalf—appropriating ICTs for social change in three different, but closely interrelated, forms of collective action:

1. *Women in community telecenters.* We describe some examples of women's empowerment using ICTs through telecenters in Latin America. A telecenter is a shared-access facility equipped with telephones, computers, television, video, and other equipment set up to provide demand-driven communication and information services for community development (Roman and Colle 2003). Telecenters have been widely promoted as vehicles to provide access and training to ICT-enabled services, especially for low-income communities.

2. *Women in social movements.* We look at the ways in which women are advancing their rights through active participation in social movements in Latin America. Engaging in different struggles for women's rights, human rights, fair trade, indigenous rights, corporate governance, and environmental protection, among others— social movements in Latin America are key vehicles in the search for alternative routes to development. Using ICTs, these movements are establishing alliances with national and international civil society groups and are raising global awareness and support for local social struggles. We use the experience of indigenous women in the Zapatista movement in Chiapas, Mexico, to illustrate how they are advancing their struggle for equality and empowerment within the broader social focus of the movement and how ICTs are contributing to this process.

3. *Women in information and advocacy networks.* We describe some examples of strategic use of ICTs to generate and disseminate knowledge about efforts for the advancement of women's rights. Through the creation of websites, electronic forums, Internet radio, e-mail distribution lists, and Web-based publications, women in Latin America are building electronic spaces where they can

communicate, share experiences, and join forces to change discrimi-
natory public policies and collaborate toward other common goals
(Plou 2004). In this arena ICTs are providing venues for women's
voices *desde las bases* (from the grassroots) to be heard, along with
those of intellectuals and activists, thus facilitating collaboration
and understanding as well as fostering women's self-esteem.

We take a cultural approach to technology in our analysis. We explicitly recognize "the interpenetration of technology with social forms and
systems of meaning" (Pfaffenberger 1988, 244). Understanding "tech-
nology-as-culture" sees technology as embedded in a specific social system (Hafkin 2002). In this sense, technology is not value free; neither is
it independent from the society that adopts or reinvents it. Rather, technology exists and functions in dynamic interaction with the individuals
and social groups who use it. This is a particularly important consideration in the study of ICT diffusion in developing countries, where cultural norms and power and authority structures affecting the way
information is produced and shared frequently differ from communication patterns in industrialized economies (see, for example, Lind 1991;
Azad, Erdem, and Saleem 1998; Lehmann 1995; Jain 1997; Avgerou
and Walsham 2000; Loch, Straub, and Kamel 2003).

The first section of the chapter discusses the contributions of ICTs
that we consider the most relevant for women's empowerment in the
context of Latin America, along with background on the situation of
women and ICT in the region. The second part analyzes the ways in
which women in the region are appropriating ICTs to further their rights
through telecenters, social movements, and networks of information and
advocacy in the context of globalization. The third section explores some
national and regional trends that provide important lenses through which
to analyze and direct future research regarding the potential of ICTs to
further women's empowerment and economic opportunity in Latin
America.

ICTS AND WOMEN'S EMPOWERMENT—OPPORTUNITIES AND CHALLENGES FOR WOMEN IN LATIN AMERICA

As noted above, economic globalization and the development and use
of ICTs for social change are opening new opportunities and posing

new challenges for women and other groups in their quest for empowerment in Latin America. In the context of these two interrelated phenomena, the potential for women to appropriate ICTs to further their rights is determined to some extent by the way these technologies are integrated in the processes of promoting citizenship and social empowerment. The fundamental rights to education, health, and communication can be better exercised with the effective use of ICTs. The benefits of ICTs for women's empowerment are well known (see, for example, Hafkin 2002; Harcourt 2001; Bonder 2003; Huyer 2003; Plou 2004; Gurumurthy 2004). Drawing from this literature we consider the following contributions of ICTs to be the most relevant in the context of women's empowerment in Latin America:

- self-esteem and renewed self-confidence to change their own lives from access, use, and appropriation of ICTs;
- the generation and dissemination of grassroots knowledge and the provision of venues for women to collaborate, share experiences, learn from one another, and organize more effectively to secure their rights;
- the potential to advance women's economic empowerment by improving their economic productivity and creating new entrepreneurial opportunities;
- the collaboration and networking possibilities that open channels for the participation of women's groups in national and international decision-making processes.

Despite its significant progress in the last three decades, Latin America still carries "a heavy cultural weight in relation to the role of women assigned by a society that dresses itself with the make-up of modernity but still upholds traditional values especially in the relationship between genders" (Plou 2004, 1). There are many gender-related socioeconomic divides still present in the region that help to explain patterns of unequal ICT access and usage.

Bonder (2002, 1) states that "connectivity is an unavoidable, though insufficient, indicator in order to evaluate the participation of [women] in the region [in regards to ICTs]." However, a discussion of the potential of ICTs for women's development inevitably moves from the issue of access to the hardware. The percentage of those connected to the Internet in Latin America is 13 percent of the population.[2] Compared with the United States (69 percent), Europe (37 percent), and Australia (50 percent), Internet penetration in Latin America is comparatively low. When the differences among countries are considered, the access gap widens. Argentina has an Internet penetration of 20 percent; Chile, 26 percent; and Uruguay, 37 percent. Central American countries such as Guatemala, Ecuador, and Bolivia remain at less than 5 percent each (see Table 7–1 for Internet statistics of selected countries in the region). Despite the fact that usage grew by 160 percent between 2000 and 2005, more than 450 million people in the region still have no access to the Internet (Internet World Statistics 2005).

There are few data sources in the region that disaggregate the number of Internet users by sex. The estimated percentage of women among Internet users in Latin America ranges between 42 and 48 percent, the majority of whom are urban, employed, middle-class women aged thirty-five years or under, with educational levels above secondary school (Plou 2005a). The few available statistics for the percentage of women Internet users in Latin America place Chile at the top with 50 percent, followed by Mexico with 48 percent, Argentina with 45 percent, Brazil with 42 percent, and Venezuela with 30 percent (ITU 2002). Without solid gender-related ICT indicators (not only regarding the Internet, but also other relevant ICTs), it is difficult to advocate for the inclusion of gender considerations in ICT policies and development programs (Hafkin 2003).

Nonetheless, because access is a multidimensional concept (Rice, McCreadie, and Chang 2001), research needs to go beyond merely documenting women's connectivity. Besides appropriate infrastructure and a favorable policy environment, disadvantaged women's access to ICTs depends on a set of factors that can be summarized in the following categories:

- affordability
- relevance—do the ICT services respond to local women's needs?
- women's awareness of the value of information and communication services
- local political conflicts and power asymmetries—are women in the community allowed to access ICT services?

In other words, there are structural, social, and individual factors that account for women's effective use of ICTs.

Table 7-1. Internet Usage in Selected Latin American Countries (2005)

Country	Population Est. 2005 (i)	Female Pop. 2004 (ii)	Internet Users 2005 (i)	Female Internet Users 2002 (iii)	Usage Growth 2000-2005 (i)	Internet Penetration in Population 2005 (i) (%)
	(millions)	(millions)	(thousands)	(as % of total)	(%)	
Argentina	39.2	20	7,500	42	200	20
Bolivia	9.07	4.18	270	N/A	125	3
Brazil	181.8	88.34	22,320	40	346.4	12.3
Chile	15.5	7.68	4,000	49	127.6	25.8
Colombia	45.9	21.4	3,585	N/A	308.4	7.8
Costa Rica	4.3	1.98	1,200	N/A	380	27.9
Cuba	11.3	5.58	120	N/A	100	1.1
Ecuador	12	6.3	581	N/A	223.1	4.8
El Salvador	6.4	3.2	550	N/A	1,275	8.5
Guatemala	12.3	5.64	400	N/A	515	3.2
Honduras	6.6	3.21	272	N/A	580	4.1
Mexico	104	49.9	14,900	45	449	14.3
Nicaragua	5.76	2.55	90	N/A	80	4.1
Panama	3.07	1.14	192	N/A	326.9	6.2
Paraguay	5.5	2.72	120	N/A	500	2.2
Peru	28	12.93	4,510	N/A	82.8	16.3
Uruguay	3.25	1.718	1,190	N/A	221.7	36.6
Venezuela	24.8	12	3,040	30	231.2	13

Sources: (i) Internet World Statistics 2005. (ii) Economic Commission for Latin America and the Caribbean (Population Gender Statistics, 2004). (iii) ITU 2002.

LOOKING BACK, LOOKING FORWARD—
WOMEN IN LATIN AMERICAN DEVELOPMENT

In the field of international development, ICTs have almost always been considered critical agents and catalysts for social change. As early as the 1950s, when modernization approaches guided the practice and theory of development, communication technologies (particularly mass media) were seen as mechanisms to achieve economic growth, increase literacy, and spread the values of modernity within traditional societies (Lowenthal 1952/53; Lerner 1958; Rogers 1976; Schramm 1964). Since then, revisions of development theory have continued framing the way development communication scholars and practitioners approach their work and think about what they do (Wilkins and Mody 2001).

However, gender approaches to development were neglected in practice and theory until the 1970s. Two influential works represent the rise of feminist critiques of development and the gradual integration of women's needs in national and international policy agendas. First, the contribution of Ester Boserup's *Women's Role in Economic Development* (1970) "helped catalyze the 1975–1985 United Nations Decade for Women as well as the implementation of women-specific policies and programs in most aid agencies" (Steeves 2001, 398). Second, Paolo Freire's *Pedagogy of the Oppressed* (1970) was the major inspiration for a new approach to development called "participatory development." Participatory approaches to development aimed at empowering people at the community level to become key actors in the process of change, recognizing and supporting the capacity of local people to make their own decisions about their future. In participatory development practice, communication is considered a key ingredient to reach self-help goals. In the decades that followed, the role of women in this context was increasingly emphasized in every stage of the development process.

In Latin America, gender approaches to development in the 1970s centered on understanding the contribution of women's work to national economies and household welfare. Nash (2003) points out that at the start no national databases included gender breakdowns. It took almost a decade's work by feminist activists and scholars in the region to develop ethnographic studies that assessed women's contribution to gross national product. Studies undertaken in the 1980s in countries such as Brazil, Colombia, Mexico, and Peru challenged the commonly held assumptions that income was shared equally among members of the household and that women's work at home made no contribution to the economy.

During the 1980s, also known as the Lost Decade in Latin America, the social dislocations caused by the emergent global economy started to become apparent. The economic situation of women during the debt crisis of the 1980s was changed along two patterns: (1) women became the targeted labor force in development programs based on *maquiladoras* (assembly lines); and (2) driven by the need to support their families, "women invented a whole new economy as street and market vendors that created what we know as informal economy" (Nash 2003, 61). Women organized themselves in collective kitchens processing and cooking foods, selling arts and crafts for tourists, or selling fresh fruits and vegetables in the street markets, among other activities. These self-organized programs allowed women to become more autonomous (Nash 2003). Even though women increased their participation in the economy, traditional political channels remained mostly closed to them. This prompted women to participate actively in alternative social actions to an extent that led them to become the protagonists of the majority of social movements in the 1970s and 1980s in the region.

Despite the negative social impact of neo-liberal policies and adjustment programs on the majority of the population, Latin American governments continued to integrate the region's markets into the global economy throughout the 1990s. However, the growing discontent with globalization policies brought groups together in a search for alternative development options. In the last decade Latin America witnessed a resurgence of political activity on the part of civil society organizations. During the 1990s, women's movements in the region and around the world engaged in dialogue and increased cross-national collaboration, especially in conjunction with the world conferences convened by the UN. Organizing for these conferences, women began to use ICTs strategically to disseminate information about women's rights' movements around the world. As we describe in the following section, women in Latin America used ICTs to create discussion forums, e-mail distribution lists, and online publications, providing opportunities for women to collaborate toward common goals (Plou 2004).

ICTS FOR WOMEN'S EMPOWERMENT IN LATIN AMERICA

The experiences of women described below illustrate the ways in which the potential of ICTs are being harnessed to advance women's rights and economic empowerment in Latin America.

Women in Community Telecenters

Many development communication scholars study how to reach lower socioeconomic levels so that communication programs mitigate (or do not worsen) the already wide gaps between social classes existent in developing countries. Thus, many telecenter projects focus on how to offer egalitarian access to their services in order to empower the most disadvantaged in society, particularly women.

We conducted an online open-ended questionnaire survey in order to gather qualitative data on women's experiences with telecenters in Latin America.[3] Responses were received from one male and six female telecenter managers in seven countries: Mexico, Bolivia, Guatemala, Ecuador, Colombia, Venezuela, and Chile. While their responses reflect the experience of telecenters with an explicit concern for women, we have no way of knowing how prevalent such centers are in the region. The goal of the consultation was to gain a better understanding of telecenter services specifically targeted at women, the way women benefit from accessing these services, and the challenges involved in making these services work both for telecenter managers and women users. These three points are addressed in the remainder of this section.

What Services Are Telecenters Offering?

All the telecenters surveyed in our consultation provide basic ICT access services (telephone, fax, photocopying, computers, and Internet) and formal or informal training on computer use. Most important, some of these centers offer locally relevant value-added ICT-enabled services. The Apachita Indigenous Communication Network has eighty telecenters in Bolivia serving the Aymara and Quechua indigenous groups in the country. The Apachita network creates print, audio, and video news services and makes them available to these communities at its telecenters. Among other services, the telecenter established by the Association for the Integral Development of Mayan Guatemala (AIDMG) supports local microenterprises by building the capacity of local indigenous women in the use of computer and Internet resources. The Autónoma de Occidente telecenter manager in Colombia advises users about funding sources to support local community projects and organizes talks on topics of community interest, including gender.

How Are Women Benefiting from Telecenter Services?

Women in Latin America are using telecenters to communicate with people outside their communities; they are learning how to use new ICTs for different social and economic purposes and to obtain information about topics that affect their lives. The Apachita telecenters are a key resource for indigenous rural women in Bolivia who need to stay in touch with their husbands and other family members who emigrate to the cities or abroad to work or study. The AIDMG telecenter is training local Mayan women how to repair, clean, and maintain computers, and how to install hardware and software, thus opening new job opportunities for them. In addition to technical training, the telecenter offers training for indigenous women on topics such as human rights, women's rights, women's participation in civic life, reproductive health, and family violence. According to the AIDMG telecenter manager: "Our objective is to help women change their mindsets, and allow them to believe that they can have a different life. Our center is filling a gap, because indigenous women rarely have the possibility to attend school. Here women realize that they are still able to learn new things." The manager of the El Chaco telecenter in Ecuador shared a similar point of view: "I believe our services contribute to women's personal growth and self-esteem. The women who come to our center are setting an example for all the women in our community. Our telecenter helps women form their own opinions and educates them to exercise their democratic rights." In the same way, the El Encuentro telecenter manager in Chile explained that "using ICTs allows women to build their self-confidence. We notice this because once women are trained at our telecenter, they dare to do things they would have never done had not they come here, such as completing their formal education or creating microenterprises."

What Are the Challenges to Women's Use of Telecenter Services?

Telecenter managers indicated that there were sociocultural and sociopsychological obstacles originating from the social discrimination against women and *machismo* prevalent in many Latin American communities that make it difficult for many women to use telecenter services and affect ICT usage among disadvantaged women. The AIDMG telecenter manager in Guatemala explained: "There is a generalized belief that women must be subdued and accept the fate other people assign to them. There is also a cultural problem: people think of women as housewives who stay at home. It is so difficult to sit a woman in front of a computer and convince her that she can make it work." The El Chaco telecenter manager in Ecuador said that "there is a lot of *machismo*. There are very few spaces for discussion and dialogue about women's issues and a lack of capacity and education." For the El Encuentro telecenter manager in Chile, "the most complex obstacle [for women to access telecenter services] is women's technophobia, a psychological barrier that becomes more difficult to overcome if women are not supported by their families." In other words, both social norms and lack of confidence are barriers to women's access to telecenters in Latin America. In addition, it is not easy for telecenter managers to offer services specifically targeted at women. Most managers point to lack of economic resources as the main obstacle to providing telecenter services expressly for women. This obstacle is not surprising, considering that economic sustainability is a central concern in discussions about the strategic viability of telecenters (see, for example, Best and Maclay 2001; Proenza 2001).

Women in Social Movements: The Zapatista Movement

On 1 January 1994 an army formed by indigenous peasants under the name Ejercito Zapatista de Liberacion Nacional (the Zapatista National Liberation Army) took over seven towns in the southern state of Chiapas, one of the poorest states in Mexico[4] (Schulz 1998). The uprising was fueled by concern over the poverty, discrimination, and exploitation that have plagued native Mexican communities for centuries. The Zapatista revolt was timed to make headlines in the national and international press on the same date that the North American Free Trade Agreement took effect. Thus the Zapatista movement was attempting to reveal to the international community what it saw as inherent contradictions between economic globalization and the chronic deprivation of these marginalized indigenous people.

The Zapatista movement uses the Internet as a tool for global mobilization, which has brought the movement enormous international attention. A movement initiated by local indigenous people looking for solutions to local problems has become an icon for social justice for marginalized and exploited groups around the world (Cleaver 1998). Civil society groups working in areas such as human, women's and indigenous rights, fair trade, international peace, and development take their inspiration from and actively support the Zapatistas (Garrido and Halavais 2003).

ICTs have enabled the creation of a network of Zapatista supporters to generate and disseminate information about the movement's struggle and to mobilize support for the Zapatista communities.[5] The international network assists Zapatista communities in many ways: distributing information through websites and discussion lists, participating in peace camps and international meetings, aiding the Zapatistas' effort to build schools and health clinics, and providing channels to sell local products under fair-trade conditions in international markets.

Indigenous women are at the forefront of the Zapatista movement, making up about one-third of Zapatista fighters and 55 percent of its support base. The Zapatista Women's Revolutionary Law,[6] enacted in January 1994, supported women's demands for education, reproductive rights, political participation in their communities, the right to work and receive a fair salary, and freedom from domestic violence. The law also influenced other rural and urban women's movements in Mexico. As Leyva Solano points out: "The law fell on fertile ground, and it was immediately taken up by many feminists and women from grass-roots organizations. These women, who had their own histories of struggle, found that their demands were reflected in the demands of the Zapatista women" (2003, 8).

Gender roles in the communities are slowly changing, and Zapatista women are advancing their rights while becoming key participants in the economy of their communities (Nash 2003). Increasingly, women in Zapatista communities participate in meetings and decision making. They have organized themselves into women's cooperatives and collective work groups, making crafts, baking bread, growing vegetables and herbs, and producing honey and candles. They are also using ICTs to advance their empowerment.

Our Word Is Our Weapon: ICTs Enabling Zapatista Women

Indigenous women in Zapatista communities share the Zapatista slogan "Our word is our weapon," using the power of information and education to secure their rights and improve their livelihoods. ICTs support their information generation and dissemination efforts in two important ways:

- Zapatista women use ICTs to disseminate information about domestic violence and participation in the autonomous councils, discussing the right of women to own land, issues concerning reproductive rights, and relevant international news. Since access to telecommunications and electricity remains a major obstacle for almost all the indigenous communities in the area, women—and men—take advantage of a unique trait that ICTs offer: the convergence of traditional media with new information technologies. An example of this is Radio Insurgente, the official voice of the Zapatista movement. Radio Insurgente broadcasts programs and music in several indigenous languages through FM and short-wave radio, with the programs uploaded weekly to the radio website. Although Radio Insurgente broadcasting is not exclusively geared toward women, it delivers numerous programs that discuss gender and women's issues. Women also participate in reporting and editing programs concerning women's and other issues.

- ICTs have enabled women's organizations at local, national, and international levels to make use of the information coming directly from the Zapatista communities. Dozens of websites and distribution lists use this material to mobilize efforts on behalf of Zapatista women. For example, some organizations have used ICT-disseminated information to pressure the central government to end military harassment of women. Organizations such as Global Exchange, Mexico Solidarity Network, Fray Bartolome de las Casas Human Rights Center, IFCO Pastors for Peace, and the Chiapas95 distribution list feed this information into electronic forums to raise awareness and mobilize support for the Zapatista communities.

Supporting the Collective Work of Women in Zapatista Communities

Since the uprising began in 1994, many cooperatives producing arts and crafts, honey, organic coffee, bread, and vegetables have been formed, with women as key participants. Women established some of the cooperatives themselves and joined with men to start some of the others, such as the coffee cooperatives. In a recent visit to Zapatista communities in Chiapas, one of the authors of this chapter spoke to Zapatista women in the arts-and-crafts cooperatives located in Oventic (one of five autonomous councils). Pointing out the potential for ICTs to provide markets and international exposure for Zapatista women in cooperatives,[7] one woman from the Women for Dignity Cooperative said:

The cooperative was founded eight years ago, and today we have six hundred members, almost all of them are women, but there are some men too. Each week, two women attend the store, and we organize ourselves with other women who take care of our kids while they are working there. Most of the income for the cooperative comes from visitors to Oventic, but the sales are still small. We need more markets; we need more exposure to our products. We have an e-mail address, and one organization in Chiapas is helping us to attract more buyers, but it is not enough. We would like to get in touch with more organizations that support fair trade.[8]

Women in Information and Advocacy Networks

The strategic use of ICTs by women and feminist movements has dramatically increased our knowledge about different struggles to advance women's rights around the world. Plou explains:

As a result of the communication needs of these movements in relation to the world conferences organized by the United Nations in the decade of the 90s (the 1992 Conference on Environment and Development [the Earth Summit], the International Conference on Population and Development in Cairo in 1994, and the fourth World Conference on Women in Beijing in 1995), the use of ICTs to create electronic discussion lists, websites, electronic forums, publications, news, and Internet radio nurtured the environment for women to organize and work toward common goals. (2004, 3)

Further, these networks opened a space for smaller organizations to share information, join the dialogue about women's rights issues, and provide channels for the voices of women from the grassroots to be heard.

In Latin America many information and advocacy networks have emerged that work in behalf of women's participation in civic life and generating new norms for a more inclusive information society. These networks are growing more sophisticated in their use of ICTs; they generate databases, offer technical training sessions in open-source software (Free/Libre Open Source Software—FLOSS), and integrate ICTs with the use of traditional mass media (Internet radio). The following are some examples of these networks.

Association for Progressive Communications Women's Networking Support Program in Latin America (PARM-AL)

The APC Women's Networking Support Program is a global network founded in 1993 that supports women's organizations working for social change through the appropriation of ICTs. Through its website and electronic forums, PARM-AL works on issues of gender and ICT policy, develops training materials to enhance the expertise of women ICT trainers and technicians, promotes gender-sensitive evaluation methods, and provides a venue for sharing relevant resources and documents. Headed by Dafne Plou, the Latin America regional network has twenty members from countries of the region and is actively involved in promoting awareness about the importance of gender issues in ICT policies, particularly in the context of WSIS (Plou 2005b).

Independent Media Center (IMC) in Latin America

The IMC is a network of collectively run media outlets that work independently of government and corporate sponsors. IMC was born during the protests against the World Trade Organization in 1999. Since then, the IMC model, using open-source software, has been extended to more than one hundred locations, of which seventeen are in Latin America. Many IMCs have integrated traditional mass media into their websites through freely downloadable Internet radio and video documentaries. While IMCs are not geared exclusively toward women, all the centers devote considerable space to publishing and discussing gender-related issues. In IMC Mexico, for example, considerable coverage is given to the femicide in Ciudad Juarez, where five hundred to eight hundred young women have reportedly disappeared in the last ten years. IMC Argentina features articles and discussions about abortion, domestic violence, and unemployment. IMC Bolivia publishes news and discussions in Spanish, English, and three indigenous dialects—Aymara, Quechua, Guarani—on issues related to fair trade, with material on women workers and producers.

Modemmujer

Modemmujer is a communication and information network based in Mexico that works to support, disseminate, and develop activities and initiatives from women and women's organizations in Latin America. Modemmujer's strategic use of ICTs gained regional reputation in the preparation for the 1995 Beijing World Conference on Women, when the network launched an e-mail information campaign. Since then, Modemmujer has become a prominent example of women's appropriation of ICTs for political empowerment. The network fosters women's collaboration on Latin America issues and builds capacity through its training material, activities, and electronic discussion forums (Plou 2004). It has over thirteen hundred members in Mexico and elsewhere in Latin America.

Red de Información de Mujeres de Argentina—RIMAweb

RIMAweb is a communication network with over eight hundred members from nineteen provinces in Argentina, as well as elsewhere in Latin America and in Europe. The network was conceived as a communication channel for women's organizations working in Argentina to share information, collaborate, and improve the flow of information among women's groups and traditional and alternative mass media. The members of RIMAweb work to make women's experiences visible and to promote the integration of women's issues in mass media. They also try to diminish the use of sexist language in the news and legislative documents and develop campaigns to sensitize people about gender issues. RIMAweb is currently developing a network of journalists in Argentina and promoting collaboration with other women's networks in the country.

Radio Internacional Feminista (FIRE)

FIRE was founded in 1998 by a group of Latin American and Caribbean women living in Costa Rica. FIRE's objective is to advance the rights of women to communicate and to create a space for women to produce and distribute news and information. Along with other women's information and advocacy networks in the region, FIRE provides a venue where voices and stories are shared in order to advance their rights and to promote images that challenge gender stereotypes. Through its multimedia website, FIRE informs its readers of events concerning women in the Latin American region and around the world. The website provides information about conferences, seminars, protests, demonstrations, and campaigns, and posts interviews with women activists. FIRE also offers training for other women to learn the technical aspects of broadcasting on the Web (Plou 2004).

Fala Mulher

"Fala Mulher" (Women speak up) is a radio program that started broadcasting in Brazil in 1989, supported by CEMINA in Rio de Janeiro. Through its AM station and Internet radio, Fala mulher broadcasts programs about women's and feminist movements in the country. The radio programs and archived audio files available on the website include news, information, events, and thematic campaigns. In 2000 CEMINA also created Red Cyberela (Cyberela Network), whose objective is to train women as popular gender-communication specialists—*comunicadoras populares*—in radio and ICTs, to encourage them to produce content with a gender perspective, and to stimulate dissemination and use of information that supports women's activities in their communities. By 2004 the network had trained twenty-nine women and provided them with computer equipment, technical maintenance, and broadband Internet connectivity. Red Cyberela has helped launch several women-run and women-focused radio stations that broadcast their own programs on the Internet.

FUTURE DIALOGUE AND RESEARCH

The profound economic, social, and cultural transformations in Latin America in the last two decades have created opportunities for women's social development. We consider the following national and regional trends to be important lenses to understand and direct future dialogue and research regarding the potential of ICTs to further women's empowerment and economic opportunity in the region.

Women and Economic Globalization: Empowerment and Disempowerment

Neo-liberal globalization has had a negative impact on the majority of people in Latin America. The free-market policies advocated by the International Monetary Fund and the World Bank have exacerbated poverty, exclusion, and exploitation, and created new challenges in the region. Progress in the advancement of women's rights must be measured against both the opportunities that are steadily being opened and the ways that these opportunities are generating new challenges or perpetuating old ones. In recognition of its paradoxical nature, we call this process *disempowering empowerment*. The situation described in 2005 by an indigenous woman, Clotilde Marquez Cruz, working in a community telecenter in Bolivia illustrates the inherent contradictions of empowerment in the context of globalization:

> I work as a volunteer in the telecenter to help my sisters [indigenous women] overcome the terrible economic situation we live in. The administration of the telecenters in the communities is under the responsibility of women because all the men have left their communities in the search for jobs in the cities. Many of them have migrated to other countries: Chile, Argentina, and Brazil because of the difficult economic situation that Bolivia is enduring. This is the reason why there is so much poverty in our communities.[9]

On the empowerment side, women are participating more actively in the activities of their communities, seeking venues to communicate, collaborate, and organize, often with the use of new ICTs. On the disempowering side, the migration of men to the cities or to other countries is creating new challenges for women and is increasing what is known as the feminization of poverty.

Increased Collaboration among Civil Society Groups Working for Social Change

In the last decade civil society in Latin America has become more involved in economic and social development issues. Nurtured by the growing democratization of the countries in the region and aided by the appropriation of ICTs, civil society groups are finding alternative communication spaces to voice their concerns and raise awareness of their local struggles beyond their borders. Today, civil society organizations (NGOs, social movements, and voluntary associations) are key actors in the search for alternative routes to development. The Zapatistas are the most widely known of such groups, but there are others as well, including, notably, the Landless Rural Worker's Movement in Brazil. As these movements develop with women in the region as key participants, it will be interesting to see to what extent the movements and the women in them incorporate ICTs into their activities.

CONCLUSION

In this chapter, we described the different ways in which women in Latin America are using ICTs to advance their rights, foster social and economic empowerment, and create bridges across communities, countries, and regions to disseminate information about women's social struggles. Even though the experiences and efforts described here have accomplished a great deal, there are daunting obstacles that prevent women from fully harnessing the potential of ICTs for social and economic empowerment. Rampant poverty, unemployment, wage and labor discrimination, lack of access to education and resources, cultural stereotypes, and poor access to communication infrastructure remain some of the critical challenges hampering the development of women in the region.

Globalization and ICTs are the main engines paving the development of the so-called knowledge society. The extent to which these two interrelated factors work to increase equality and social justice for women will depend on the implementation of mechanisms that expand access to ICTs and create enabling environments for access to open economic, social, and political opportunities for women and other unrepresented and under-represented groups. Access within this context must be defined as the appropriation of the technological tools and requisite skills to manage them, as well as a nurturing socioeconomic and cultural environment that allows women to use them to further their empowerment and to become active members of the knowledge society (Menou 2005). We have emphasized some of the challenges and opportunities women in Latin America face today. While ICTs are important tools, they are not enough in themselves to bring women's empowerment, given the depth and extent of the situations they face. It is clear that information and communication, and the tools that bring them, are necessary but not sufficient conditions for the advancement of women in Latin America and elsewhere in the world.

NOTES

[1] Women in Latin America were granted the right to vote in Brazil in the 1930s; in Argentina, Chile, Costa Rica, Ecuador, Jamaica, Mexico, Panama,

and Venezuela in the 1940s; in Colombia, Honduras, Nicaragua, and Peru in the 1950s; and in El Salvador and Paraguay in the 1960s.

[2] http://www.internetworldstats.com/stats.htm.

[3] Since the sample was not necessarily representative, no attempt was made to use the data as the basis for generalizations about women in telecenters in Latin America.

[4] Mexico has the largest population of indigenous people in Latin America— around 12 million from different ethnic groups. Chiapas is one of the three poorest states in Mexico, with an indigenous population of around 1.2 million people of Mayan descent. Despite the fact that 55 percent of Mexico's hydro-electric energy is produced in Chiapas, seven out of ten homes there lack electricity, while nine out of ten have no access to water. Wages in Chiapas are estimated to be one-third of the national average, and 20 percent of these people are without jobs or regular income. Infant mortality is double the national average, and it is estimated that 66 percent of the population suffers from malnutrition, one of the highest causes of death there. http://flag.blackened.net/revolt/mexico/comment/women_jul98.html.

[5] The Zapatista communities are organized in five autonomous councils called Juntas de Buen Gobierno (Good Government Juntas) comprised of representatives elected by women, men, and children of the communities. Since the Zapatista communities accept no support from the government, JBGs were created to build an autonomous government structure for community political participation, to coordinate national and international civil society support, and to find communal ways to address the needs of the Zapatista communities. For more information on JBGs, see Martinez 2003.

[6] See: http://flag.blackened.net/revolt/mexico/ezln/womlaw.html.

[7] More information on the Zapatista women's cooperatives is available from mujeresporladignidad@laneta.apc. DESMI, a local NGO, trains indigenous women to become entrepreneurs and supports their work in Zapatista and non-Zapatista communities in Chiapas. See: http://www.laneta.apc.org/desmiac/. The website of the Human Bean Company that markets coffee and honey produced in the Zapatista cooperatives is http://www.caferebelion.com.

[8] Translated from the Spanish by the authors.

[9] Translated from the Spanish by the authors.

REFERENCES

Avgerou, C., and G. E. Walsham, eds. 2000. *Information technology in context: Studies from the perspective of developing countries.* Burlington, VT: Ashgate.

Azad, A. N., A. S. Erdem, and N. Saleem. 1998. A framework for realizing the potential of information technology in developing countries. *International Journal of Commerce and Management* 18, no. 2: 121–33.

Badshah, Akhtar, Sarbuland Khan, and Maria Garrido, eds. 2003. *Connected for development: Information kiosks and sustainability.* Vol. 4. New York: UN ICT Task Force.

Bennett, L. 2003. Communicating global activism: Strengths and vulnerabilities of networked politics. *Information, Communication, and Society*, 6 no. 2: 143–68.

Best, Michael, and Colin Maclay. 2001. Community Internet access in rural areas: Solving the economic sustainability puzzle. In *The global information technology readiness report 2001–2002*, ed. G. Kirkman, P. K. Cornelius, J. D. Sachs, and K. Schwab. New York: Oxford Univ. Press.

Bonder, G. 2002. From access to appropriation: Women and ICT policies in Latin America and the Caribbean. Paper presented at the UN Division for the Advancement of Women Expert Group Meeting on ICTs and Their Impact on and Use as an Instrument for the Advancement and Empowerment of Women. Seoul, Korea, 11–14 November. http://www.eclac.cl/mujer/noticias/noticias/4/12634/GBonder.pdf (accessed 30 June 2005).

———. 2003. *The new information technologies and women: Essential reflections.* Santiago, Chile: United Nations Economic Commission for Latin America and the Caribbean, Women and Development Unit. http://www.eclac.cl/publicaciones/UnidadMujer/2/LCL1742/lcl1742i.pdf (accessed 25 June 2005).

Boserup, E. 1970. *Women's role in economic development.* New York: St. Martin's Press.

Chase, Jacquelyn. 2003. The spaces of neoliberalism in Latin America. In *The spaces of neoliberalism: Land, place and family in Latin America*, ed. Jacquelyn Chase. Bloomfield, CT: Kumarian Press.

Cleaver, H. 1998. The Zapatista effect: The Internet and the rise of an alternative political fabric. *Journal of International Affairs* 5, no. 2: 621–40.

Diani, Mario. 1992. Analyzing social movement networks. In *Studying Collective Action*, ed. Mario Diani and Ron Eyerman. London: Sage.

Freire, P. 1970. *The pedagogy of the oppressed.* New York: Herder and Herder.

Garrido, Maria, and A. Halavais. 2003. Mapping networks of support for the Zapatista Movement: Applying social network analysis to study contemporary social movements. In *Cyberactivism: Online activism in theory and practice*, ed. M. McCaughey and M. D. Ayers. New York: Routledge.

Gumucio-Dagrón, Alfonso. 2001. *Making waves: Stories of participatory communication for social change.* New York: Rockefeller Foundation.

Gurumurthy, A. 2004. Gender and ICTs: Overview report, Bridge Cutting Edge Pack. Brighton: Institute of Development Studies. http://www.bridge.ids.ac.uk/reports/cep-icts-or.pdf (accessed 5 May 2005).

Gwyne, R., and K. Cristobal, eds. 2004. *Latin America transformed: Globalization and modernity.* 2nd ed. London: Oxford Univ. Press.

Hafkin, Nancy J. 2002. Are ICTs gender neutral? A gender analysis of six case studies of multi-donor ICT projects. UN/INSTRAW Virtual Seminar Series on Gender and ICTs. Seminar One: Are ICTs Gender Neutral? http://www.un-instraw.org/en/docs/gender_and_ict/Hafkin.pdf (accessed 10 May 2005).

————. 2003. Some thoughts on gender and telecommunications/ICT statistics and indicators. Presented to Third World Telecommunication/ICT Indicators Meeting. 15–17 January. Geneva. http://www.itu.int/ITU-D/ict/wict02/doc/pdf/Doc46_Erev1.pdf (accessed 25 June 2005).

Hafkin, N., and N. Taggart. 2001. *Gender, information technology, and developing countries: An analytic study.* Washington, DC: Academy for Educational Development (AED). http://learnlink.aed.org/Publications/Gender_Book/Home.htm (accessed 10 May 2005).

Hall, G., and A. H. Patrinos. 2005. Executive summary: Indigenous peoples, poverty and human development in Latin America: 1994–2004. Washington, DC: The World Bank Group. Worldbank.org website (accessed 10 September 2005).

Harcourt, Wendy. 2001. Rethinking difference and equality: Women and the politics of place. In *Places and politics in an age of globalization*, ed. R. Prazniak and A. Dirlik. Lanham, MD: Rowman and Littlefield Publishers.

Huyer, Sophia. 2003. Globalization and poverty reduction: Gender dimensions of the knowledge society. Part II. Gender equality and poverty reduction in the knowledge society. Gender Advisory Board, United Nations Commission on Science and Technology for Development (UNCSTD). http://gab.wigsat.org/partII.pdf (accessed 12 May 2005).

ITU (International Telecommunication Union). 2002. Female Internet users as percent of total Internet users, 2002. Telecommunication Development Bureau. http://www.itu.int/ITU-D/ict/statistics/at_glance/f_inet.html (accessed 16 July 2005).

Internet World Statistics. 2005. Internet usage statistics for the Americas. http://www.internetworldstats.com/stats2.htm (accessed 17 August 2005).

Jain, R. 1997. A diffusion model for public information systems in developing countries. *Journal of Global Information Management* 5, no. 1: 4–15.

Kirkman, G., P. K. Cornelius, J. D. Sachs, and K. Schwab, eds. 2001. *The global information technology readiness report 2001–2002.* New York: Oxford Univ. Press.

Lehmann, H. 1995. Towards an information technology management framework for developing countries: Investigating the Keiretsu model. *Journal of Global Information Management* 3, no. 3: 16–24.

Lerner, D. 1958. *The passing of traditional society.* New York: Free Press.

Leyva Solano, Xochitl. 2003. *Neo-Zapatista advocacy networks, from local to global experience.* Paper presented at the conference on Global Protest Movements and Transnational Advocacy Networks, Dublin, Republic of Ireland. http://www.dsckim.ie/conference.html (accessed 20 January 2005).

Lind, P. 1991. *Computerization in developing countries: Model and reality.* London: Routledge.

Loch, K. D., D. W. Straub, and S. Kamel. 2003. Diffusing the Internet in the Arab world: The role of social norms and technological culturation. *IEEE Transactions on Engineering Management* 50, no. 1: 45–63.

Lowenthal, L. 1952/53. Introduction to the special issue on international communication research. *Public Opinion Quarterly* 16, no. 4: v-x.

Mansell, Robin, and Uta Wehn. 1998. *Knowledge societies: Information technology for sustainable development*. Oxford: Oxford Univ. Press.

Martínez, J. C. 2003. Las juntas de buen gobierno: Autonomía y gobernabilidad no estatal. *Chiapas al DIA. CIEPAC, 379*. Chiapas, Mexico. 17 October. http://www.ciepac.org/bulletins/301-%20500/bolec379.htm (accessed 25 February 2005).

Menou, Michel. 2005. Las mujeres y las TICs en América Latina. E-mail communication received 27 June.

Nash, J. 2003. Indigenous development alternatives. *Urban Anthropology and Studies of Cultural Systems and World Economic Development* 32, no. 1: 57–99.

Pfaffenberger, B. 1988. Fetishized objects and humanized nature: Towards an anthropology of technology. *Man* 23, no. 2: 236–52.

Plou, Dafne. 2004. Mujeres y nuevas tecnologías de la información y la comunicación. *Cuadernos Internacionales de tecnología para el desarrollo humano* 2, November. http://www.cuadernos.tpdh.org/file_upload/02_Dafne_Sabane.pdf (accessed 14 July 2005).

———. 2005a. Estadísticas de mujeres usuarias de Internet en América Latina. E-mail communication received 30 June.

———. 2005b. Las mujeres y las TICs en América Latina. Interview with Maria Garrido. 12 June.

Proenza, F. 2001. Telecenter sustainability: Myths and opportunities. *Journal of Development Communication* 12, no. 2: 4–109.

Rice, R. E., M. McCreadie, and S. L. Chang. 2001. *Accessing and browsing information and communication*. Cambridge, MA: MIT Press.

Roman, Raul, and Royal Colle. 2003. Content creation for information and communication technology development projects: Integrating normative approaches and community demand. *Journal of Information Technology for Development* 10, no. 2: 85–94.

Rogers, E. M. 1976. Communication and development: The passing of the dominant paradigm. *Communication Research* 3, no. 2: 213–41.

Schramm, W. 1964. *Mass media and national development*. Stanford, CA: Stanford Univ. Press.

Schulz, M. 1998. Collective action across borders: Opportunity structures, network capacities, and communicative praxis in the age of advanced globalization. *Sociological Perspectives* 4, no. 3: 597–610.

Sen, Amartya. 1999. *Development as freedom*. New York: Anchor Books.

Sivard, R. L., A. Brauer, and R. J. Cook. 1995. *Women, a world survey*. Washington, DC: World Priorities.

Steeves, L. 2001. Liberation, feminism, and development communication. *Communication Theory* 11, no. 4: 397–414.

Stiglitz, J. E. 2003. *Globalization and its discontents*. New York: Norton.

Veltemeyer, H., and J. Petras. 2000. *The dynamics of social change in Latin America*. New York: St. Martin's Press.

Warschauer, M. 2003. *Technology and social inclusion: Rethinking the digital divide.* Cambridge, MA: MIT Press.

Wilkins, K. G., and B. Mody. 2001. Reshaping development communication: Developing communication and communicating development. *Communication Theory* 11, no. 4: 385–96.

Zermeño, S. 1996. *La sociedad derrotada: El desorden mexicano del fin de siglo.* Mexico City: Siglo veintiuno editores.

8

Empowerment of Women through ICT-enabled Networks

Toward the Optimum ICT-impact Model

Vikas Nath

THE ICT–GENDER EQUALITY CHALLENGE

People have always sought to communicate and to gain information that will sustain their livelihoods, increase their opportunities, and improve the quality of their lives. ICTs can provide the tools to do this. From the woman in rural South Africa who spends the equivalent of $1.90 a month for five minutes of airtime to speak to her husband working in Johannesburg (LaFreniere 2005), to the businesswoman in Europe who spends several hundred euros monthly to maintain business relationships with clients via the telephone, ICTs fulfill a basic need for all. People around the world understand the value of ICTs and *on their own initiative* make an effort to use devices such as mobile phones or land lines. They engage in both voice and text-based communication, depending on what they can afford and what is accessible to them.

From a development perspective, the challenge is *not* in simply helping people connect with each other, as this is largely a self-driven outcome of the penetration of ICTs within a society. The challenge instead is *to transform these new forms of communication into real opportunities for growth and development, especially for those who are most likely to be bypassed*

This chapter is written by the author in his individual capacity and does not represent the views of the organization that he may be working for or is associated with.

in the absence of a concerted effort to include them in ICT-enabled networks. This group comprises people who are marginalized financially, socially, politically, and geographically, and includes more women than men.

Empowering Women through ICT-enabled Knowledge Networks

Empowerment of women through ICTs can be understood as the use of ICTs by or for women to develop further their skills and abilities to gain insight about actions and issues that affect them (positively or negatively), as well as to build their capacity to be involved with, voice their concerns about, and make informed decisions on these issues. This entails building the capacities that will allow women to overcome social and institutional barriers to strengthen their participation in economic and political processes and bring an overall improvement in the quality of their lives.

Figure 8–1. Empowering Women through ICT-enabled Networks

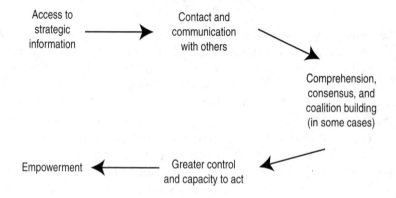

ICTs can also support women to broaden the scope of their actions to include issues that they were previously unable to address in an individual capacity. ICT-enabled knowledge networking allows one woman or one women's group to link up with others and form coalitions to influence decision making and strengthen local and national democratic processes, while also encouraging awareness of the political power of women (see Figure 8–1).[1] It can extend the range of decision-making mechanisms to all levels of society, including women in low-income and rural households, where implementing alternative mechanisms to replicate this activity would require substantially greater amounts of time, resources, and effort.

A range of ICT-based models has been used to support the empowerment of women around the world. In Africa, groups such as the Africa Women's Network of the APC have conducted training workshops to support electronic networking among women's groups in different countries. In Uganda, the Forum for Women in Democracy finds information for female members of parliament on the Internet to support their contribution to parliamentary debate and investigate issues around new bills introduced in the House (Opoku-Mensah 1999). Women'sNet in South Africa uses ICTs to advance women's equality by providing gender-sensitive training and support; linking projects, people, tools, and resources; and creating a platform for women's voices and issues. In this way, the "engendering" of ICT knowledge networks can empower women and their representatives, and encourage their informed and active participation on issues that influence their lives directly. These kinds of networks form the base from which women can overcome the constraints of isolation from the wider economy and society; mobilize support, advice, and resources; and open up avenues for lifelong learning.

The challenge for ICT-based development is to build on examples such as these and others in this book to ensure that women can benefit equally from the benefits and opportunities offered by ICTs and to implement ICT projects that will significantly increase the representation of women in all aspects of their societies. This chapter addresses these issues by assessing how ICT-enabled networking can promote women's participation in the public sphere in the form of participation in governance, access to improved government service delivery, and mobilization and public advocacy. It then suggests a set of impact and assessment models for visualizing the effect of ICTs on women.

USING ICTS TO ENTER THE PUBLIC SPHERE

Traditionally, the participation of women in the public sphere is limited. Here the public sphere encompasses activities performed by women outside the household production sector and includes trade, commerce, and political activities. Women's contributions in these areas are limited by the greater demand on their time of household or farm chores, limitations that may be compounded by difficulties in maintaining long absences from their families, lack of access to outside information, the dominance of men in public-sphere decision making, and socioreligious customs that discourage or prohibit the active participation of women outside the home. Women affected by one or more of these factors will be less able to influence decisions at different levels of their society, including election of local government representatives, district-level development planning, local NGO activities, agendas for village-level meetings, or even location of community wells.

Any action to overcome the segregation of women from public decision making will also need to provide a means for the inclusion of women's concerns and interests. ICTs have the potential to fill this role. Theoretically, any woman with an ICT access point can connect to the outside world. Even within the confines of their homes or village, women can use ICTs to find information, interact with others, and publish or broadcast their views.

Recent cases suggest that in households where women are active users of ICTs, they will have the potential to express their views and participate actively in activities and decision making in their communities, thus breaching the traditional boundaries between the private and public spheres. A case in point is the Nabanna project in West Bengal, India, which has shown that ICTs can promote respect for women's knowledge in the public sphere. The goal of the project was to encourage information and knowledge exchange among the women of Nabanna Municipality. Two to three women from each of the municipality's seventeen wards were identified as information agents and trained in basic computer skills. These women continue to participate in ongoing information and communication training, forming the core of the community networks. Each information agent leads a weekly information group meeting, comprised of ten women recruited from the local area. The participants report feeling empowered through an increased capacity to learn and a sense of ownership over new networking spaces. Nabanna activities have motivated and supported self-reflection, expression, and creativity among the women in the community. They are respected in the community at large for their computer skills and knowledge on a range of issues that in some cases have given them a greater voice in their families and ushered in changes in gender dynamics in the larger community. The project has led to increased solidarity among women who now share a space for communication and learning (Ghose and Ghosh Ray 2004).

Empowerment through Participation in Governance

The ability to influence external decisions that affect our lives is a sign of empowerment. Women face more barriers and restrictions than men in influencing governance. Politics at all levels is more biased toward the participation of men,[2] and in some countries women are still barred from voting in elections, let alone standing as electoral candidates. Recognizing this situation, governments in some developing countries are taking steps to encourage the involvement of women in governance processes through such strategies as electoral reservation,[3] creation of separate departments or ministries to focus on women's and gender issues, and initiating women-specific governance projects. Nevertheless, we know that even when women are elected as government representatives, they can experience a range of difficulties and barriers, both physical and social. A woman representative at the district level may find it more difficult to fulfill her responsibilities effectively if she is not able to attend village-level meetings held during evening hours or in remote locations. Women can also experience "indifferent attitudes" of their male colleagues and constituents, as well as apathy on the part of government officials (Mohapatra 2001). In such cases ICT tools can open up alternate channels for communication with colleagues and constituents, both male and female.

ICTs can also support communication and capacity building within decision making and electoral frameworks. This is seen in Women Mayors' Link, an initiative of the Stability Pact Gender Task Force (SPGTF). The project was developed in 2002 in the twelve countries and territories of the SP region in South Eastern Europe. The network, which largely communicates through e-mail, was established to strengthen women mayors' leadership skills, lobby for the better representation of women in local government, promote cooperation between women mayors and local women's networks in designing projects to improve the quality of life of women and children, and to exchange best practices with other groups regionally and internationally.[4]

Empowerment through Better Government Service Delivery

Public services, such as primary education; primary health care, hygiene, and immunization; information on seed storage, food processing, and animal husbandry; information on credit availability for enterprise creation; and information about government services can tremendously improve the lives of women. However, many government services simply do not reach women, especially those living in poor and remote rural communities. When women are able to access government services, in many cases the benefit of these services is lessened by corruption, inefficiency, and disorganization, so that they fail to have a real or lasting impact.

In some regions, particularly in Asia, governance processes are increasingly being transferred online. This trend poses the potential to transform the woman-government interface. Electronic governance, for instance, enables access to government services from home or the nearest ICT terminal. It is no longer necessary in each case to travel to a government office (many of which are located far from rural communities) to stand in line. Online governance services allow users to access government websites on their own time and according to their particular interests in order to find the names and contact information of local officials and their roles and responsibilities; working hours of government offices; application forms available by download; rules and regulations; and so forth. Women stand to benefit tremendously from this kind of transformation. The existence of online government services allows them to interact with the government online and with local electoral representatives on issues such as redressing grievances, information on new services or on the status of existing services, reporting cases of corruption and harassment, and job applications.

In this way governance mechanisms are brought closer to women. They can open up new channels for interaction that do not require either extensive travel or representation of women by family members. This immediate access to information by women can encourage greater awareness and understanding of political and governmental processes, which can lead to greater participation in these processes. In short, the ICT-enabled governance model can open up avenues for direct interaction of women with their governments and local representatives.

E-seva in West Godavari district, Andhra Pradesh, India, is an example.[5] The project was initiated to introduce citizen-to-citizen and citizen-to-government services in rural areas, particularly to women. Internet kiosks or e-seva centers at the block level were put under the control of women's self-help groups. Over time, women managers became active users of the services and technologies offered at the centers, while the kiosks became an important interface for communication and transactions between the local administration and the community. Since the inception of the project in 2002, over a million transactions involving local communities have been conducted, ranging from payment of bills to delivery of government certificates to information sharing among different village communities. Twelve thousand grievances have been filed, of which, according to the local government, over eleven thousand have been redressed to date. The women managing the e-seva centers have become information intermediaries and information leaders in their villages, with improved standing and increased influence as a result.[6] Increased independence is another outcome of the project, since the women participants feel that e-mail and the Internet offer them greater autonomy and more opportunities to make choices in their lives.

ICT-enabled governance models can open up avenues for the direct participation of women in the governance of their societies, including in areas where they have previously been insufficiently engaged. Further, these new models can lead to a more interactive and active form of communication with officials in local governance that are characterized by greater transparency and accountability.

The online service delivery approach can also be applied outside government institutions for the benefit of women. For example, the computerization of the Self Employed Women's Association (SEWA) Bank in India—the largest women's bank in the country—has promoted the involvement of self-help groups in the provision of financial services at the village level. In other examples, the use of computers in district level organizations allows up-to-date maintenance of records, supporting increased efficiency. Computers have provided access to new markets for more than forty thousand craftswomen at Banaskantha and Kutch in India, who display their products on the Internet. Their products now command higher prices.

Empowerment through Mobilization and Public Advocacy

The most widely known use of ICTs to promote women's participation in governance relates to the building of alliances and the development of issue-based solidarity among women's groups as a prerequisite for concerted action. A local women's group protesting environmental degradation caused by the practices of government or a transnational company no longer finds itself waging battle alone. Instead, it can strike alliances with groups located across the country or even across regions to raise a common voice against these kinds of unsustainable practices.

Virtual communities are another powerful force by which women's groups form collaborations around a common viewpoint and value framework. The virtual community movement is directed at providing individuals, local communities, and regional groupings with the ability to advocate policies that protect and further their interests and promote better governance at all levels. In this way such communities push to create spaces within existing governance mechanisms for democratic decision making that is governed by welfare and human rights principles, sustainability, and social-development objectives. In Africa, Fahamu mobilized mobile phone users to send SMS text messages in support of a petition to lobby African governments to sign the Protocol to the African Charter on Human and Peoples' Rights on the Rights of Women in Africa. The petition can also be signed online through the Internet. At the time of printing, 3,626 signatures were collected, 468 of them through SMS, and fifteen countries had ratified the agreement, the minimum number to put the protocol into force.[7]

These kinds of virtual communities can be very effective in influencing transnational polices and debates that require strong and persistent lobbying at the global level for change to occur. ICTs can facilitate the creation of alliances among women that are based on common value frameworks and objectives rather than determined by geographical boundaries.

VISUALIZING THE IMPACT OF ICT MODELS ON WOMEN: AIMING FOR THE OPTIMUM IMPACT MODEL

There is no single or simple model to assess either the impact of ICTs on women or whether ICTs promote or discourage the empowerment of women any differently from other technologies. Instead, we need to develop creative models and approaches to help us understand:

- in what ways ICTs are integrated in the lives of women;
- the impact of this integration; and
- whether the impact is different from that of other technologies.

Only when we are able to answer these questions will we have a clear picture of how ICTs support the empowerment of women, and if they are a catalyst in the overall improvement of women's situation.

In general, it is recognized that the increased penetration of ICTs worldwide has initiated a substantial increase in *information access* and *information flows*, defined as follows:

- *Information access:* Opportunities or avenues that allow individuals to seek information from different sources, such as other individuals or institutions, public-domain resources or databases, websites, news groups, e-mails, chat sessions, or blogs.
- *Information flow:* The supply and availability of information within a society. Information flows may be "restricted" in some societies and "open" in others. Greater use of ICTs has generated new content in the form of text, photographs, and movies that can be accessed through the Internet, mobile phone calls, and text messages.

However, if we are to assess in particular the relation of ICT information access and flows in relation to women's empowerment, it is important to look at the *geometry of information flows* in order to understand how increases in information access and information flows influence women and their participation in the public sphere. The geometry of information flows provides a detailed "human-centric" picture of information flows in a society. It focuses on identifying who is connecting and who benefits when there is an increase in information access and flows. The aim is to understand the distribution of information and information flows in the society (Digital Governance Initiative 2005), instead of focusing solely on enhancing communication. Some of the questions the study of geometry of information flows should answer with respect to the empowerment of women follow:

- Which new constituencies or target groups of women are participating in ICT networks?
- Has any relevant content started to flow to women or women's groups as a result of their connection to ICT networks?
- Do information flows to women in lower socioeconomic levels increase when there is a *total* increase in information access and flows?

Figure 8–2 and Figure 8–3 model several scenarios for women's participation in the public sphere before and after the introduction of ICTs. Figure 8–2 represents the situation of women in a society prior to the introduction of one or more ICTs. It illustrates the existing situations, in which only a few women in the society are able to benefit from useful public or private services *(information flows)*. This may have been possible by other means; for instance, some women may not face social barriers to physical travel and will be able to visit government offices for information on public programs and services. Others may have some prior experience of dealing with government offices. However, the number of such women is low in many regions, and once they arrive at the office, only a small number of services or programs may be accessible.

Figure 8–2. Situation before Introduction of ICT

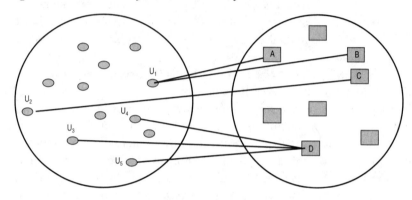

After the introduction of ICTs in a society, several possibilities can develop:

Case A: Information flows have increased only among those already connected (U_1-U_5)—a situation that tends to exclude certain social groups, including women. This means that while the society on the whole will register an increase in the magnitude of information exchanged among its population, most of this information will be exchanged among those who already had access to information prior to the introduction of ICT. In this situation the gap between the information *haves* and the *have nots* is widened, and women will not tend to benefit. In fact, they may end up at an even greater disadvantage as a result of increased disparity in information access and use, especially as information flows may increase exponentially as a result of the introduction of ICT.

An example can be seen in relation to employment: if women do not have access to online job databases, employment ratios may become increasingly skewed to the disadvantage of women. This kind of result is most likely to occur when ICTs are introduced as a communication and entertainment medium rather than as a tool for social development and growth. A quick peek inside many privately run internet cafes in developing countries will reveal the low number of girls and women who use them. In short, as demonstrated in the analysis of national-level statistics in Chapter 2, integrating ICTs in the lives of disadvantaged women calls for *planned intervention;* it will not occur simply as a result of the increased penetration of ICTs within a society.

Case B: Information flows have increased, accompanied by a substantial change in the geometry of information flows to include more women as users (U_1-U_8), but no new women-targeted services or activities have been implemented (that is, services provided remain limited to A, B, C, and D). This is a likely situation in societies where ICTs have been integrated in a planned manner, for instance, through interventions of government agencies, NGOs, and the private sector to provide affordable or universal access to ICTs. In such cases there is certainly an increase in the number of women using ICT tools, and they may start using these tools to improve their quality of life. For instance, they may be able to find information on new employment opportunities, or government services, or they may communicate with other women, or learn about household-level economic enterprises such as food processing or handicraft production. However, as other studies indicate, women's opportunity to benefit from ICT projects is less than men's unless specific gender-specific actions are taken and services provided.

Figure 8–3. ICT-Women Optimal Impact Situation

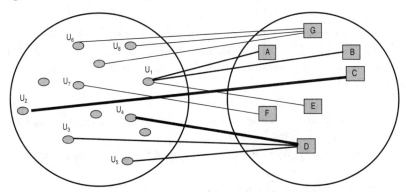

Case C: In this case, women are most likely to benefit from the introduction of ICTs. There is a substantial change in the geometry of information flows as a result of an increase in the number of women users (U_1-U_8) *and* through a significant increase in women-specific information flows (A-G) (see Figure 8–3). This involves the design or customizing of services that are accessible and of use to women in a society or community, and can be delivered online or through a hybrid online-offline model. Services may include:

- Identifying specific information needs of women, such as information on health (including reproductive health), employment opportunities, and government programs directed to or relevant to women.
- Creating women-specific products and services, for instance, online training courses on obtaining loans to start an enterprise or credit facilities for women entrepreneurs.

This model for ensuring the value of ICTs to women and their opportunity to benefit will be realized only when there is political will on the part of government bodies to work with one another, NGOs, and the private sector to target women in poor and remote communities. Careful planning and ongoing monitoring is required to ensure that ICT interventions do not bypass women but instead provide substantial benefits to women who would not otherwise gain access.

PARTNERSHIPS TO ENSURE WOMEN EXPERIENCE THE BENEFITS OF ICT

Partnerships to alter the geometry of information flows in society to achieve Case C (which sees an increase in the number of women users as well as an increase in gender-specific information), would use four main approaches:

- provision of affordable ICT access and connectivity to women and women-linked institutions;
- creation of women-relevant content or provision of relevant experts and expertise;
- training and capacity building; and
- reaching targeted communities.

Partnerships to Provide Affordable ICT Access and Connectivity

Partners can collaborate to enable women and women-linked institutions to *access* ICT tools at an *affordable cost*. Partnership support could consist of providing hardware and software applications, telephone main lines, wireless connectivity, broadband networks, or access to existing telecenters.

- *Access* provided by these partners may be exclusively through women's institutions, self-help groups, or institutions such as schools, telecenters, and research stations that provide a safe environment for women.
- *Affordable cost* implies access that is either free or available at rates that easily can be managed by women, even those with low incomes.

Partnerships to Provide Relevant Content or Content Experts

Providing affordable access and connectivity by itself will not ensure the flow of information that is useful and relevant to women's interests and concerns. Content that relates to the situation of women and women's groups and can be communicated to them is necessary.

Partners under this category will need to:

- provide content of value to women in a format that is comprehensible to them, that is, that is practical, useful, and available in local languages; or,
- provide experts who are knowledgeable in issues and areas relevant to women's concerns and who can communicate this knowledge in a comprehensible format.

Comprehensible format implies that the content or knowledge that is transmitted is in the language of end users and specific to local requirements. The content may be created in-house, based on the specific needs of the community, or sourced from outside. Partners will have the expertise to search for content and experts from available public-domain information and to create new content specific to the local situation.

Partnerships to Support Training and Capacity Building

Partners in this category should be able to deliver training and build capacity among women to use effectively ICT tools such as computers, word-processing applications, databases, HTML applications, e-mail and the Internet. This role could be filled by private agencies or training institutes run on a nonprofit basis. It is important that these partners be experienced in creating conditions that would encourage ICT use by women, for instance, by providing customized training in a safe and accessible environment. Studies show that the presence of women trainers and managers, both as role models and to make women users more comfortable with the technology, tends to increase the number of women users.

Partnerships to Reach Out to Communities

This is the most important category of partnerships, and development agencies should select partners for this category with great care. Partners should have an experience of working with women, preferably with an explicit mandate to work toward women's development as part of their regular activities. In addition, they should be able to identify and address the specific information, technical, and input needs of women participants, for instance, those who are unemployed, who face social and household discrimination that hinders their participation in the economic and political front, or who are from low-income households. These partners should be an established source of information for women's groups, as this will allow them effectively to integrate ICTs in the lives of women and create greater opportunities for women to use them as tools for empowerment and growth.

The key roles of partners are to extend available online products and services to women; customize or translate available information for local users; provide assistance in searching for information, technical inputs, and financial advice; and sensitize women about potential uses of ICTs for empowerment and economic benefit. Examples of prospective partners are women-focused NGOs, women's departments in local government offices, and women's self-help and savings groups.

CONCLUSION

Empowerment of women through ICTs will need to be a directed change. The introduction of ICTs in a community will not naturally bring about benefits to women, especially those women in low-income groups. *Planned intervention* is required to create conditions and avenues that will encourage women to participate more fully. Such interventions need to be made in both the public and private sectors, as some initiatives will be best undertaken by the "public hand," while others may be better provided and sustained by market forces.

The public hand can ensure that government offices (including local and district offices) provide information conducive to improving women's situation and addressing their concerns—for instance, ensuring that social security, employment, or education programs are available online. This will allow women who are unable to travel and those whose cultural norms prevent them from traveling unaccompanied to obtain access to this information. Information should be made available in vernacular languages, and online services should include government employment databases and the ability to file and redress grievances electronically.

The private sector can create special services for women, such as online training and education courses that are sensitive to the needs of women with families, or organizing credit facilities for women's ICT-based enterprises. However, encouraging private-sector intervention in this sector will require governments to implement the right incentives and conditions for action.

The year 2005, which marked the tenth anniversary of the Beijing World Conference on Women, brought renewed energy and commitment, but it also called for revised thinking by policymakers, NGOs, and donor agencies. Political willingness and a commitment to public-private partnerships can create new opportunities for women to benefit from the ICT revolution. The implementation of gender-sensitive and women-targeted ICT-enabled networks can provide women with the tools to participate actively in political and governance frameworks that affect their lives.

NOTES

[1] "Unrestricted and continuous sharing of global and local knowledge between policy-makers, public and private sectors, and the civil society heralds the way forward to an empowered knowledge society which can efficiently manage the development change process. Thus, in a knowledge society, there is not only an efficient transfer of knowledge but also a greater likelihood that such knowledge will be used effectively for empowerment and reducing inequality and poverty" (Nath 2000).

[2] Data show that women's political representation is lower than that of men in all countries.

[3] Allocating a specific number or percentage of electoral seats to be held by women.

[4] Gender and ICT Awards. 2003. Romania: Women Mayors' Link. http://www.genderawards.net/winners/wml.htm.

[5] http://www.westgodavari.org.

[6] "IT for Development: E-services in India." http://www.pstm.net/article/index.php?articleid=533.

[7] "Africa mobile phone users rally for women's rights." Joint agency press release. http://www.pambazuka.org/en/petition/index.php.

REFERENCES

Digital Governance Initiative. 2005. The geometry of information flows. http://www.DigitalGovernance.org (accessed 30 November 2005).

Ghose, Jhulan, and Jhumpha Ghosh Ray. 2004. Nabanna: Empowering woman? *i4d Online.* May. http://www.i4donline.net/issue/may04/empowering_woman_full.htm (accessed 30 November 2005).

LaFraniere, Sharon. 2005. Cellphones catapult rural Africa to 21st century. *The New York Times.* August 25. http:// www.lirneasia.net/2005/08/nyt-article-cellphones-catapult-rural-africa-to-21st-century (accessed 30 November 2005).

Mohapatra, Ajaya Kumar. 2001. Putting women in their place? Participation in Indian local governance. In *Development in Brief: Gender and Participation* 9. (BRIDGE/IDS). http:// www.bridge.ids.ac.uk/dgb9.html (accessed 5 October 2005).

Nath, Vikas. 2000. Heralding ICT-enabled knowledge societies: The way forward for developing countries. Sustainable Development Networking Program/UNDP), India. http://216.197.119.113/vikas/heralding.htm (accessed 30 November 2005).

Opoku-Mensah, Aida. 1999. Democratizing access to the information society. *African Development Forum 1999.* Addis Ababa: United Nations Economic Commission for Africa.

Contributors

Shoba Arun, after completing three degrees in economics from India, did her doctoral studies at the Department of Sociology, University of Manchester, on gender, development, and agriculture in the southwest state of Kerala, India, examining the gendered economy during structural adjustment in Kerala, a region with a reputation for social development, particularly for women. During this time she also taught social policy at the University of Salford and sociology/development studies at the University of Manchester. After completing her Ph.D., she moved to Northern Ireland, where she worked for the Women's Opportunities Unit in the University of Ulster. In 2001 she joined the UNESCO Centre in the University of Ulster, where she coordinated a DFID grant to strengthen the global dimension in teacher education in Northern Ireland. In 2002 she joined the Department of Sociology at Manchester Metropolitan University (UK). Her primary research interests are globalization and gender, work and society, women and the labor market, poverty, and the implications of information and communication technologies. She has worked in collaboration with NGOs, governments, companies, and multinational corporations in the UK, Europe, and Ireland, as well as in southern countries. Her e-mail address is S.Arun@mmu.ac.uk.

Maria Garrido is a Ph.D. candidate in the Department of Communication and a research assistant for the Center of Internet Studies at the University of Washington. Her research explores the role of information technology in fostering economic development in low-income communities in Latin America. She has published research on how grassroots organizations make use of new media as a tool to mobilize and create networks of support on a global scale to generate social change. She earned her bachelor's degree in international relations at the Universidad Iberoamericana in Mexico City and a master's degree in international relations at the University of Chicago. She can be contacted at migarrid@u.washington.edu.

Nancy J. Hafkin has been working on issues of gender and information technology and development for more than three decades. In 1976 she co-edited *Women in Africa: Studies in Social and Economic Change* (Stanford University Press). From 1976 to 1987 she worked as chief of research and publications at the African Training and Research Centre for Women of the United Nations Economic Commission for Africa (Addis Ababa, Ethiopia). In the area of information technology at ECA, Hafkin headed the Pan African Development Information System (PADIS) from 1987 until 1997 and served as team leader for promoting information technology for African development from 1997 to 2000, where she was coordinator of the African Information Society Initiative (AISI). In 2000 the Association for Progressive Communications established an annual Nancy Hafkin Communications Prize competition, with the first prize allocated to women-led initiatives. In 2001 she co-authored *Gender, Information and Developing Countries*. Retired from the United Nations since 2000, Nancy works as a consultant on gender and information technology through her consultancy Knowledge Working. She has a Ph.D. in history (Africa) from Boston University. She can be contacted at nhafkin@comcast.net.

Richard Heeks is a senior lecturer in information systems and development at the Institute for Development Policy and Management, University of Manchester. He has an M.Phil. in information systems from the University of Leicester, and a Ph.D. on Indian IT industry development from the Open University. His book publications include *India's Software Industry* (1996), *Reinventing Government in the Information Age* (1999), and *Implementing and Managing eGovernment* (2006). His research interests are IT industry development, information systems and corruption, informatics in remote regions, and health information systems. His online materials are available at http://www.manchester.ac.uk/idpm/dig, and he can be contacted at richard.heeks@manchester.ac.uk.

Sophia Huyer is executive director of Women in Global Science and Technology (WIGSAT) and senior research adviser with the Gender Advisory Board of the United Nations Commission on Science and Technology for Development (GAB-UNCSTD). Her recent publications include "Women in the Information Society" in *From the Digital Divide to Digital Opportunities:Measuring Infostates for Development* (Orbicom), "Overcoming the Digital Divide: Understanding ICTs and Their Potential for the Empowerment of Women," a synthesis paper of the INSTRAW Virtual Seminar Series on Gender and ICTs, and the UNESCO/GAB Toolkit on Gender Indicators in Engineering, Science, and Technology. She was also a co-organizer of the recent international symposium Women and ICT: Creating Global Transformations, at the Center for Women in Technology, University of Maryland, Baltimore County (USA). She has a Ph.D. in environmental studies and international development from York University, Toronto, Canada. She can be contacted at shuyer@wigsat.org.

Shafika Isaacs is executive director of SchoolNet Africa. Based in Johannesburg, South Africa, she was previously senior program officer with the International Development Research Centre (IDRC) Acacia Program, where she promoted the SchoolNet Africa initiative and supported youth, gender, and schoolnet projects in Africa. She is formerly director of the Trade Union Research Project

(TURP), a labor research service organization in South Africa. She is a founding member of the Cape Town–based Primary and High School Schools Tuition Program and the Skills Training and Education Centre. A finalist for the World Technology Network Award in 2003 and recipient of the Mandela Scholarship to the University of Sussex, she serves on the boards of directors of OneWorld Africa, Ungana Afrika, and SchoolNet South Africa; on the Steering Group of the United Nations ICT Task Force Global eSchools Initiative (GESCI); and on the Council of the Free and Open Source Software Foundation for Africa (FOSSFA). She also served as interim co-ordinator of the WSIS Gender Caucus in 2003 and was chairperson of the United Nations Division for Advancement of Women (UNDAW) Expert Group Meeting on ICTs as an Instrument for the Advancement of Women. Shafika can be contacted at s.isaacs@schoolnetafrica.org.

Sonia N. Jorge has been an international consultant in communications policy and regulation and gender and development for over fifteen years. Her recent work has focused on ICT policy, universal access in the context of development, and gender analysis and awareness in the process of planning for ICTs. Recent projects include the rural ICT development policy for Indonesia, a region-wide study of universal access in Latin America, preparation of the UN Task Force on Financial Mechanisms report on financing ICT for development, development of training materials on ICT policy, a gender curriculum for the ITU, and national sector policies in Ghana, Mozambique, Sri Lanka, Dominican Republic, and South Africa. Jorge has published and presented various papers in international conferences, primarily focusing on gender and ICT issues. She holds a master's in public policy (Tufts University) and a B.A./B.S. in economics and business finance (University of Massachusetts). She was raised in Angola, is a Portuguese citizen, and is based in Boston (USA). She can be contacted at sjorge@att.net.

Sharon Morgan is a graduate teaching fellow at the Institute for Development Policy and Management, University of Manchester (UK), where she is doing research on women in the ICT professions in the Development Informatics Group. After working in the software industry in the UK, she taught computer science at universities in the UK and Botswana, focusing on human-computer interaction and widening access to technology. She has also worked as an adviser with NGOs in Sri Lanka and Botswana. She can be contacted at sharon.morgan@postgrad.manchester.ac.uk.

Vikas Nath, an e-entrepreneur, is the founder of several ICT4D initiatives, including http://www.DigitalGovernance.org and http://www.KnowNet.org, aimed at bringing good governance to developing countries through knowledge, technology, and e-governance applications. He is the founder of the http://www.DevNetJobs.org and http://www.DevNetJobsIndia.org jobs portal, an electronic gateway for job opportunities in international development that serves eighty thousand people and eighteen hundred organizations. Nath has been involved with research, designing, monitoring, and evaluation of projects relating to application of information technology in agriculture, small and medium enterprises, public-sector reform, good governance, and rural development in over thirty-five developing and developed countries. Nath is an Inlaks Scholar at the London School of Economics (UK). He holds two master's degrees, in environment and development from the London School of Economics and in natural resources management from the Indian Institute of Forest Management, and is a consultant to several international organizations. Nath formerly worked as a policy analyst with UNDP in New York, where he did research on provisioning and financing of ICT global public goods. He has also worked with the Government of India on environment and sustainable development issues. He can be contacted at http://www.vikasnath.org or vikas.nath@gmail.com.

Raul Roman is a research associate at the Annenberg Research Network on International Communication, Annenberg School for Communication, University of Southern California, and a nonresident research fellow at the Center for Internet Studies, University of Washington. His research focuses on social and economic effects of ICT in communities of the developing world. He has conducted research and consulted with international organizations, governments, and the private sector on information technology and international development programs in South Asia, Latin America, and sub-Saharan Africa. Roman publishes widely and regularly presents his work at meetings and conferences. He serves as regional editor for Latin America for the journal *Information Technologies and International Development*. Roman received a B.A. in journalism and mass communication from the University of Seville, Spain, and M.S. and Ph.D. degrees in communication and international development from Cornell University. He can be contacted at raul.roman@usc.edu.

Index

Also from Kumarian Press...

New and Forthcoming

Development Brokers and Translators: The Ethnography of Aid and
Agencies
Edited by David Lewis and David Mosse

Transnational Civil Society: An Introduction
Edited by Srilatha Batliwala and L. David Brown

Non-State Actors in the Human Rights Universe
Edited by George Andreopoulos, Zehra Kabasakal Arat, and Peter Juviler

The Great Turning: From Empire to Earth Community
David Korten

Peace Operations Seen from Below: UN Missions and Local People
Beatrice Pouligny

Of Related Interest

Women and the Politics of Place
Edited by Wendy Harcourt and Arturo Escobar

Progress of the World's Women 2005
Edited by Martha Chen, Joann Vanek, Francie Lund, James Heintz with Renana Jhabvala, and Christine
Bonner

Policy, Politics & Gender: Women Gaining Ground
Kathleen Staudt

Development with Women
Edited by Deborah Eade

Visit Kumarian Press at **www.kpbooks.com** or
call **toll-free 800.289.2664** for a complete catalog.

Orbicom: Women in the Info Society
Tech. is not neutral

Kumarian Press, located in Bloomfield, Connecticut, is a forward-looking, scholarly press that promotes active international engagement and an awareness of global connectedness.